PARKLANDS
of the MIDWEST

Celebrating the Natural Wonders
of America's Heartland

Midwest Living® name and logo are trademarks of the Meredith Corporation, used under license by Morris Book Publishing, LLC.

Cover photos: Sleeping Bear Dunes National Lakeshore, Michigan. By Jason Lindsey.

Cover design: Diana Nuhn.

Text and layout design: Geri Boesen, Terri Ketcham.

Map illustrations: Bill Reynolds.

Midwest Living® project team: Geri Boesen, Creative Director; Nancy Singh, Project Coordinator; Nancy McClimen, Contributing Copy Editor; Rob Kaercher, Travel Assistant; Karen Ziebarth and Tiffany Cleghorn, Transcriptionists.

Photographers: Bob Stefko, Jason Lindsey, Clint Farlinger, John Noltner, Randall Lee Schieber and Per Breiehagen.

Midwest Living® magazine: Greg Philby, Executive Editor; Trevor Meers, Managing Editor; Barbara Morrow, Senior Travel Editor; Joan Lynch Luckett, Project Manager; Diana McMillen, Senior Food Editor; Terri Ketcham, Associate Art Director; Brenda Kienast, Photo Researcher; Judy Cordle and Merrie Tatman, Administrative Assistants.

Contributing Editors and Writers: Barbara Humeston, Linda Ryberg, Debbie Miller and Sandra Granseth.

Fact Checking and Research: Kelly Meade, Deb Smith, Brooke Bates and Angela Kennebeck.

Library of Congress Cataloging-in-Publication Data is available.

ISBN: 978-0-7627-4370-4 (Hardcover) ISBN: 978-0-7627-4300-1 (Paperback).

Printed in the United States of America.
First Edition/First Printing.

PARKLANDS
of the MIDWEST

Celebrating the Natural Wonders
of America's Heartland

By Dan Kaercher

The
Globe
Pequot
Press

GUILFORD, CONNECTICUT

Contents

This book combines Dan's travel essays with practical information about visiting more than 130 parklands in the 12 Midwest states. While by no means a comprehensive listing, these parklands are among Dan's Midwest favorites. Each was selected to help portray the diversity that exists throughout the region and within each state. State-by-state chapters include Dan's reflections about the parks he visited during the summer of 2006, including detailed travel advice about those stops, as well as contact information and suggestions for lodging, dining, shopping, related events and other area attractions. The "More Parks" section summarizes additional recommended parklands in each state. A recipe sidebar in each chapter brings to life another dimension of Dan's trip: the great food to be enjoyed. All of those recipes have been tested for flavor and practicality in the *Midwest Living*® Test Kitchen.

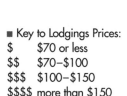

■ Key to Lodgings Prices:
$ $70 or less
$$ $70–$100
$$$ $100–$150
$$$$ more than $150

Dan traveled 11,118 miles through 12 Midwest states during the summer of 2006, visiting more than 40 parklands.

My amazing summer in the great outdoors

Shawnee National Forest, Illinois.

THE SEEDS OF THIS JOURNEY were planted in a North Woods Wisconsin tavern over beer and walleye at a Friday-night fish fry. Our crew was taking a break from filming *Taste of the Midwest*. Although that book-, magazine- and television project focused on food and dining, we all agreed it would be wonderful to feature the great parks of the region—and in *Parklands of the Midwest* that's just what we've done.

As with my two previous road trips—each a collaboration among my own magazine, *Midwest Living*®; the publishers of this book, Globe Pequot Press; and Iowa Public Television—this foray was an opportunity to showcase yet another aspect of what makes me so proud to live in the nation's Heartland: our beautiful and largely unspoiled outdoor surroundings. Within these pages, you'll also see how these natural areas relate to our region's culture, history and people.

I've also spotlighted worthy efforts at preservation and restoration of the environment, as well as outdoor education, recreation and tourism opportunities.

I chose the word "parklands" over "parks" in the title to acknowledge the incredible range that exists in these areas, both in oversight—national, state, county, city—and type: park, forest, preserve, wilderness, refuge, grassland, byway, river, lakeshore. What diversity! Surely the pundit who labeled the middle of the United States "flyover country" never saw the rumpled, tree-covered Ozarks and Black Hills...the raw, rugged shores of Lake Superior and the colossal dunes of Lake Michigan...the serene grasslands of the Great Plains...the eerie landscapes of the Dakota Badlands.

In preparation for my task, I read the works and biographies of great Midwesterners who focused on the topic at hand. I

wish to acknowledge four in particular: preservationist John Muir (1838–1914), wildlife advocate Aldo Leopold (1887–1948), environmentalist Sigurd Olson (1899–1982) and agrarian reformer Louis Bromfield (1896–1956). My guiding lights also included Ernest Oberholtzer, May Thielgaard Watts, J.N. "Ding" Darling and many other Midwest conservation pioneers.

Before I proceed, I have a confession: I love the outdoors on the hiking/biking/swimming/nature-watching level, but I am the antithesis of a rugged camper/hunter/fisherman/survivalist type. I'm also rather phobic. Heights, even when scenic, do not appeal. Confined spaces, especially dark caves, make my palms sweat. And though I am an avid exercise swimmer, I have a pronounced aversion to situations that could lead to drowning or getting nibbled to death by tiny fish lurking in the depths.

Despite all that, this book unexpectedly brought the most inspiring and fun summer of my life. I hiked, bicycled, canoed, sailed, kayaked, climbed and "spelunked" my way across all sorts of Midwest parks. I experienced searing heat, oppressive humidity, torrential rains and drought—a reminder that when it comes to weather, and everything else, nature rules and humanity adapts.

I had a near miss with a series of tornadoes that ripped across eastern Missouri and encountered another illustration of Mother Nature's changeability when sudden 8-foot waves almost swamped our fishing boat on Lake Michigan. My accommodations were as diverse as the weather: cabins and cottages, gracious inns and bed and breakfasts, a guest ranch, a lockkeeper's house, a tent in a wilderness area. Regardless of the accoutrements, the settings were universally splendid.

As always, I returned with a head (and several worn spiral notebooks) full of observations, a good many of which comprise this book. If I were to condense some of the more significant epiphanies into several lessons, they would include these:

■ All environments constantly are evolving; in some instances, humanity can moderate the pace of change, but ultimately, we can never cosset nature. Our planet is remarkably durable at the core but highly fragile on the surface. That said, I learned fire can be a friend to both forest and grassland.

■ Hiking over rocks billions of years old and admiring trees that date back more than three centuries testifies that our perception of our own significance, mine included, is laughably inflated. We would all get along better if we simply would apply the brakes to our lives now and then and experience the natural world together. Embracing nature in an unhurried manner can heal and restore us when we feel weary or broken.

■ The Midwest is far richer in biodiversity than is widely appreciated, and having four distinct seasons only serves to amplify that splendid outdoor symphony.

■ Our parks are increasingly and tragically threatened by funding cuts, overuse (in some instances) and encroaching development. If nothing is done, we risk irreversible losses that will unforgivably deprive future generations of their environmental birthright. Volunteering time and making a financial gift to various "friends of the parks" organizations are two ways we can help. We still owe a great debt to the legacy of Depression-era CCC and WPA park-development projects.

■ Littering or otherwise abusing our parklands is rude; obey the rules. By applying wise management practices, parks and public lands can be husbanded for seemingly divergent yet ultimately compatible purposes, such as conservation, preservation and recreation.

■ Parks should be free to all. Instituting fees or raising existing ones is unfair to some patrons. Many worthy parks are underutilized because we simply don't seek out their charms. We need to create more opportunities for persons with disabilities to enjoy the outdoors.

■ When you visit a park, always begin by checking in at the visitors center to get oriented, pick up a map and flyer and ask the staff any questions. When hiking, biking or otherwise experiencing the great outdoors, be sure to take plenty of water, sunscreen, insect repellent, comfortable layered clothing, a wide-brimmed hat or helmet and a good pair of hiking shoes or boots.

Some of you may challenge my selection of the venues in this book, especially the 40-odd parks I was able to visit personally (one featured parkland per state, as well as several more scouted briefly en route). I want you to know how I arrived at my final destination list:

As much as possible within time and route constraints, I attempted to show the widest range of parks in the region as a whole. This pertained to types of parks as well as to their topography, ecosystems, geology, plant life and wildlife. Activities, amenities, interpretive resources and sheer uniqueness also were criteria. In addition, I tried not to revisit stops from my first two books (and I succeeded in most, but not all instances). Selection of the abbreviated entries in the "More Parklands" section at the end of each chapter adhered to the same principles.

What memories I have! During most of my journey, I relied on a knotty cedar hiking stick acquired at a gift shop in Badlands National Park in South Dakota. That amber-colored talisman now occupies a place of honor in my home. Every time I look at it or pick it up, I recall yet another moment from my great parklands journey. I hope you'll enjoy reading about my adventures and, more important, try to experience firsthand—and to help preserve for future generations—the natural treasures I've tried to describe on these pages.

Dan Kaercher

Dan Kaercher, Editor-in-Chief
Midwest Living® Magazine

ILLINOIS

Garden of the Gods, Shawnee National Forest.

A surprising woodland treasure

THINK "ILLINOIS" and you visualize Chicago and skyscrapers, right? Wrong—at least when it comes to parklands. Stretching about 400 miles from head to toe, this state will give me a glimpse of contrasting environments found in the Midwest Corn Belt and the fringe of the heavily wooded South (after all, the bottom tip of the state is farther south than Louisville and Richmond and closer to Atlanta than Chicago).

Forests are the exception to the rule in the generally flat farm country of north-central Illinois. There, three miles south of I-80 along the Illinois River at Utica (population just under 1,000), I'll stop at one of the Midwest's oldest and best-known state parks, Starved Rock. Then I'll buzz "downstate" via I-57 just past Mount Vernon (population 16,300) to 20-mile-long Rend Lake, a U.S. Army Corps of Engineers recreational paradise that's a regional camping favorite. Finally, almost as far south as I can go and still be in the Midwest, I'll roam the rocky vistas, woodland trails and drowsy Ohio River Valley towns that mark Illinois' sprawling, off-the-beaten-path parkland jewel, Shawnee National Forest.

Starved Rock State Park

My first reaction as I drive the winding entrance road to the rugged, wooded splendor of 2,800-acre Starved Rock State Park? *What's this state park doing here, where there*

Photography by Bob Stefko

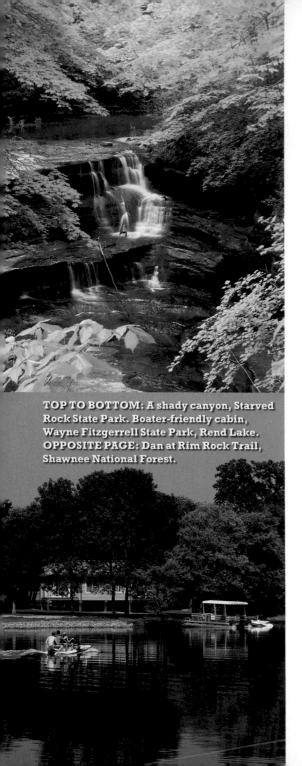

TOP TO BOTTOM: A shady canyon, Starved Rock State Park. Boater-friendly cabin, Wayne Fitzgerrell State Park, Rend Lake. OPPOSITE PAGE: Dan at Rim Rock Trail, Shawnee National Forest.

should be yet more rolling farm fields? I'm mesmerized by craggy, 450 million-year-old St. Peter sandstone bluffs shaped by glacial melt waters that once raced through these canyons and ravines on their way to what's now the Illinois River.

Starved Rock takes its name from an unconfirmed Native American legend: In the 1760s, a band of luckless Illinois Indians was trapped by avenging Ottawa and Potawatomi warriors atop a massive 125-foot bluff overlooking the river valley. When the Illinois' food ran out, they chose to die of thirst and hunger rather than surrender.

At the visitors center, Site Interpreter Toby Miller tells me that Starved Rock was established in 1911. It's on the south bank of the river now tamed by Starved Rock Lock and Dam, visible far below the sandstone outcrops that tower over the valley. Nearby is 2,000-acre Matthiessen State Park, a less-visited but still-worthy geologic and recreational treasure.

On a short and often steep loop that begins near the visitors center, I weave over, through and around some of the park's signature shady canyons. From vistas atop Starved Rock and Eagle Cliff, I gaze down upon the valley that French explorers such as Marquette, Jolliet and La Salle canoed in the late 1600s. A promontory called Lovers Leap memorializes another unsubstantiated but irresistible legend: A young Native American couple from opposing tribes plunged to their deaths rather than part.

Trails here are carefully marked; the environment is fragile. No climbing is permitted. I pass summer-dry waterfalls that I'm told gush forth in spring and after heavy rains. Toby explains that, in environmental terms, this is a relict community, with white pine and white cedar—an ecosystem left behind by retreating glaciers.

This is a busy park, with picnicking, camping, horseback riding, canoeing and

bird-watching. Toby tells me that in January visitors often spot as many as 100 bald eagles feasting in the free-flowing water just below the dam. It's hard to believe I'm just 90 miles from those "urban canyons" of the Chicago loop. Accessibility is one reason this park attracts up to 2 million national and international visitors annually.

I peer down French Canyon, one of 18 such sandstone-sided ravines here, some up to 90 feet deep. They're dense with cold-climate trees, including Canada yew and northern white cedar that appear to cling to bare rock. Ferns, mosses and lichens contribute to the mysterious mood. I'm told that long ago the park's tall white pines were harvested for totem poles and ship masts.

My hike completed, I return to the park's rambling lodge built by the Civilian Conservation Corps (CCC), opened in 1939 and renovated in 1989 (with an indoor pool and sauna). I like the knotty-pine feel still apparent in many of the 71 rooms and 22 cabins—especially the grand original dining room with its huge stone fireplace. Here, three flags hang from the rafters, recalling the nations that have claimed this ground: France, Britain and the United States.

Rend Lake

Rend Lake, just off I-57 at Benton (population 6,900), offers camping as well as water sports, hunting and a host of other outdoor activities. It's 20 miles long and a reliable 10 feet deep on average, 30 feet tops. The reservoir, created by the U.S. Army Corps of Engineers in 1965 primarily to provide potable water and flood control, soon became a recreation magnet that also encompasses the 3,300-acre Wayne Fitzgerrell State Park and the State Fish and Wildlife Area.

Rend Lake Operations Manager Jim Lynch drives me past some of the lake's 700 beautifully groomed campsites. It's generally flat here, but the landscape is accented by native oak, hickory and other trees, plus prairie grasses and wildflowers along an 18-mile hiking and horseback-riding trail. I see RV sites complete with electricity, water and waste hookups; nearby showers and bathrooms; and adjoining pontoon boat landings. The RV area is popular with retirees, youth groups, families here for reunions and weekend campers. On some summer weekends, this area hosts 5,000 campers (private campsites are available, too), among 3 million visitors annually.

At the visitors center, I learn about the U.S. Army Corps of Engineers, who proudly proclaim they are the nation's largest provider of outdoor recreation thanks to projects such as this one (they manage 11 million acres at 460 sites nationally). Dating back to 1775 and the Battle of Bunker Hill, the Corps completed the Panama Canal in 1914 and constructed many locks, dams and levees on the Mississippi and Ohio rivers after the disastrous floods of 1927.

Additional exhibits spotlight the area's mammals, birds, reptiles, amphibians and other critters (Illinois hosts 17,000 kinds of insects alone!). We head to the marina for a boat ride on glassy waters, passing families wading at sandy South Sandusky Beach and anglers trolling in an area where trees were deliberately left in the water for aquatic habitat. Anglers converge here for catfish, crappie, bass, bullhead, carp and sunfish. Other wildlife include white-tailed deer, wild turkeys, pheasant, bobwhite quail, rabbits and squirrels, as well as shorebirds and waterfowl in autumn. Back on shore, we drive over the two-mile-long earthen-embankment dam atop the Big Muddy River, one of the lake's five tributaries.

Jim tells me about the 15,000-square-foot Illinois Artisans Shop nearby, which features arts and crafts made by more than 900 Illinois artisans. Other attractions include a 27-hole golf course, antiques stores and wineries. If camping isn't your style, there's 105-room Rend Lake Resort, within the Wayne Fitzgerrell State Park, where you can lodge in a "hostel" unit that permits you to dock your boat just steps from your room and enjoy a gourmet meal at the classy resort restaurant.

Shawnee National Forest

En route to Shawnee National Forest, named for a Native American tribe that once roamed these hills, I see signs indicating I'm in Little Egypt (also known as Greater Egypt or Egypt): Lake Egypt, the Little Egypt Off Road Motorcycle Club, the Egyptian Health Department and the Greater Egypt Regional Planning Commission. Towns here have names such as Thebes, Karnak and Cairo.

The geographic theory claims the nickname most correctly applies to the flat alluvial floodplain at the southernmost tip of Illinois, where the Ohio meets the Mississippi. The historical explanation is that after a disastrous harvest and severe winter in 1830, settlers from upstate Illinois were forced to travel to this region for grain, just as in the Bible the Israelites trekked to Egypt for food. Nowadays, aside from agriculture (corn and soybeans, mostly) and coal mining, the major industries in the region are outdoor recreation and six prisons.

My first destination is the sleepy Pope County Seat of Golconda (the name purportedly means town of gold, probably referring to prosperity once derived from river trade). The town was founded in 1816 when the Ohio River, now girded by a massive levee, was America's primary route west. These days, the entire hamlet of 750 is listed on the National Register of Historic Places, its almost two-century history serving as a reminder that, unlike most Midwest states, Illinois was settled from the bottom up, not from east to west.

I check out my unique lodging: a former lockkeeper's house perched beside a tranquil lakelike stretch of the river known as the Smithland Pool, which extends 40 miles north of the Smithland Locks and Dam, itself about 18 miles south of here. It's one of four such residences built from 1928 to 1930 and later abandoned (along with Lock and Dam No. 51) upon completion of the new Smithland project in 1980.

Across the river, to the east, are the green hills of Kentucky. At daybreak, a big orange sun will set those hills and the river ablaze. The sturdy brick lockkeeper's house, restored in 2001 and now managed by local tourism volunteers, is cozily furnished in the new-old manner you might find in your grandmother's house (although I doubt she'd have that inviting hot tub on the screened front porch).

I enjoy the front-row view of the Ohio River barges chugging past, scudding as far as Pittsburgh upriver and downriver to New Orleans on the Mississippi, loaded with coal, grain, gravel and chemicals. At one time, fluorspar (Illinois' official mineral) was mined nearby and shipped on those barges for use in aluminum, steel, enamel, glass and toothpaste. In 1803, Explorers Lewis and Clark and their men passed this spot.

After my typical hearty breakfast at the Dari Barr cafe on Main Street, I rendezvous with my tourism-volunteer hosts at the Pope County Historical Museum, housed in a former hardware store on Main Street. Jovial Sharon Tuttle tells me she and her husband, who came here from east-central Illinois, started vacationing here after a 1987 *Midwest Living*® article spotlighted the Shawnee region. They decided to take the early-retirement plunge here in 2000. Louise Burkhart is another "newcomer" who came here with her husband from Kentucky about 30 years ago. Both clearly can't wait to show off the place, starting

with the museum, jam-packed with hand-stitched quilts, vintage photos, antiques and other memorabilia—as well as a giant mastodon tusk uncovered in 1926 during the construction of Lock and Dam No. 51.

Golconda's streets are quiet on weekdays, but its marina draws hundreds of weekend visitors. Fall brings hordes of deer hunters. This area is Illinois' self-proclaimed deer-hunting capital; drivers should be alert, especially at dusk when it's feeding time, and hikers need to check for ticks. History is evident on Main Street in the square-steepled 1869 Presbyterian church, the third edifice built by the state's first Presbyterian congregation, organized in 1819. The 1872 brick courthouse presides just a block away. Around a corner, there's the 1837 Buel House, a partially restored, clapboard-faced log home, the only surviving structure in town that witnessed a great tragedy during the winter of 1838–39:

Thousands of Cherokee Indians from the Southeast passed through Golconda, having been forced to relocate to eastern Oklahoma. The civilized Cherokees had been cruelly displaced by the federal government, which confiscated their highly coveted lands in North Carolina and Georgia. Many of them froze, starved or died of disease just across the river from Golconda, unable to secure passage on the ferry from Kentucky. Today, that heartrending trek is appropriately known here and elsewhere as the Trail of Tears.

A Multifaceted Forest

It's going to be over 100 degrees today! "And weather isn't the only thing that can make life interesting here," Sharon says. "We're on the New Madrid Fault—you know, the one that caused the earthquake that made the Mississippi flow backward back in 1812," she reminds me. "But I've only felt one tremor so far." The New Madrid

quakes during the winter of 1811–12, centered in Southeast Missouri, would have measured 8.0 on today's Richter scale and were felt over an area of 1 million square miles. "We're supposed to have another big quake one of these days," Sharon says, nonplussed. Hmmm....

The hodgepodge that is Shawnee National Forest and adjoining state parks and historic sites encompasses 285,000 acres across parts of 11 Illinois counties, covering 150 miles from the Ohio to the Mississippi. A painterly canvas of trees and rocks veils 1,250 miles of paved and unpaved roads and trails that thrill hikers, campers, climbers, mountain bikers, horseback riders, hunters, anglers and nature lovers in general. The federal government first began acquiring depleted land hereabouts from Depression-battered farmers back in 1933; President Franklin D. Roosevelt signed the official national forest designation in 1939. I'm concentrating on the more-visited eastern part of the forest in two counties: Pope and Hardin.

The many types of parklands in the Midwest include national scenic byways, lakeshores and rivers; state and national parks, forests, preserves and grasslands; and recreation areas, wildlife refuges, and U.S. Army Corps of Engineers reservoirs. To many, it may not be apparent that there is a noteworthy distinction between national parks and national forests such as Shawnee.

It all dates back to before the turn of the 20th century, when the federal government first began setting aside large tracts of land for the public good. Conflict emerged between "preservationists"—personified by Wisconsin native John Muir, who ultimately became known as the father of our national parks system—and "conservationists"—led by Gifford Pinchot of Pennsylvania, later the nation's first Forest Service director. Preservation advocates

CLOCKWISE, FROM TOP LEFT: (All taken at Shawnee National Forest) Sunrise on the Ohio near Golconda. A red-spotted purple butterfly. View from Trigg Tower. Young trail riders near Elizabethtown.

wanted those federal lands left intact as much as possible. Conservationists wanted the land managed for a variety of uses, such as mining and lumbering, in addition to preservation and recreation. The National Forest Service was founded in 1905, the National Park Service in 1916.

Fortunately, both camps seem to be getting along relatively well now. America's national forests alone currently number 155, with 20 related national grasslands. That's 190 million acres, an area larger than Texas—and 8.5 percent of the United States. Like most national forests in the eastern half of the country, Shawnee was created long after settlement and still is acquiring public land from private owners. A number of existing parks, attractions and small communities also lie within what's broadly termed the forest.

First is Dixon Springs State Park, about 10 miles east of Golconda, once the site of a small frontier settlement (named for an early resident) and, later, a Victorian-era resort hotel. The springs, known as "Great Medicine Waters" by warring Native Americans who considered this neutral ground, were thought to cure everything from physical ailments to frayed nerves. Three small country churches still stand near ghosts of a general store, post office, blacksmith shop and gristmill; these days there's also a campground and a swimming pool.

Among the trees I see in this region are oak, hickory, cypress, gum, pine, sycamore, beech, walnut, persimmon, birch, maple, willow and Kentucky coffee. Louise tells me I should visit in springtime, when dogwood, redbud and catalpa bloom like mad, along with wildflowers such as jack-in the pulpit, violet, lady's slipper, sweet William, May apple and foxglove. I'd give my eye-teeth to see it all ablaze in autumn as well.

More Forest Surprises

Next, we take in a sweeping high-rise view of the forest from Trigg Tower, a slowly rusting defunct CCC fire tower. Then Louise proclaims, "We're going to see a cypress swamp!" We pull off State-146 and, at the Grantsburg Ecological Area, view a spooky world of cypress, tupelo, oak, birch and willow trees standing in water carpeted with neon-green duckweed, created several years ago by the beaver dams I spot. A great blue heron flaps away from a gnarly tree limb. Captivated, I vow to make time on my next visit for the larger Little Black Slough in the Cache River State Natural Area near Vienna, about 40 miles from here.

Soon, we're bobbing up and down country roads past small farmhouses and pointy-leafed mimosa trees laden with rose-colored blossoms on our way to the northwest corner of Pope County. At the forest's Bell Smith Springs (named for another early settler), I descend a narrow stone staircase between high rock walls to a spot where four streams converge. In this scenic canyon thrive many of the area's 700 species of plants and a lot of butterflies. "That's 20 percent of all types of plants found in the entire state of Illinois!" Sharon exclaims.

We head to Bear Branch Horse Resort in the Lusk Creek Canyon area, one of about

10 such "horse camps" hereabouts. Over a dessert of delicious blackberry cobbler in the resort's rustic Log Cabin Restaurant, I chat with cowboy-outfitted owner Dick Manders, another former visitor who relocated to the area—he's from Milwaukee.

Trail riding is one of Shawnee's star attractions, the focus of a nine-day confab each summer that draws thousands of horse enthusiasts from throughout the United States. "We're the fifth-ranking state in the nation when it comes to horses, with 77,000 horse owners, 350,000 riders and almost 220,000 horses. That's even more than in Kentucky!" Dick says. "It's all very important to our economy." Dick's property, which adjoins the forest, offers 80 campsites, seven cabins and a 40-stall horse barn. With 250 miles of trails, you and "Old Paint" can escape the modern world for days on end in the Shawnee region.

Back to my own trail! Human habitation in Shawnee National Forest has been traced as far back as 11,500 years. I'm visiting a spot called Millstone Bluff, hiking a one-mile trail atop a 320-foot wooded sandstone escarpment. Interpretive signs explain the sights. I'm moved by one of 20 crude limestone coffins buried here by Mississippian-culture Native Americans sometime between 1250 and 1450 A.D. Sadly, many of the graves were vandalized long ago for their pottery and other artifacts.

There's an embankment of hand-laid rocks designed as a bulwark. Shallow depressions denote what was a small village of pole-framed, grass-covered family homes with a community building and plaza. Archaeology students from the University of Illinois are excavating a nearby dig to piece together the area's story. Before I leave, I stop at an overlook and gaze upon some petroglyphs carved into a flat stone, which along with such relics as arrowheads and stone tools, offer more clues. The faintly visible line drawings depict a spider, thunderbirds, pipes and axes, a turkey and tracks, an athlete and a circle and cross.

Time to call it a day, but not before a refreshing stop at the Lake Glendale Recreation Area, where the Forest Service offers campsites, a bathhouse and a big swimming beach. I nudge a paddleboat out onto the water and enjoy a frozen-pickle-juice snack, which apparently was just an off-the-wall idea that caught on here. Especially on this sweltering afternoon, I heartily approve of the cold and tangy concoction.

Dazzling Garden of the Gods

My second fabulous sunrise along the Ohio portends another scorcher, as I begin the Hardin County segment of my Shawnee National Forest visit. My host is Rhonda Belford, an energetic country-western singer/songwriter who also is running for the Illinois state legislature. I'm delighted she can take time to show me around the hills where she's lived all her life, as has my other host, Bob Winchester, a genial former state legislator and deputy governor.

Rhonda and Bob are on the board of the Ohio River National Scenic Byway, yet another of the myriad parkland entities hereabouts. The byway extends 967 miles

Country Apple Cobbler

Donna Norton, owner along with her husband Don of Bay City General Store & Lodging near Golconda, prepares this cobbler using strong tea, because "that's the way my Granny Ann and great-grandmother made it."

½ of a 15-ounce package refrigerated
    rolled, unbaked piecrust (1 crust)
1 cup all-purpose flour
½ cup packed brown sugar
1½ teaspoons ground cinnamon
¼ teaspoon ground cloves
½ cup butter
1 cup granulated sugar
1 teaspoon ground nutmeg
¼ teaspoon salt
10 cups sliced, peeled tart apples
3 tablespoons butter, cut into small pieces
2 tablespoons strong tea, cooled
    Powdered sugar icing (optional)

Roll piecrust into a 13-inch circle; trim to 10×10 inches. Place piecrust in 9×9×2-inch baking pan; prick. Line with double thickness of foil. Bake in a 450° oven 8 minutes. Remove foil. Bake 5 minutes more or until golden. Cool. Reduce oven to 350°.

For topping: In a small bowl, combine flour, brown sugar, ½ teaspoon of cinnamon and cloves. Cut in ½ cup butter until mixture resembles coarse crumbs; set aside.

For filling: Combine granulated sugar, 1 teaspoon cinnamon, nutmeg and salt. Add apple slices. Gently toss until coated.

Transfer apple mixture to pastry-lined baking pan; dot with the 3 tablespoons butter. Pour tea over apples; sprinkle with topping. Bake about 60 minutes or until apples are tender, filling is bubbly and topping is golden. Remove from oven. Cool on a wire rack for 30 minutes. If you like, drizzle icing over warm cobbler. Serve at room temperature. *Makes 9 servings.*

through Ohio, Indiana and Illinois, 188 miles of it here in Illinois, and much of that threading through Shawnee National Forest. It passes through a fascinating collection of parks and forests, sleepy river towns, prehistoric Native American archaeological sites, Underground Railroad stops and other natural and historic attractions.

Soon I'm viewing a sign that reads "Caution: High Cliffs Ahead," announcing the forest's premier scenic attraction—a jumble of weathered, knobby sandstone outcrops collectively known as Garden of the Gods. I've long looked forward to seeing the panorama in person—but I didn't realize I'd be so spellbound by these rumpled, tree-covered hills that draw my eyes 25 miles off into the misty horizon.

Rhonda introduces me to District Ranger Jeff Seefeldt, a Wisconsin native and 20-year Forest Service veteran, who offers a brief geology lesson about how aeons ago this was a vast ocean bottom carpeted with sediment, sand and mud that eventually turned into rock. About 320 million years ago, that sedimentary rock was uplifted into mountains that in turn eroded into the 130-foot-high, multilayered knobs here today.

After I rip myself from the breathtaking view, I study the shapes of these crags, some named for the figures they resemble, such as Camel Rock, Anvil Rock and Devil's Smokestack. Jeff points out how one rock resembles a monkey's face, another a turtle, yet another an old man's profile. "Just gaze at them, the way you'd look up at clouds in the sky," he advises. Jeff is right!

I coax myself out to the edge of several of the round-shouldered rocks. It's a long way down! A short walk takes me through a narrow passage called Fat Man's Squeeze (yes, I make it through). Nearby, Jeff points out a sandstone rock face textured with intriguing reddish-brown whorls called "oyster-shell swirls" (scientifically known as liesegang

bands), formed by streaks of iron oxide that have weathered through the ages.

I ask Jeff about the plant and animal life in this junglelike world. It's primarily an oak-hickory forest ecosystem, with about 50,000 acres of nonnative white pine planted by the CCC mainly for erosion control. "This is where the North meets the South in botanical terms—we have incredible diversity. There are white-tailed deer, bobcats, foxes, skunks, possums, raccoon, squirrels, wild turkeys, quail and songbirds, and plenty of bass, bluegill, crappie and catfish. Hunting and fishing are big here." What does Jeff like best? "Just exploring the woods. And the history," he says. "Once, I came across an elaborate carving in stone done by a man who'd lived here back in 1861. I did some research. He fought on the Union side in the Civil War."

Just 15 miles east of Garden of the Gods, there's another natural area my hosts want me to see: 230-acre Pounds Hollow. Soon I'm hiking a flagstone walkway on the Rim Rock Trail in the Rim Rock National Recreation Area to a secluded valley formed by yet more sandstone monoliths that sheltered the forest's early inhabitants. The basin later attracted settlers who used Oxlot Cave, a high-walled rock canyon, as a natural corral for their horses, cattle and oxen.

Pirates! Murder! Mayhem!

We're back near the Ohio in 200 acres of emerald bluffs and hills just east of the village of Cave-In-Rock (population 310). Before we visit the legendary cave that gave the town and this state park their names, I sample a local signature: succulent fried catfish, followed by another sweet-tart fresh blackberry cobbler and ice cream at Kaylor's Restaurant in the park. (Berry picking and mushroom hunting are two favorite Shawnee pastimes.) The restaurant and four newer duplex state-park cabins here offer

CLOCKWISE, FROM TOP: (All taken at Garden of the Gods, Shawnee National Forest) Hikers savoring the view. Ranger assisting a climber. Aerial perspective. Liesegang bands resembling oyster-shell swirls.

splendid views of the Ohio River below.

Soon, Rhonda nudges Bob and me toward steps that lead down an embankment and path to the 55-foot arched opening of the infamous Cave-In-Rock. Rhonda shares the cave's story of "pirates, murder and mayhem," describing scoundrels Samuel Mason, the Harpe brothers and a band of counterfeiters, among other miscreants who often were abetted by the townspeople.

From 1797 to the 1830s, the rogues lured unsuspecting emigrants traveling down the Ohio in flatboats into their lair with promises of libations, food and lodgings, then robbed and murdered them (even stuffing the bodies with stones and dumping them into the river!). The legend lives on in movies such as *How the West Was Won* (1962) and Disney's *Davy Crockett and the River Pirates* (1956). Rhonda leads us into the limestone cave, which is 500 feet deep and 25 feet high. There's a big natural skylight, but it's still damp and spooky inside.

Back in daylight, we head to Elizabethtown (population 360), another historic village on the Ohio. Here I spot the five-room, state-owned Rose Hotel, high above the river, with an inviting Southern-ish, double-tiered veranda and a gazebo on the lawn. We're on our way to a final historical site in the forest, a 1967 reconstruction of a towering (42 feet high) limestone, charcoal-fired 1839 pig-iron furnace, the first one built in the state. During the Civil War, much of its output was shipped upriver to become Union cannonballs.

There's not much going on here now, but I study the interpretive signs to better understand the iron-making process. Not far away, swimmers giggle and shout in a gently flowing creek, as each takes a turn at holding onto a fat rope and swinging over the water. If only I could join them here in yet another magical corner of Shawnee National Forest…

THIS PAGE: (Both taken at Shawnee National Forest) Sunset near Golconda on the Ohio River. **OPPOSITE PAGE:** Dan as Atlas, Bell Smith Springs.

Dan's Travel Journal

FEATURED STOP

Shawnee National Forest 280,000 acres between the Mississippi and Ohio Rivers in southern Illinois. This oasis amid farmlands harbors treasures from ancient bald cypress swamps and magnificent bluffs to backcountry wildernesses and a wealth of wildlife, including 250 bird species and 109 kinds of fish. Trek the forest on foot (the popular trail network at Garden of the Gods fits any skill level), on horseback (250 miles of horse trails) or drive along the 70-mile stretch of the Ohio River National Scenic Byway that traverses it. Other outdoor options include a dozen campgrounds, fishing in streams or 2,700 acres of lakes, swimming at beaches, birding, boating and hunting. Get maps and information at forest headquarters in Harrisburg (800/699-6637) or at ranger stations in Jonesboro and Murphysboro (western) and Vienna (eastern).

Lodging, Dining and More

Bay City General Store and Lodging Bay City (10 miles south of Golconda). This refurbished 1915 general store with original potbellied stove stocks bulk candy, antiques, collectibles and gifts. Lodgings upstairs or in a cabin overlooking the Ohio River (618/683-4305).

Bear Branch Horse Resort Eddyville. Named for a creek in Shawnee National Forest, Bear Branch features one-stop accommodations for horse and rider, including trail rides, box stalls and corrals, 80 campsites, seven cabins and great grub in the hilltop Log Cabin Restaurant (618/672-4249).

Cave-In-Rock State Park Cave-In-Rock. This 320-acre, heavily wooded park, named for its intriguing limestone cave, climbs high bluffs overlooking the Ohio River. Full-service restaurant and eight guesthouses on-site, plus hiking trails, fishing, boating and modern campsites (618/289-4325).

Dari Barr Golconda. Situated at Main Street's four-way stop, serving daily breakfast, plate-lunch specials and dinner, cooked for two decades by owner Clara Warfield (618/683-4878).

Dixon Springs State Park Ten miles west of Golconda. Once a favorite Native American camping grounds and a 19th-century health spa, this 800-acre park still draws a following with its rock formations, cliffs, canyons, springs and giant century-old trees, along with campsites, hiking trails, hunting and a swimming pool with waterslide (618/949-3394).

Lake Glendale Recreation Area Twelve miles west of Golconda. Eighty-acre lake offering swimming, fishing, hiking and bicycling trails, boat rental and 60 campsites (618/949-3807).

Lock & Dam 51 Homes Golconda. Overnight lodging along the Ohio River in four antiques-furnished lockkeepers' homes built in the 1920s. $$–$$$$ (618/683-6702).

Ohio River Scenic Byway. Starting at the southernmost border of Illinois in Cairo and passing through Shawnee National Forest, this 967-mile paved route flows alongside the Ohio River to New Haven and on to Indiana and Ohio (800/248-4373).

Pope County Historical Museum Golconda. In a 1906 hardware store, historic artifacts trace the county's past as a bustling early-20th-century river port (618/683-9702).

The Rose Hotel Elizabethtown. Owned by the Illinois Historic Preservation Agency, a five-room hotel built in 1812 on limestone river bluffs; country breakfast included. $$ (618/287-2872).

Related Area Event

Nine-Day Trail Ride Pope County, last Saturday in July—More than 1,000 horses and mules, along with their riders, gather at a base

camp in the heart of the Shawnee National Forest (near One Horse Gap Lake) for trail riding. Groups set out on their own day trips (maps available) and meet back at the camp for live music and food, tack vendors, horse shows and overnight camping (618/683-2105).

More Information

Golconda Main Street (618/683-6246, www.mainstreetgolconda.net).

Illinois Bureau of Tourism (800/226-6632, enjoyillinois.com).

Southernmost Illinois Tourism Bureau (800/248-4373, www.southernmostillinois.com).

DAN'S OTHER STOPS

(See also More Parks section that follows.) Rend Lake Benton (618/439-7430) and Wayne Fitzgerrell State Park Whittington (681/629-2320), Starved Rock State Park Utica (815/667-4726).

Lodging, Dining and More

Southern Illinois Art & Artisans Center Rend Lake. Fine crafts for sale by 900 Illinois artisans, plus workshops, changing exhibits and annual festivals (618/629-2220).

More Illinois Parks

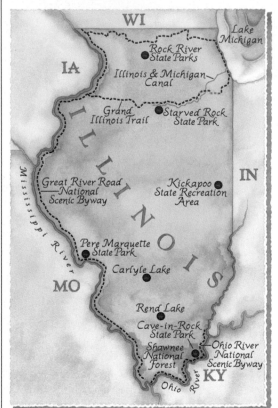

Carlyle Lake

The almost endless blue waters of Illinois' largest man-made lake seem like a mirage amid the Illinois prairie and farmland (50 miles west of St. Louis). At this popular getaway, sailboats and powerboats glide across 15-mile-long Carlyle Lake, and houseboats anchor in quiet coves.

Along the shore, you'll find swimming beaches, forested nature trails and campgrounds at two state parks (Eldon Hazlet and South Shore) and two state recreation areas. Eldon Hazlet State Park claims the largest campground in Illinois' state park system (364 sites on 3,000 acres). Visitors also stay in modern cabins. As another option, try renting a houseboat. You can swim, fish and sightsee along the lake, then overnight in an out-of-the-way spot.

Thanks to the wide-open water and reliable winds, sailing is outstanding at this U.S. Army Corps of Engineers' reservoir. On some summer days, spectators line the shore to watch regattas, some Olympic-sanctioned events. Marinas around the lake rent various craft, including sailboats. Just south of the lake, the bustling town of Carlyle draws visitors for dining and golf.

Contact: Carlyle Lake Chamber of Commerce (618/594-4015, carlyletoday.com). Carlyle Lake Corps of Engineers (618/594-2484, carlylelake.com). Nearest lodgings: in Carlyle (contact above).

Grand Illinois Trail

More than a decade ago, visionaries began planning to link existing bicycle trails and develop new ones from Chicago to Illinois' western state line and back. Between Lake Michigan and the Mississippi, the Grand Illinois Trail makes a nearly 500-mile loop across northern Illinois. When completed, the trail will be among the nation's longest.

Today, cyclists can pedal 320 miles on established trails and another 150 miles along country roads. The route follows existing bike trails along Chicago's riverfront and the Illinois & Michigan Canal State Trail, where you can savor history and stop at six state parks. Other segments travel through rural landscapes. Beside the Mississippi, north from the Quad Cities to Savanna, sheer palisades edge the roadway.

You can ride a segment of the trail or the whole route, stopping at restaurants, accommodations and campgrounds in cities, small towns and state parks along the way. For the past four years, bicycle enthusiasts have gathered in June to pedal portions of the loop on the seven-day Grand Illinois Trail and Parks Ride.

Contact: IDNR Grand Illinois Trail Coordinator (815/625-2968). League of Illinois Bicyclists (630/978-0583, bikelib .org). Nearest lodgings: all along the route (800/226-6632, enjoyillinois.com).

Great River Road National Scenic Byway

Illinois' section of this national scenic byway traces the ever-changing Mississippi River landscape. The 557-mile route links memorable vistas with the region's heritage, intriguing towns and cities.

Toward the southern end of the byway, plan to visit the ancient burial sites at Cahokia Mounds State Historic Site. Then, journey on to Nauvoo near the route's midsection to tour a refurbished Mormon community. Near St. Louis, you'll pass soaring riverside cliffs. Traveling north, bluffs hug the road at Mississippi Palisades State Park near Savanna. Homes in Quincy showcase historical architecture. In picturesque Galena, bed and breakfasts abound, plus more than 100 shops and historic sites such as the home of Ulysses S. Grant.

Short detours lead to historic villages such as Maeystown, a German settlement where 60 stone buildings date to the 1800s. But best of all, you're never far from the river. Pick a park for a picnic with a view, or just gaze at the water and boats passing by.

Contact: Great River Road Scenic Byway in Illinois (877/477-7007, greatriverroad -illinois.org). Cahokia Mounds State Historic Site (618/346-5160, cahokiamounds .com). Galena (877/464-2536, galenaorg). Maeystown (618/458-6660, maeystown .com). Nauvoo (877/628-8661, beautiful nauvoo.com). Quincy (800/978-4748, quincy- cvb.org). Nearest lodgings: in communities all along the byway (contacts above); for others, Illinois Bureau of Tourism (800/226-6632, enjoyillinois.com).

Illinois & Michigan Canal

In the mid-1800s, the Illinois &Michigan (I&M) Canal, a 96-mile waterway joining the Illinois River and Lake Michigan, put a small trading center called Chicago on the map. Today, a 61-mile state trail follows the canal's old towpaths, linking parklands and towns. To explore the I&M, head for Lockport, home of Lock No. 1 and the canal's original offices, plus a museum tracing the waterway's past. The nearby Gaylord Building houses a visitors center for the trail, which cyclists, hikers and cross-country skiers travel year-round. The path stretches from Channahon State Park southwest of Lockport to near LaSalle and Lock No. 14, restored to its 1848 working condition.

Just west of Joliet at the town of Channahon, anglers line up along Locks 6 and 7. Nearby, the restored lockkeeper's cottage provides a peek at 1850s life. From Channahon, the trail links a series of state parks. Goose Lake Prairie State Natural Area, a 2,500-plus-acre enclave accessible from the trail at Morris, includes the largest stand of tallgrass prairie in Illinois.

Contact: Illinois Department of Natural Resources (815/625-2968, dnr.state.il.us).

TOP TO BOTTOM: Up a lazy river, Sugar River Forest Preserve. Autumn-burnished bluffs at Mississippi Palisades State Park.

LEFT TO RIGHT: Black Hawk Statue, Lowden State Park. Bridge spanning the Illinois & Michigan Canal. "Boatel" accommodations, Wayne Fitzgerrell State Park, Rend Lake.

Nearest lodgings: in LaSalle (815/223-0227, ivaced.org), Lockport (815/838-0549, lockport.org) and Morris (815/942-0113, city.mornet.org).

Kickapoo State Recreation Area

Strip mining in the late 1800s scarred land along the Middle Fork of the Vermilion River in east-central Illinois. More than 2,800 acres have been reclaimed as a state recreation area just west of Danville. It took nature—and humans—years to create the first park in the nation on strip-mined land. Cottonwood, ash and cherry trees have obscured the naked ridges, and stagnant waters are clear again. Surrounded by prairie, the recreation area includes 22 deepwater ponds for fishing, forested uplands and bottomlands. Wildlife and wildflowers attract hikers to 15 miles of trails.

Canoeing the Middle Fork of the Vermilion River, designated a federal and state scenic river, is a popular pastime (canoes for rent). It's an easy paddle, with limestone and sandstone bluffs towering along the banks. In bottomlands, you might spot herons and wild turkeys. The park office supplies a birding list. Visitors can picnic at sites with shelters and stay at two campgrounds.

Contact: Illinois Department of Natural Resources (217/442-4915, dnr.state.il.us). Nearest lodgings: in Danville (800/383-4386, danvillecvb.com).

Pere Marquette State Park

The name of this wooded, bluff-filled park honors Father Jacques Marquette. In 1673, he and Louis Jolliet became the first Europeans to set foot on this land, which would become a playground for vacationers not far from the confluence of the Illinois and Mississippi rivers near Grafton (30 miles northeast of St. Louis).

History runs deep at the 8,000-acre park, where the Civilian Conservation Corps built the huge timber-and-stone Pere Marquette Lodge. Stay in modern hotel rooms there or at park campgrounds. You can dine on home-style fare such as fried chicken and catfish dinners before settling in beside the massive fireplace in the lodge great-room or challenging other players on the world's largest chessboard (12 feet square).

Though almost everyone explores the shops in nearby Grafton, it's easy to fill your days at the park. Visitors hike 12 miles of forested trails and ride horses from the stables. An indoor swimming pool, sauna and whirlpool, plus exercise and game rooms provide other options. You also can learn about the Illinois River, its wildlife and local history at the visitors center.

Contact: Pere Marquette State Park (618/786-3323, dnr.state.il.us). Nearest lodgings: in Alton, Elsah and Grafton (800/258-6645, visitalton.com).

Rend Lake

This huge U.S. Army Corps of Engineers' reservoir, developed as a water source for southern Illinois, has become a favorite for fishing, boating, swimming and camping. Some 20,000 acres of public lands, including five state recreation areas and a state park, surround the 19,000-acre lake (15 miles south of Mt. Vernon).

Three-quarters of Wayne Fitzgerrell State Park, where hickory forests intersperse with farmland, borders the lake. At the heart of the 3,300-acre park, the Rend Lake Resort and Conference Center includes a restaurant, pool, cabins and lodge rooms, where you can cast fishing lines from your deck.

Everything from rafts and personal watercraft to powerboats and houseboats is for rent at lake marinas. Swimmers head for two public beaches. Hiking, cycling and equestrian trails run through the recreation areas. At Gun Creek State Recreation Area on the lake's east side, visitors can play 27 holes at the Rend Lake Golf Course, rated among the Midwest's best public courses. Towns around the lake, including Benton and Whittington, cater to vacationers with shopping, dining, lodgings and more golf.

Contact: Rend Lake Resort and Conference Center (800/633-3341, dnr.stat.il.us). Rend Lake Tourism Bureau (618/439-7430, rendlake.com). Nearest lodgings: in Benton, Sesser, West Frankfort and Whittington (800/661-9998, enjoyillinois.com).

Rock River State Parks

The forested tapestry that Sauk Chief Blackhawk once called home endures in Illinois' rugged northwestern corner. Three state parks supply a spectacular look at nature not far from the Rock River near Oregon (30 miles southeast of Rockford). From a wooded bluff in Lowden State Park, a 50-foot-tall sculpture known as Black Hawk Statue honors the region's first residents. Visitors can camp, hike four miles of trails and boat on the Rock River at this small park (boat rentals in Oregon).

Just downriver, plan to climb the 200 steps at Castle Rock State Park for far-reaching river valley views. You can picnic riverside and hike six miles of trails through ravines and forests at this 2,000-acre park (no camping). Spring and Pine creeks run past moss-covered bluffs west of Oregon at smaller White Pines Forest State Park. Seven miles of trails lead through the woods. You can camp or stay in cabins amid one of the state's last stands of virgin pines. The lodge restaurant serves meals.

Contact: Castle Rock State Park (815/732-7329, dnr.state.il.us). Lowden State Park (815/732-6828, dnr.state.il.us). White Pines State Park (815/946-3717, dnr.state.il.us). Nearest lodgings: in Oregon (815/732-2100, oregonil.com).

Shawnee National Forest

(See previous section of this chapter.)

Starved Rock State Park

You might not expect to see deep ravines and tumbling waterfalls tucked into the Illinois prairie, but this popular state park includes both. Southeast of the central Illinois communities of LaSalle and Peru near I-80, 18 canyons dramatically slice through tree-covered sandstone bluffs along the Illinois River.

Melting glaciers and water erosion formed the natural wonders at this 2,700-acre park. Along four miles of trails amid moss-covered sandstone walls, hikers feel the mist from waterfalls. You're bound to see wildlife and lots of birds as you walk an additional 15 miles of trails. Visitors can camp but often choose modern hotel rooms at the stone-and-log Starved Rock Lodge and Conference Center. Built in the 1930s, the lodge includes an indoor pool and giant lobby fireplace, along with Native American artifacts, rugs and artwork. The decor seems fitting: The park takes its name from a legendary tale about a band of Illiniwek starving atop a bluff here while under attack by a rival tribe.

Contact: Starved Rock State Park (815/667-4726, dnr.state.il.us). Nearest lodgings: outside the park in LaSalle (815/223-0227, ivaced.org).

INDIANA

Dan hiking waterlily-carpeted Blackwell Pond in Hoosier National Forest.

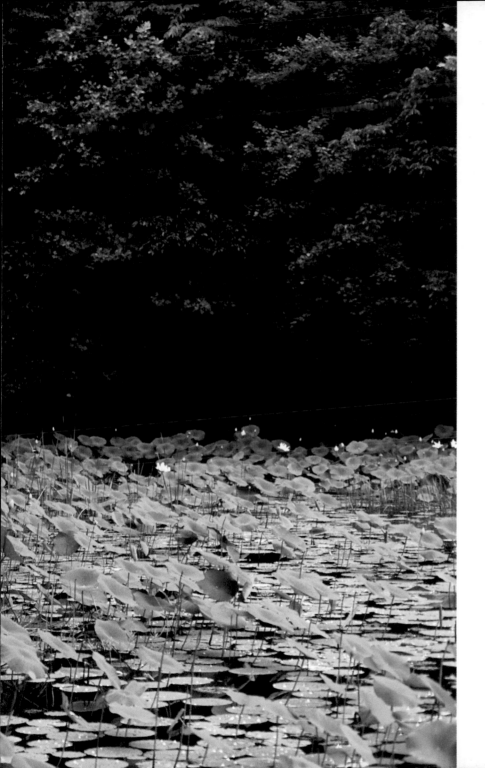

Wilderness camping adventures

TWISTING BYWAYS. Scruffy pastures and checkerboard fields. Barely standing barns. Country hamlets. Hardwood trees everywhere. Southern Indiana is one of my favorite Midwest escapes. On this trip, its backroads will lead me to secluded corners of far-flung Hoosier National Forest, whose jagged boundaries encompass a good share of nine south-central Indiana counties.

Indiana is (just barely) a Great Lakes state: About 40 miles of sandy Lake Michigan beaches take a watery bite out of its northwest corner; half of that densely populated corridor hosts Indiana Dunes National Lakeshore, where I'll begin my journey. Some 330 miles later in the far-south end of the state, I'll complete my Hoosier sojourn at a pair of parks honoring the great leader who spent most of his boyhood here.

Indiana Dunes

Arcing eastward from Chicago, northwestern Indiana's Lake Michigan shore is a labyrinth of highways that whizzes travelers past Gary (population 102,700) and other sometimes gritty communities still struggling to reverse a half-century of industrial decline. I turn off congested I-80 at Porter and head several miles north to explore an unexpected 15,000-acre petri dish of biodiversity: beaches, dunes, forests, wetlands and prairies in America's first national lakeshore, which was established in 1966.

Photography by Bob Stefko

LEFT TO RIGHT: Nancy Hanks Lincoln's grave site, Lincoln Boyhood National Memorial. Indiana Dunes National Lakeshore. (Both taken at Hoosier National Forest) Nebo Ridge Trail. Lake Monroe shore, Hardin Ridge Recreation Area.

I make an informational stop at the Dorothy Buell Memorial Visitors Center near the heart of the elongated park, which also enfolds the smaller Indiana Dunes State Park. Then Chief Ranger Mike Bremer and I drive toward Michigan City (population 32,900) at the east end. Minutes later, we're climbing the gentler, greener south slope of Mount Baldy, the park's tallest dune at 126 feet. From the lofty summit, a favorite of hang gliders, we look northward across fine, off-white sand beaches dotted with windblown marramgrass to the foot of 300-mile-long Lake Michigan.

Proximity to metro Chicago, 50 miles northwest, makes Indiana Dunes one of the Midwest's most popular national parks; 2.2 million visitors annually relax and play on these relatively uncrowded beaches and 14 miles of trails. I find it hard to believe that 5 million people reside within 50 miles of these vast dunes!

Our hike up the woodsy back side of the sand monolith leads us past white oak and cottonwood trees and holly bushes. This is a living dune, constantly reconfiguring from the onslaught of waves, wind—and people. "We want people to enjoy the lakeshore, but we don't want them to love this environment to death," Mike says. "We have a great environmental-preservation and -education program." He cites a rookery that hosts great blue herons and the fact that threatened species such as the Karner blue butterfly and pitcher's thistle thrive here within view of Chicago's distant skyline on the west and a giant Michigan City power plant to our east.

Soon I'm on a prearranged tour with 15 other park visitors, led by Interpretive Park Ranger Jeff Kissell. We caravan about eight miles inland from the visitors center, as our destination isn't contiguous with the rest of the lakeshore. We park and enter a fragile, fenced-off wonderland: Pinhook Bog, named for the local township. One of two bogs that are part of the lakeshore, it is, in effect, a highly acidic, 50-foot-deep clay-lined bowl, or kettle, created when a huge chunk of ice broke off from a glacier and melted. Jeff explains that a bog such as this is virtually sealed off, unlike a swamp that replenishes itself as water flows in and out. The result is a realm of quirky plants that have adapted and now thrive here.

Our group slowly walks the "floating," jiggling boardwalk to the center of the bog, which Jeff tells us is a 4-foot-thick mat of sphagnum moss and peat. From that acidic moss—so absorbent when dry that Native Americans used it for diapering their babies—sprouts a dense, eerie assortment of trees (tamarack, pine, larch and oak), shrubs (wild blueberry and poison sumac) and flowers, including the sundew plant, which traps insects in a sticky goo it secretes, then "digests" them.

Jeff talks about the perfectly preserved human remains, such as those of Denmark's famous 2,350-year-old Tolland Man, that have been recovered from bogs like this in northern Europe. He speculates that the word "bog" may be where the term "boogeyman" originated. Hmmm…now I'm thinking it's time to move on!

Lincoln Park and Memorial

I love forested 1,747-acre Lincoln State Park, founded in 1932 and located four miles west of Santa Claus in southwest Indiana, home of Holiday World and Splashin' Safari, a popular theme park. From a recreation standpoint, the park, which many families include in a Holiday World getaway, boasts 270 modern and primitive campsites and a pleasant 58-acre lake ideal for bathing, fishing and boating. This is second-growth

forest; the original trees were cleared by settlers in the early 1800s.

At one time, the area was scarred by strip-mining for coal. I hike around a former mining pit known as Weber Lake, now revivified by the creation of an adjoining marsh, which acts as a water filter; it's teeming with stocked largemouth bass, bluegill and sunfish. Ten miles of hiking trails wind through dense stands of tulip poplar, black walnut, sycamore and white ash, in addition to the area's signature white oak and hickory. The woods host white-tailed deer, wild turkey, red fox and raccoon. Many more species ran free hereabouts—bison, cougar, black bear, elk and timber wolf—in the days when Abraham Lincoln lived here as a boy (1816–1830).

Most people think of Illinois when they think of Lincoln, which irks Hoosiers. Lincoln was just 7 years old when his ever-restless father ferried the family across the Ohio River here from Hardin (now LaRue) County, Kentucky, about 139 miles southeast. I'm learning all I can about the park's added historical dimension from Assistant Manager Michael Crews, who grew up near this park, as did his father and grandfather—five generations, all told. We stop by the handsomely restored and furnished 1834 Colonel William Jones Home, which reminds me of houses I've seen in Colonial Williamsburg, complete with a rooftop widow's walk. Michael tells me an ancient-looking red cedar on the front lawn was already mature when Lincoln did farm chores here for Colonel Jones.

We head to the quiet, shady Old Pigeon Cemetery beside a simple country Primitive Baptist church. Here, Lincoln's sister, Sarah Lincoln Grigsby, and her infant were buried after she died in childbirth at age 20 in 1828. "Abraham Lincoln's boyhood years here were very hard," Michael says. "He lost both his sister and his mother." The grave of Lincoln's (by all accounts) gentle and loving mother, Nancy Hanks Lincoln, is just across State-162 from the state park at the 200-acre Lincoln Boyhood National Memorial, so designated in 1962 (it was managed by the state prior to that).

The 1943 U-shaped memorial building is decorated with limestone bas-reliefs depicting various periods in Lincoln's life, including his years in Indiana, Illinois and Kentucky. Inside are biographical exhibits, a beautiful chapel and even an imposing cabinet believed to have been crafted by Lincoln's father, Thomas, who was a furniture maker as well as a farmer. We walk up a hill to Lincoln's mother's grave site, where I toss the customary penny over the black iron fence. "She died a painful death of what was then called 'milk sickness,'" Michael tells me. "At the time, nobody knew the cause, which turned out to be dairy cows grazing on the white snakeroot plant."

Lincoln's father married another kind-hearted Kentucky woman, Sara Bush Johnson, a widow with three children, and brought her here. Another short walk takes us to a representation of the small, dark Lincoln log cabin the family occupied on the 80-acre Lincoln farm within the memorial property. The home is part of a bare-bones farmstead with split-rail fences and outbuildings enclosing livestock. A costumed interpreter in the yard explains her quilting to a group of children, and I'm reminded of the humble Indiana boyhood roots of the man who became our 16th president.

Hoosier National Forest

My primary host at Hoosier National Forest is Recreation Program Manager Les Wadzinski, a native Hoosier who's a cut-to-the-chase kind of guy. Like other dedicated

CLOCKWISE, FROM THIS PHOTO: (All taken at Hoosier National Forest) Meandering Lake Monroe shoreline. Woodland view from Hickory Ridge Tower. Mule hauling crushed rock for trail, Charles C. Deam Wilderness.

forest- and park-service professionals, Les even volunteers to help fight forest fires in the West each summer. We plot out the next two days over a forest map spread out on a picnic table at the Hardin Ridge campground at the north end of the forest, about 12 miles south of Bloomington (population 69,300, about half of whom are Indiana University students). I soon realize we're just a stone's throw from rustic Brown County and its popular state park.

Les tells me a national report rates Hardin Ridge as one of America's top 100 campgrounds, based on its accessibility, amenities and activities. The appeal stems from the fact that this section of the forest abuts much of the shoreline of multi-tentacled Lake Monroe, created in 1965 by the U.S. Army Corps of Engineers. Hoosier is a patchwork-quilt national forest, where 200,000 acres of public land and more than three times that much private property hopscotch the wooded hills that characterize the southern one-third of the state, as far south as the Ohio River. More private land continually is being acquired, a process that began when the forest was launched in 1934. Much of the national forest was purchased after subsistence farmers abandoned their land during the Depression.

The natural hallmark of Hoosier National Forest definitely is the hardwoods, mainly oak and hickory, that made Indiana a leading furniture manufacturer a century ago. Firms such as the Tell City Chair Company and, well, the Batesville Casket Company (America's leading producer of hardwood caskets, among other models) carry on the manufacturing tradition. Oh, and that name "Hoosier"? The best guess is that it's some sort of corruption of "Who's yere?"

I'm about to begin the big camping adventure of my journey, and I can hardly wait (the hot, humid weather and threat of thunderstorms notwithstanding). Part of my objective on this trip is to experience the wide range of accommodations available to those who visit the Midwest's parklands. I'm lodging in places from convenient chain motels and no-nonsense cabins to cozy country inns, condominiums, guest ranches and historic hotels—even a houseboat and a lockkeeper's house. Later today, I'll tent in an honest-to-gosh wilderness area.

Cherished Recreation Land

As we head to our first stop, Les explains why Hoosier National Forest is so important to Indianans from a recreation standpoint. Only 4 percent of this state of just over 6 million inhabitants is publicly held land (Nevada, at the other end of the spectrum, is about 75 percent federally owned).

Neither is Indiana overly blessed with public-access lakes, which is what makes 10,000-acre, scenic Lake Monroe so prized by the state's anglers and other water-sports enthusiasts. The other end of the forest adjoins another large U.S. Army Corps of Engineers reservoir, even less crowded 8,800-acre Patoka Lake. Throw in diversions such as hiking, horseback riding, camping, hunting, climbing, caving, wildlife-watching, visiting archaeological and historic sites, and you have Indiana's Elysian Fields when it comes to outdoor recreation.

Still, in the conservation tradition of national forests (as opposed to more preservation-focused national parks), this is a working forest, where visitors see examples of carefully managed harvesting of renewable timber resources. In 1800, Indiana had 20 million acres of woodlands, but only a tenth of that amount a century later. Now its forests have rebounded to 4.5 million acres, or almost one-fifth of the state; 83 percent of those are privately owned. Today the national forest draws about 660,000 visitors annually. "We're a popular, close-to-home getaway, especially when gas prices

are high," Les says. "We're within a day's drive of Indianapolis, Chicago, Cincinnati and Louisville."

Soon I'm chatting with Cal and Grace Reddick, a Florida couple who tell me Indiana is usually much more temperate than the Sunshine State at this time of year. They help manage Hardin Ridge's 200-plus campsites (most with electricity and many with RV hookups) and two new cabins during summer. The Reddicks work with a handful of other retirees who help oversee campgrounds here and at four other national forests under the auspices of the nonprofit Cradle of Forestry, based in North Carolina. That organization originated in 1898 with the forester at Biltmore, the Vanderbilt estate in North Carolina's mountains.

Cal proudly shows me around Hardin Ridge: campsites, a picnic area, a boat ramp and an amphitheater for interpretive programs. I'm impressed by the new no-frills cabins (each sleeps seven for less than $50 per night) just yards from a Lake Monroe cove. We stroll down to the lake, where a fawn grazes and drinks as it moseys along.

It's lunchtime, and I need to stock up on a few incidentals for camping, so Les suggests a stop at Krazy Joe's Hardin Ridge Trading Post, distinguished by two giant tepees out front. I order a deli sandwich and pick up some insect repellent and snacks, but I'm quickly engaged by matching Amish wooden coffins flanking the fireplace in Krazy Joe's adjoining counter and dining area. "They're his-and-hers. All handmade. $850 each. Interested?" the owners inquire. "Not at the moment," I reply as I walk away.

After lunch, Les and I whip by the 1890s Brooks Cabin, typical of the bare-bones homes occupied hereabouts as recently as the early 1900s. Relocated here in 1994 from a site 60 miles distant, the cabin now serves as a visitor center and gateway to the

Charles C. Deam Wilderness, where we'll be camping tonight. Behind it is a dreamy pond, its calm surface crowded with lily pads, where I'd love to spend the afternoon…but I'm meeting some mules.

At the Blackwell Trailhead, we drop in on a group of Youth Conservation Corps high-school students working here for the summer. They're loading gravel into big saddlebags to be ploddingly hauled by a team of eight mules into the designated wilderness area, where no motorized vehicles are permitted. The gravel will help stabilize a muddy section of the trail. Finally, we climb the Hickory Ridge Fire Tower, built by the Civilian Conservation Corps in 1939. No longer used to spot fires, the tower still affords a 360-degree view of the green Hoosier hills as far as Lake Monroe, Bloomington and Brown County.

S'mores around the Campfire

Time for our wilderness camping adventure. But first a couple of confessions: Although we're tenting it tonight, it's with the able assistance of two savvy camping instructors. And while experiencing nature on many levels is one of the great joys of my life, my wife, Julie, and I are not campers. I camped occasionally as a kid, and I dutifully camped with my offspring. But somehow I've developed an affinity for flush toilets and my every-morning coffee-shop lattes. Nevertheless, we park our vehicles at the John Grubb Trailhead and, with our backpacks and gear secured, head off on the one-mile hike to our campsite. Ominous black thunderheads loom in the distance, but by some miracle we won't see a drop of rain during the night.

Leaves and twigs crunch underfoot during our hike over gentle ridges and through a few soggy swales. Before we know it, we spot our blue dome-type tents, already set up by our two trip leaders, Indiana University staff member Ryan Ridge and recent graduate Mary Williams. They're native Hoosiers and avid lifelong campers, now with Indiana University Outdoor Adventures, which sponsors outings for college students and other groups to travel all over the United States as well as to Mexico and Central America.

Outdoor Adventures is affiliated with the international, nonprofit Leave-No-Trace program, which promotes basic wilderness-camping principles governing the disposal of trash and waste, campsites and campfires, interaction with wildlife and other campers, and generally pursuing outdoor activities in ways that won't harm the environment. "The basic idea is to leave things just as you found them," Ryan explains. Hear! Hear!

Ryan gives me the lowdown on some wilderness basics, such as how to read a topographical map of the area as well as a compass. Soon I'm ready to head off on my own to experience one of the main attractions here: solitude. I follow the fading ruts of what once was one of the almost 60 miles of roads that laced this area. Until just 50 years ago, there still were more than 80 small farms within the 13,000-acre Deam Wilderness, and these woods were fields of corn and hay—that is, what wasn't barren after years of poor farming practices. Now the reborn forest shrouds me in an eerie silence. I keep deciding I'll turn back, but then my curiosity draws me farther down the path.

I think about two men who spent a good share of their lives on solitary forest walks. Charles C. Deam (1865–1953) would have been pleased to have his name attached to this, Indiana's only federally designated wilderness. A pharmacist whose true passion was botany, he probed the woods in every township and county of Indiana and authored books about the state's trees and plant life. Eventually, he became Indiana's first state forester and founder of the state's forest system.

Although Indiana proudly can claim Charles Deam as a native son, few people realize that the man most widely acknowledged as the father of America's national park system had an Indiana connection as well. Scotland-born and Wisconsin-raised John Muir (1838–1914) is commemorated with a plaque, dedicated by local Sierra Club members in 2004, at the intersection of South Illinois and Merrill streets in downtown Indianapolis.

An inventor as well as a naturalist, Muir signed on as an industrial engineer for an Indianapolis carriage-materials company in 1866. It's said he was drawn to the area by the hardwood forests nearby (Indianapolis is just 65 miles north of Hoosier). Tragically, when a power belt pierced his right eye, he was faced with a long sightless recovery that thankfully led him to pledge his first love, nature. When his sight returned, Muir began his worldwide explorations and crusades.

Thanks to men like Muir and Deam and organizations such as the Sierra Club and the Wilderness Society, today more than 106.7 million U.S. acres (more than half in Alaska) are protected in 687 designated wilderness areas found in national forests such as this one, as well as in parks, refuges and other public lands. Although this sounds like a lot of land, if you exclude Alaska, that's just 2 percent of the United States, and the percentage is even lower east of the Rockies. To meet the criteria and be afforded the highest level of environmental protection under the 1964 Wilderness Act, a wilderness must be, among other things, free of roads, vehicular traffic and permanent structures.

Not all wilderness areas are virgin in the natural sense, and rules aren't uniformly

CLOCKWISE, FROM TOP LEFT: (All taken at Deam Wilderness, Hoosier National Forest) Orienteering lesson. Turning up the heat. Campout pancakes. Campsite inspection.

Hoosier Campout Caviar

Backpacking in Hoosier National Forest doesn't mean you can't enjoy gourmet camp food. Mary Williams of Indiana University Outdoor Adventures loves serving this refreshing salsalike appetizer alfresco.

1 15-ounce can black-eyed peas, rinsed and drained

1 11-ounce can white (shoepeg) corn, drained

2 medium tomatoes, seeded and finely chopped

2 medium avocados, halved, seeded, peeled and finely chopped

4 green onions, finely chopped

¼ cup snipped fresh cilantro

¼ cup red wine vinegar

¼ cup olive oil

2 cloves garlic, minced

2 teaspoons Mexican or fajita seasoning

¼ to ½ teaspoon ground cumin

¼ teaspoon salt

   Scoop-shaped tortilla chips, corn chips or assorted crackers

In a large bowl, combine black-eyed peas, corn, tomatoes, avocados, green onions, cilantro, vinegar, oil, garlic, Mexican seasoning, cumin and salt. Cover and chill for at least 2 hours or up to 4 hours. Serve salsa with tortilla chips. *Makes 5½ cups dip (22 appetizer servings).*

Tip: To tote, place a tightly covered container of chilled mixture in an insulated cooler with ice packs. Pack chips in a separate container.

rigid. Many, especially in the eastern half of the United States, still are being nursed back to their original states. Today I'm one of 12 million Americans who annually get to experience just a taste of what the Wilderness Act itself defines as wilderness: "an area where the earth and its community of life are untrammeled by man, where man himself is a visitor who does not remain." Many wilderness areas, particularly in the West, never have been settled, but others, like the Charles C. Deam Wilderness, gradually are being restored. And although some wilderness areas are more restrictive about activities, this one permits horseback riding, hunting, fishing and climbing in addition to the usual primitive camping, hiking and, of course, savoring solitude.

By the time I return to camp, Ryan and Mary have prepared a wonderful fresh salsa appetizer (see the recipe at left). In a big Dutch oven over a fire, they expertly make a vegetable lasagna with tofu, mozzarella, spinach, onions and a white sauce. After dinner, we bask in the campfire camaraderie while enjoying delectable s'mores we toast over the fire. Everyone seems to have a hilarious camping memory to share—whether it's the raccoon that got into camp or the night the tent blew down.

Mary, who spent a month camping in Washington state, talks about cooking in the wilderness. "You have to plan ahead. Organize what you're going to make and be sure that, without going overboard, you bring everything you need. Freeze-dried and dehydrated foods are easy to carry. You also have to learn to improvise. A Frisbee makes a great plate and cutting board."

The next morning, I wake up feeling surprisingly refreshed and secretly relieved that I haven't been mauled by any rogue forest critters. I set off on a prebreakfast hike down another overgrown trail. I keep watching for landmarks, but all these trees look alike—luckily, the dawning sun playing peekaboo behind the endless tree trunks beside the trail tells me which way is east. The aroma of Ryan and Mary's campfire breakfast lures me back to the campsite to eat before we pack our gear and hike back to the trailhead to meet Les. Hearing of my hikes, Les wisely remarks, "The main point is to experience true solitude. It's reassuring just to know that places like this *exist.*"

Trees, Sandstone and Humanity

Indiana's backcountry charms reveal themselves even more in the southern part of the forest. I love these towns with names such as Ethel, Bacon, Sulphur, Sassafras and Magnet (not to mention French Lick, the site of a venerable resort hotel and the home of basketball great Larry Bird)—all adjoining the forest. An occasional Amish buggy slows us down; beside a field of haystacks, I spot an authentic Mail Pouch Tobacco sign painted on a weathered barn. Several quarries remind me that Indiana's limestone helped build such landmarks as the Empire State Building and the Pentagon.

Our first destination here is Hemlock Cliffs, a box canyon of limestone and sandstone, much of the latter honeycombed by weathering veins of iron ore. Les tells me even many locals don't know the canyon is here. We hike just over a mile to a shady and thankfully cooler world with plants including wintergreen, wild orchids, wild geranium, French's shooting star, mountain laurel and liverwort. But the real star here is a dribble of a waterfall that Les tells me becomes a torrent in springtime; it tumbles off a cliff right in front of an arcing overhang big enough for us to stand in. "It's quite a sight in the wintertime, too, when the water freezes," he says. The gaping overhang was used by pre-Columbian Native Americans for shelter and defense.

Next stop: an 88-acre forest saved in 1941

by a group of women who belonged to the Pioneer Mothers Club. Here, undisturbed by loggers since before 1816, are Indiana's oldest trees—soaring beeches and maples, some 300 years old, still thriving in a forest setting that recalls how much of this state looked when the first settlers arrived. An interpretive sign announces a 14th-century Native American stockaded village located by archaeologists nearby (however, there's little for the untrained observer to discern).

Time to say good-bye to Indiana's remarkable Hoosier Forest, but not before one last rendezvous at the Indian-Celina Recreation Area. Angie Krieger is the forest's heritage resource specialist. A native Iowan, she studied anthropology at the University of Minnesota Duluth and really knows history and archaeology. We tour the sandstone Jacob Rickenbaugh House, which served the tiny Winding Branch community that once existed here as a post office, church and gathering place.

Jacob was a local tanner and farmer who commissioned a crew of Belgian stonemasons to construct his imposing home—with 20-inch-thick walls—for just $1,000 in 1874. Rehabilitated in 2002 primarily by volunteers, the Rickenbaugh House now is on the National Register of Historic Places and presides near the shore of man-made, 164-acre Celina Lake.

Behind the house, Angie guides me down a forest trail that's been in use for thousands of years. We're on our way to one of 1,600 documented archaeologically or historically significant sites within the forest dating back as many as 12,000 years. Just outside an overhang, overlooking a wooded ravine, is a rock with a bowl-shaped indentation, used as a primitive mortar for cracking nuts and grains. I'm awed by the evolving human endeavors and sheer passage of time this forest's rocks and hardwoods have witnessed through the ages.

CLOCKWISE, FROM TOP LEFT: (All taken at Hoosier National Forest) Moss-covered rocks, Indian-Celina Recreation Area. Historic 1874 Jacob Rickenbaugh House, Indian-Celina Recreation Area. Woodland view from inside an overhang, Hemlock Cliffs.

TOP TO BOTTOM: (Both taken at Hoosier National Forest) Naturally air-conditioned accommodations. Brooks Cabin Visitor Center adjacent to Deam Wilderness. OPPOSITE PAGE: Chicago skyline from Indiana Dunes.

Dan's Travel Journal

FEATURED STOP

Hoosier National Forest Four parcels from Brown County on the north to the Ohio River near Tell City on the south. Outdoor adventures abound at this 200,000-acre forest that branches out across the hills of south-central Indiana: hiking, bicycling and horseback riding on 265 miles of trails, plus primitive and modern camping, hunting, fishing and boating. Wildlife watchers spot some of the forest's 50 types of mammals and 142 bird species. Along forest roads, signs identify prime wildlife-viewing sites, including Buzzard Roost and Paw Paw Marsh. The panoramic Ohio River Scenic Byway through the southern forest, State-446, goes from Bloomington to east of Bedford; other scenic routes showcase fabulous fall color and springtime's blooming dogwoods and wildflowers. Maps and information available at U.S. Forest Service offices in Tell City and Bedford (812/275-5987).

Lodging, Dining and More

Capers Tell City. Specialties include Gulf shrimp dishes, New Orleans po'boy sandwiches and live acoustic music (on weekends) in a historic 1890s former IOOF lodge (812/547-3333).
Fairfield Inn Bloomington. Minutes from Indiana University and a half-hour drive from Brown County and the northern section of Hoosier National Forest. Indoor pool/spa, fitness center, wireless high-speed Internet and free breakfast. $$$ (812/331-1122).
Holiday Inn Express Hotel & Suites Tell City. Near the southern tip of Hoosier National Forest, with indoor pool, exercise room and complimentary breakfast. $$ (812/547-0800).
Indiana University Outdoor Adventures Bloomington. Affordable outdoor trips headed by trained leaders for students and the public, including caving, kayaking and rock-climbing day trips, plus weeklong outings such as Baja surfing and Yellowstone backpacking (or customize your own adventure). Complete gear rental (812/855-2231).
Krazy Joe's Hardin Ridge Trading Post Lake Monroe. Just south of Lake Monroe to Hardin Ridge Campgrounds, a down-home convenience/gas stop and eatery with jumbo tenderloin sandwiches, homemade biscuits and gravy and live music (812/837-9388).

Related Area Event

Brown County Wildflower Foray Brown and Monroe counties, last full weekend in April—Wildflower and bird walks, boat trips and hikes throughout both counties, including the northern Hoosier National Forest (812/988-2785).

More Information

Indiana Office of Tourism Development (800/677-9800), www.visitindiana.com).

DAN'S OTHER STOPS

(See also More Parks section that follows.)
Indiana Dunes National Lakeshore between Gary and Michigan City (800/959-9174),
Lincoln Boyhood National Memorial Santa Claus (812/038-4541), **Lincoln State Park** Santa Claus (812/937-4710).

Lodging, Dining and More

Buffalo Run Farm, Grill & Gifts Lincoln City. One mile east of Lincoln State Park, order buffalo burgers and "buffalo chip" ice cream at the grill, and view the buffalo herd, log cabin and Native American tepee (812/937-2799).
Hilton Garden Inn Chesterton Chesterton. Minutes from Indiana Dunes National Lakeshore (one hour from Chicago); opened in 2001 with 120 rooms, restaurant, indoor pool and fitness center. $$ (219/983-9500).
Strongbow Inn Valparaiso. Fifteen miles south of Indiana Dunes National Lakeshore, this US-30 landmark opened in 1940 on a turkey farm and still features its signature hot turkey sandwiches and dinners, plus beef, chicken, seafood and a full bakery (800/462-5121).

More Indiana Parks

Brown County State Park

A weathered covered bridge marks the entrance to 16,000-acre Brown County State Park (55 miles south of Indianapolis). Indiana's largest state park, it lies at the center of Brown County just southeast of the history-rich artists' colony of Nashville. Ribbons of blacktop wind and climb through the park's hills and woods. At Hesitation Point, trees part to reveal a grassy clearing. Below, hills roll to the horizon, and a blue mist floats in the shadowy valleys. No wonder this area often is called "Indiana's Little Smokies."

Picnic tables perched on grassy hillsides make perfect spots to glimpse deer grazing in the woods and listen to songs of black-throated green warblers. Eighteen miles of hiking trails scale the hills and descend into the hollows. You also can fish, swim, play tennis, go horseback riding, camp and visit the nature center. Since 1932, the park's Abe Martin Lodge, with hand-hewn beams and fireplaces, has welcomed guests. Visitors dine in the restaurant there and stay in rooms at the lodge and its newer addition, along with housekeeping cabins.

Contact: Brown County State Park (812/988-6406, dnr.in.gov; 877/563-4371 for lodging). Nearby lodgings: in Nashville (800/753-3255, browncounty.com).

Hoosier National Forest

(See previous section of this chapter.)

Hovey Lake Fish & Wildlife Area

A massive wrenching of the earth's surface some 5,000 years ago changed the course of the Ohio River, leaving behind this primordial bog at Indiana's remote southwestern tip (10 miles southwest of Mt. Vernon). Shaggy trees enclose the narrow road into the Hovey Lake preserve, which encompasses 6,900 acres of sloughs, marshes and hardwood forests in the floodplains of the Ohio and Wabash rivers.

Egrets, jays and blackbirds shriek and chatter at this bird-watchers' haven, which boasts the northernmost natural stand of bald cypress trees (some 500 years old) in the United States. Startled blue herons rise, furiously beating their wide wings, and turtles kerplop off cypress stumps.

For bird-watching, fishing and secluded canoeing, paddle the 1,400-acre oxbow lake (bring your own boat). Gliding along the wooded shores of the lake's many isolated

LEFT TO RIGHT: (Both taken along the Ohio River National Scenic Byway) Old Iron Bridge, Blue River, Harrison-Crawford State Forest. Ohio River scene. Rustic covered bridge, Brown County State Park.

fingers, you'll see areas resembling swamps of the Deep South. The only access to the lake and adjacent unmarked hiking and hunting areas is from the park office at the end of State-69. Secondary roads, with turnouts for parking, run through the preserve, where you can climb the observation tower for panoramic views.

Contact: Hovey Lake Fish & Wildlife Area (812/838-2927, dnr.in.gov). Nearest lodgings: in Mt. Vernon (812/838-3639, mtvernonposeycochamber.com) or 30 miles northeast in Evansville (800/433-3025, evansvillecvb.org).

Indiana Dunes National Lakeshore

Along Indiana's Lake Michigan shore, lofty sand dunes crown a landscape of beaches, marshes, open prairie and hardwood forests at Indiana Dunes National Lakeshore. The 15,000-acre preserve, surrounding smaller Indiana Dunes State Park, stretches 24 miles between Gary and Michigan City, spanning three counties. US-12 travels through the national lakeshore and lakeside

communities. Wide beaches attract swimmers and sunbathers. Some 45 miles of hiking and biking trails, including the nine-mile Calumet Trail, skirt the dunes.

You can camp, fish, prowl the sands and join nature programs. Near the visitors center, meander through an early trader-trapper's homestead and an 1870s Swedish immigrant's farm. A quaking boardwalk runs through Pinhook Bog, an ancient wilderness of wispy tamarack trees, tiny orchids and insect-eating plants. The state park, with three miles of beach, claims three of the area's highest dunes, all topping 170 feet. Near the lakeshore's northeastern end, vacationers scurry up the shifting sand slopes of Mount Baldy. From atop, they can see Chicago's skyline.

Contact: Indiana Dunes National Lakeshore (800/959-9174, nps.gov/indu). Indiana Dunes State Park (219/926-1952, camp .in.gov or dnr.in.gov). Nearest lodgings: along or near US-12 in Portage, Porter and Chesterton (800/283-8687, indianadunes .com) and in Michigan City (800/685-7174, visitlaportecounty.com).

Jasper-Pulaski Fish & Wildlife Area

For a wildlife spectacle you'll always remember, journey to these 8,000 acres of shallow marshes and prairie straddling the Jasper and Pulaski county lines near Medaryville (90 miles northwest of Indianapolis). Every fall, thousands of sandhill cranes stop here on their migration south. The giant birds, some with 7-foot wing spans, roost in the marshes and fill the skies at sunrise, as they head out to feed in surrounding fields and swamps. Around sunset, they "kite" back from every direction to socialize before roosting in the marshes at dusk.

You can see the creatures, along with flocks of Canada geese, from observation towers and platforms in the preserve, which also includes picnic sites. Platforms in the Goose Pasture area make some of the best viewing spots. Late September through early December is prime viewing season, with birds peaking in mid-November. Smaller numbers of sandhill cranes return in spring. Visitors also hike and fish in the wetlands, where catfish, bluegill and large-

mouth bass rank among prime catches.

Contact: Jasper-Pulaski Fish & Wildlife Area (219/843-4841, dnr.in.gov). Lodgings: twelve miles northeast in North Judson (877/733-2736, explorestarkecounty.com).

Lincoln Boyhood National Memorial and Lincoln State Park

Drive 15 miles north of the Ohio River to Lincoln City and the early years of our 16th president come to life at these two sites (35 miles northeast of Evansville). In 1816, at the age of 7, Lincoln settled with his family on a farmstead here, where he matured from a skinny kid into an educated young man.

On the site where Lincoln grew up, the Lincoln Boyhood National Memorial includes his home and the Memorial Visitors Center, with a museum and orientation film. In summer, interpreters help guests do chores such as splitting wood and making butter at the living-history farm. You also can view the grave of Lincoln's mother. Surrounded by hills and shady woods

across the road, vacationers camp and stay in cabins at 1,700-acre Lincoln State Park. A summer concert series plays at the park's 1,500-seat outdoor amphitheater. Visitors also fish, swim and boat in Lake Lincoln; visit the nature center; and hike the trails.

Contact: Lincoln Boyhood National Mem-orial (812/937-4541, nps.gov/libo). LincolnState Park (812/937-4710, dnr. in.gov). Nearest lodgings: more options four miles west in Santa Claus and 12 miles north in Dale (888/444-9252, legendar places.org).

Mississinewa Lake

Even on summer afternoons, only a handful of pleasure boats ply the broad 20-mile-long channel of this U.S. Army Corps of Engineers' lake, created along the Mississinewa River 40 years ago. Four state recreation areas (Frances Slocum, Miami, Red Bridge and Pearson Mill) ring the forested shores, creating an oasis of more than 14,000 acres amid north-central Indiana farm country (60 miles southwest of Fort Wayne).

Campers almost always can find spots

among the 450 sites at the Miami Recreation Area. Ten miles of loop trails thread through surrounding woods. You can launch boats at four ramps for sightseeing, fishing and water-skiing. Fishing piers extend into the lake at the Miami area, which includes a broad stretch of cream-colored beach. Or pack a picnic and head for one of the shelters overlooking the lake.

To learn about this area's rich Native American heritage, sign up for guided hikes or other summer naturalist programs. The Miami-area headquarters provides maps pinpointing landmarks such as the Cliffs of the Seven Pillars, arches of limestone that once were the site of tribal ceremonies.

Contact: Mississinewa Lake (765/473-6528, dnr.in.gov). Nearest lodgings: seven miles northwest in Peru (765/472-1923, miamicochamber.com).

Ohio River National Scenic Byway

Rediscover the aura of the Ohio River, once the nation's highway west, traveling Indiana's 303 miles of this byway. Natural attractions and communities etched by the river beckon amid woods and bluffs tracing the state's southern border.

Sycamores arch above the Blue River at 26,000-acre Harrison-Crawford State Forest, which neighbors Hoosier National Forest (see page 19). Within the state forest, O'Bannon Woods State Park is the centerpiece for recreation. You can camp, canoe, backpack a 24-mile trail and tour the subterranean world at Wyandotte Caves.

Rock walls and waterfalls make Clifty Falls, a 1200-acre state park, a hiker's paradise. An inn overlooks the river and the city of Madison, with almost its entire downtown on the National Register of Historic Places. Other towns, including Aurora and Newburgh, entice you with shops and 1800s architecture. Swiss heritage lives on at Tell City and Vevay. In Corydon, visit the State Capital Historic Site and nearby Squire Boone Caverns.

The byway harbors surprises, too, such as the world's largest fossil bed at Falls of the Ohio State Park and remote Hovey Lake (see Hovey Lake Fish & Wildlife Area, page 27).

Contact: Historic Southern Indiana (812/465-7014, ohioriverscenicroute.org). Lodgings: all along the byway, including in Evansville (800/433-3025, evansville cvb.org), Jeffersonville and New Albany (800/552-3842, sunnysideoflouisville.org).

Pokagon State Park

As part of a treaty, the Potawatomi Indians, who once ruled this region of northeastern Indiana, transferred a million acres, including land that became this year-round state park, to the federal government for 3 cents an acre. What a bargain! Bordering Lake James and Snow Lake, nearly 1,300-acre Pokagon State Park satisfies even ardent outdoor enthusiasts, in a region blessed with natural lakes (50 miles north of Fort Wayne). The Civilian Conservation Corps built most of the roads and shelters at the park, which includes seven hiking trails and a bicycle path. Hell's Point Trail winds through a forest so thick it blocks the sun.

Tudor-style Potawatomi Inn, opened in 1928, has been refurbished with 138 comfortable rooms and a lodgelike restaurant. Guests also stay in modern cabins. You can fish, swim in the lakes and an indoor pool, relax at two beaches, boat (pontoons and small boats for rent) and take guided trail rides from the stables. In winter, visitors zip down the park's quarter-mile toboggan run, cross-country ski, ice-skate and ice-fish.

Contact: Pokagon State Park (260/833-2012, dnr.in.gov). Potawatomi Inn (877/768-2928, indianainns.com). Nearest lodgings: a couple of miles from the park in Fremont and Angola (800/525-3101, lakes101.org).

Turkey Run and Shades State Parks

Wending toward the Wabash River, languid Sugar Creek links ruggedly beautiful Turkey Run and Shades state parks in west-central Indiana's covered-bridge country (75 miles west of Indianapolis). Grab your paddle for a 16-mile trek amid woods and ravines, where featherlike ferns line the ridges. You can stop to sun and picnic along the way (canoe liveries serve the area).

Since its lodge opened in the 1920s, Turkey Run State Park has bustled with visitors. Now, trees nearly hide the sprawling inn, with guest rooms and a restaurant. You also can camp in the 2,300-acre park and stay in cabins, swim, hike, join naturalist programs, fish, ride horses and play tennis. Or simply let the gentle river carry your craft beneath historic covered bridges and past cliffs where the park's namesake turkeys roost.

At larger and less-developed Shades State Park, sunlight barely splinters through dense woods. Trickling springs once led to a booming health resort amid this wilderness. But hiking, camping, canoeing and pure solitude attract outdoor lovers today.

Contact: Turkey Run State Park (765/597-2635, dnr.in.gov). Shades State Park (765/435-2810, dnr.in.gov). Lodgings: fifteen miles northeast of Shades in Crawfordsville (800/866-3973, crawfordsville.org); 10 miles south of Turkey Run in Rockville (877/500-6151, coveredbridges.com).

Versailles State Park

Slated to become a national park during the Depression, Indiana's second largest state park (75 miles southeast of Indianapolis) never lived up to those expectations. In fact, half of the park's nearly 6,000 acres remain undeveloped. But that leaves a generous 3,000 acres devoted to outdoor recreation.

Gargantuan catfish, along with bluegill and bass, flop and splash in 230-acre Versailles Lake, centerpiece of the park. At the swimming pool complex near the lake, where you can rent paddleboats, rowboats and canoes, take a turn on the 100-foot-long waterslide. Summer activities range from stargazing hikes with naturalists to bluegrass concerts. The nature center showcases the park's wildlife, history and fossils. You might even discover a few fossils of your own along Laughery Creek and other streams crisscrossing the park.

Trails for hiking and guided horseback rides from the stables pierce the woods. The 97-mile Hoosier Hills Bike Route also runs through the park, where you can pick between two campgrounds.

Contact: Versailles State Park (812/689-6424, dnr.in.gov). Nearest lodgings: limited a mile west in Versailles (888/747-5394, ripleycountytourism.com); more options 25 miles north in Batesville (contact above).

CLOCKWISE, FROM TOP LEFT:
Swimming beach, Lincoln State Park.
Turkey Run State Park. Frances
Slocum State Recreation Area. Hovey
Lake Fish & Wildlife Area.

IOWA

Rumpled Loess Hills ridges and the flat Missouri River Valley

Enchanted hills sculpted by the wind

I THINK IT SUBLIMELY FITTING that one of Iowa's primary natural wonders is…well…dirt. Soil is Iowa's gold, mined by farmers for a century and a half for the prolific crops it yields—today mainly corn and soybeans. Iowa's Loess Hills have a magic all their own. (Loess, pronounced Luss, is a German word for "loose" or "crumbly," referring to the 200-plus-foot piles of silt prehistoric winds deposited here.) On cross-country airplane flights, I've readily identified this narrow, 3- to 15-mile-wide eruption of ridges and valleys that snakes along the east side of the broad, flat Missouri River Valley for 200-odd miles.

Iowa is my home state, and I spent a good deal of my growing-up years in the Loess Hills, in Council Bluffs (population 58,300). Yet I have much to learn about this topographical marvel and the unique ecosystem it spawned. I'll spend several days hiking ridgetop trails and sightseeing along a 100-mile stretch of the Loess Hills National Scenic Byway between the region's largest community, Sioux City (population 85,000), on the north and the village of Honey Creek, just 11 miles north of Council Bluffs on the south.

Although Iowa boasts a number of worthy smaller parks, it lacks a signature parkland on a par with, say, neighboring Minnesota's Voyageurs National Park. That's partly a byproduct of Iowans' zeal for tilling their

Photography by Clint Farlinger

ultrafertile topsoil, which encourages cultivation on an astounding scale. En route to the Loess Hills, I'll visit two very different reminders of what Iowa may have looked like prior to wall-to-wall farming in the mid-1800s: northeast Iowa's Yellow River State Forest and Neal Smith National Wildlife Refuge in central Iowa.

Yellow River State Forest

Yellow River State Forest, established in 1935, is named for a tributary that joins the Mississippi at Effigy Mounds National Monument in the northeast corner of the state (the huge burial mounds created by native peoples a millennium ago were part of the forest until 1949). At 8,600 acres, Yellow River is the smallest—and the wildest—of Iowa's four primary state forests. It's part of what geologists call the Driftless Area, encompassing corners of Iowa, Illinois, Wisconsin and Minnesota.

Iowa's "Little Switzerland" somehow escaped leveling by the Midwest's last glacier 10,000 years ago. That ice floe left the forest's tree-crowned bluffs, up to 400 feet tall along the Mississippi, and secluded hollows now laced by 25 miles of trails, most of them open to horseback riders, mountain bikers, hikers and backpackers.

The forest offers primitive camping, tubing and canoeing. Hunters come to bag wild turkey, white-tailed deer and waterfowl, bird-watchers to spot bald and golden eagles, cerulean warblers and scarlet tanagers. The streams hereabouts, notably Big Paint Creek and Little Paint Creek, tantalize anglers with stocked brown, brook and rainbow trout. Trout fishing in Iowa? It's just one more of Yellow River's surprises. "This isn't what people expect Iowa to look like at all," says my host, Forester Bob Honeywell. "Flatlanders just love it here."

As we bounce across rocky creek beds, skirt steep ravines and slowly ascend the old Fire Tower Road, Bob explains that most of the trees lining this lane are oak and hickory, which gradually will evolve into a climax community of maple and basswood. I'm amazed at the variety he points out: aspen, elm, ash, cherry, butternut, walnut, locust and red cedar. Years ago, cordwood cut in this forest fueled steamboats that plied the Mississippi just east of here.

We see pockets of nonnative white pine planted in the 1940s for harvestable lumber and erosion control. Nearby is an outdoor sawmill, where timber, mostly red oak, is milled for use at this and other state properties. Plants and wildflowers dot the forest floor: ferns, yellow lady's slipper, jeweled shooting star, snakeroot, ginseng and spring ephemerals. Our final stop, Larkins Overlook, dazzles me with one last view of the forest's valleys and cushy green blanket of treetops.

Neal Smith Wildlife Refuge

On to central Iowa and the three-by-five-mile, gently rolling Neal Smith National Wildlife Refuge, a haven for several hundred species ranging from buffalo to tree frogs. I've visited here several times with my grandson, Luis, to drive the wildlife loop for a glimpse of the 40-odd buffalo in residence.

This prairie "Noah's ark" also hosts elk, white-tailed deer, red fox, coyote, mink and otter; winged critters such as wild turkey and grassland birds including the short-eared owl, bobolink and Henslow's sparrow; and reptiles such as snakes, toads and salamanders. Butterflies galore—including rare Monarch-like, orange regal fritillaries—flutter in a colorful wildflower garden just outside the visitors center. But I'm here to focus on something else today: the prairie ecosystem.

At one time, 85 percent of what's now Iowa was tallgrass prairie, proportionately more than in any other state. Now, less than 0.1 percent of that prairie survives. Barely 15 miles east of the state's capital and largest city, Des Moines (metro population 477,000), a team of prairie enthusiasts, biologists, botanists and other scientists and researchers have launched the nation's largest prairie-restoration project on 8,600 acres of former farmland and a few small pockets of remnant prairie.

In the late 1980s, the land that's now the refuge was about to become the site of a nuclear power plant project! That's when activists spearheaded the refuge, named for a popular 20-term Iowa congressman who owned a farm just eight miles west.

I meet my hosts at the low-rise, $7 million Prairie Learning Center and begin with a compelling three-screen film that portrays the many aspects of a prairie ecosystem, both natural and cultural. One unforgettable exhibit illustrates how preventable erosion has robbed as much as 5 feet of Iowa's topsoil since settlement began, to a depth of just 1 foot in many places.

I'm learning all I can about prairies from Pauline Drobney, land-management and research-demonstration biologist, and several of her colleagues. "This is one giant laboratory," Pauline tells me on one of our walkabouts off the main loop drive. She eagerly points out some of the 450 varieties of prairie plants, grasses and grasslike sedges found here: big and little bluestem grass, switchgrass, goldenrod, bottlebrush grass, silky rye, butterfly and purple milkweed, several species of orchids, leadplant, brown-eyed Susan and gnarly bur oak trees that shade a savanna grove. In one field, we wade into waist-high big bluestem, cardinal flower and great blue lobelia. Here, Pauline and her colleagues are researching the hydrology of the prairie, which I learn is an excellent water filter and purifier.

Before I leave, Pauline takes me to her

inner sanctum at the learning center: a solarium/greenhouse where volunteers, including schoolchildren, help staff researchers clean, identify and catalog seeds collected here and elsewhere. Eventually, those seeds will be planted here, bringing new life to the almost-vanished prairie.

The Loess Hills

Just like the pioneers, I'm headed west across Iowa, although my trek is quicker (five hours on I-80 these days, versus weeks by covered wagon in pioneer times). My Loess Hills adventure begins off busy I-29 in the Missouri River Valley town of Mondamin (population 420), where Area Forester Brent Olson maps out my itinerary over meatloaf and mashed potatoes at Mama Keri's Diner.

Soon I'm three miles east, climbing the steep ridge of an unnamed hill. My reward is a panoramic view of a scene unlike any other in the Midwest: Flat farm fields abruptly erupt into bluffs created between 14,000 and 18,000 years ago, when prevailing westerly winds dropped tons of silt to form the 664,000-acre Loess Hills.

That same fine, café au lait-colored quartzite glacial runoff dusted most of Iowa, but nowhere to the depth it did here. Approximately one-third of the world's grain crops grow in loess-soil regions in places such as Iowa, Argentina and southern Russia. But only in Iowa, Germany's Rhine River Valley and, even more notably, China's Yellow River Valley does this type of soil define the horizon so emphatically. If the Loess Hills resemble a long snake, here in Harrison County they're a python that swallowed a pig, reaching their maximum width of 15 miles.

Brent is a native Iowan who served at 18 U.S. Forest Service sites across the country before returning home in 1990. That was just four years after the state began acquiring land for this state forest, which many hoped would become part of Iowa's first national park. Among the challenges: skyrocketing land prices and thousands of private landowners—but some boosters still have their hopes. Today, four separate units in Harrison and Monona counties comprise the 11,000-acre forest.

Soon we're alternating between hiking narrow paths and bouncing in Brent's truck on roller-coaster trails that dip from hilltops down into ravines and valleys. We pass several farm sites and occasional contoured hillside fields filled with swirling rows of corn. "This area was settled late because of the rugged terrain, but at one time the hills were used to graze cattle as well as to grow crops," Brent says. "A lot of farmers gave up here during the dust bowl era."

As we lurch along through officially roadless wilderness, Brent explains the diverse ecosystems here. On the shadier north-facing slopes, trees and vegetation are more lush, while the sunbaked south-facing slopes, where the hillsides are more arid, are dotted with smaller flora, such as the area's signature yucca plant with its frond-like leaves and spiky cream-colored flowers. Everywhere I turn, especially at the tops of ridges, tufts of prairie grasses and wildflowers cling to the soil, helping combat erosion.

All told, 3,000 plant species, many of them not found elsewhere in the state, have adapted to the hills. There are plenty of trees, too, in this part of the Loess Hills, but not all are welcome. Brent takes me to a hollow where chain saws have marked mature trees slated for removal in an 80-acre savanna restoration. "Overgrazing depleted many of the native grasses and wildflowers that were here when the area was settled," he says. "Then trees came in to fill the void, especially the eastern red cedar; the shade choked out native grasses and plants that prevented erosion. We're

TOP TO BOTTOM: Trout fishing, Yellow River State Forest. Prairie landscape, Neal Smith National Wildlife Refuge.

trying to restore the ecosystem." Brent explains that restoration requires burning on a rotating basis; up to 2,500 acres are set ablaze here annually.

I spy a white-tailed deer and several wild turkeys, along with pheasant and quail and turkey vultures. In all, 143 bird species have been spotted in this part of the hills. Badgers, coyotes and red foxes prowl here. Other birds and animals include the brown bat, plains spadefoot toad and box turtle.

I ask Brent about natural succession, a concept I'm just beginning to grasp on this journey. "You can't freeze this or any place in natural history; ecosystems are dynamic, always changing," he says. "What we want to do is simply return the hills to something more similar to their appearance before settlement and overgrazing."

Are the Loess Hills suited for recreation? "Primitive camping, hiking, wildlife-watching and hunting—yes. But not ATVs, horseback riding or mountain biking. Plant life here is fragile, and the hills are highly susceptible to erosion." Loess soil is cohesive when it's dry, but the flat quartz particles dissolve like sugar when they get wet.

What about development, then? "That's a big issue," Brent says. "We're just about an hour from Omaha [metro population 687,000]. People want to live in the hills, and land prices have gone way up." Sadly, other threats include trash and garbage dumping and "mining" of the hills for road gravel and clay used to make bricks.

A Loess Hills Homestead

David and Lin Zahrt operate the Country Homestead Bed and Breakfast just north of Turin (population all of 75 souls). Both are native Iowans; David grew up on this farm. Their long careers in nonprofit community development took them from Chicago to the Australian Outback and Kenya. Then David's roots beckoned, and they settled back here. "We like showing people the hills, so we opened our home to guests," David says. The Zahrts' restored Victorian house perches at the base of the hills, overlooking Nebraska on the other side of the broad river valley.

Over a breakfast of coffee and Lin's unsurpassed Loess Hills French Toast, David says he's roamed these 160 acres

since he was a boy, when his family raised cattle here, unknowingly contributing to the overgrazing that drastically altered the hills' appearance. "My family left Mother Nature with a bare hind end on our farm, grazing the hills down to the nubbins," he says. "So Mother Nature covered herself with trees [mainly pesky eastern red cedars], which she normally would have controlled with fires that we, of course, suppressed."

Now, the hills behind David and Lin's home, like much of the region, are a mix of prairies threatened by encroaching woodlands. David—on his own and with the assistance of volunteers and groups such as The Nature Conservancy and the Iowa Natural Heritage Foundation—is gradually restoring his land to savanna and prairie.

On a postbreakfast hike, David shows me some pastureland that's returning to its prairie state, now cloaked in grasses whose tenacious roots are anchored as deep as 10 feet. "Do you know about *kindshen*?" he asks me as he picks up a fist-sized chunk of calcium carbonate exposed by erosion. The hollow curiosity, also known as "pop rock" because of the way it shatters, was formed

LEFT TO RIGHT: Grassy ridges and wooded ravines, Loess Hills State Forest. Bell-shaped yucca blossoms. A winding country road probing the Loess Hills. Ingemann Danish Church, a pioneer Loess Hills landmark west of Moorhead.

by minerals that filtered down into the loess soil. "The term comes from the German word for 'little people,'" David says. "Pioneer children would dress these rocks up as dolls."

David's index finger darts from plant to plant as he points out species that have returned here: prairie flax, purple and white prairie clover, leadplant, purple and yellow coneflower, ground plum and pasqueflower. Prairie violet. Penstemon. Skeleton weed. The landscape is a canvas of vivid yellow, orange, red, blue, purple and white flowers. "I've counted 80 wildflowers and grasses in just this field alone!" David says.

Inside the "Bald-Pated Hills"

With 220 miles of paved roads and 15 side-excursion loops on mostly paved county roads, the Loess Hills National Scenic Byway is a great way to experience this twisting terrain—as long as you get out of your vehicle for a hike occasionally. David and two other knowledgeable guides, Abby Lowe and Linda Herman of the Loess Hills Hospitality Association, are my hosts on a tour of attractions in three Loess Hills counties (Monona, Woodbury and Harrison).

Passing through Turin, we pause briefly at a large pit where fill dirt and gravel once were dug—a sad but all-too-common sight in the hills. Back in 1955, a human skull fell "kerplunk!" down a hillside onto an excavator. That skull and other remains (which eventually were properly reinterred elsewhere) indicate human habitation here as long as 6,500 years ago. Side roads lead us to sites associated with a French fur trader who lived here in the 1850s and past a one-room schoolhouse being restored.

Former stagecoach roads slice through the sheer cuts in the hills. We wend past secluded farmsteads, fishing ponds, unexpected overlooks, apple orchards and pioneer cemeteries. At the bucolic, white-steepled 1884 Ingemann Danish Church, I observe two plein air painters with easels, palettes and brushes poised.

The serene, gently sloping churchyard is filled with tombstones bearing Danish surnames such as Andersen, Hansen, Jensen, Jorgensen, Neilsen, Pedersen and Sorensen. I'm touched by the hardship revealed by one family plot where seven children of eight lie buried. Tragically, they all died of diphtheria within just 13 days in the late 1800s. Life was hard here.

My crew and I are off to tidy Moorhead for lunch (roast beef at Rex and Danita's Feedbunk Cafe) and a quick tour of the cozy Loess Hills Visitors Center, housed in the relocated former one-room Cover Schoolhouse. Soon we're whizzing north along the Missouri on busy I-29 to 1,100-acre Stone State Park in bustling Sioux City, where the 1995 Dorothy Pecaut Nature Center celebrates the area's wetland, prairie and woodland environments.

At Dakota Point Overlook, one of several scenic vistas, I drink in a commanding view of the lush Big Sioux and Missouri River valleys. Lewis and Clark passed near this very spot on August 21, 1804, and again on their return journey, September 4, 1806. On the west side of Sioux City, just off I-29 at the acclaimed Sioux City Lewis & Clark Interpretive Center, built a stone's throw from the Missouri in 2002, I study dioramas with eerily lifelike animatronic figures and stroll the extensive wildflower gardens outside.

Concord Grape Pie

Grape vineyards are reappearing in the Loess Hills, and their juicy Concords are ideal for pie making.

1   15-ounce package refrigerated rolled, unbaked piecrust (2 crusts)
7   cups Concord grapes (about 2 pounds)
1   cup sugar
¼   cup cornstarch
2   tablespoons butter, cut into small pieces
1   teaspoon finely shredded lemon peel
1   tablespoon lemon juice
½   teaspoon salt
½   teaspoon ground cinnamon
¼   teaspoon ground nutmeg

Let piecrusts stand as directed on package. Line a large baking sheet with foil; set aside.

For filling: Remove skins from grapes by gently pressing each grape between your fingers. (Skins slip off easily.) Set skins aside. In a 4- or 5-quart Dutch oven, bring grape pulp to boiling; reduce heat. Simmer, uncovered, for 5 minutes. To remove seeds, press pulp though a food mill or a coarse sieve (should have about 1¾ cups pulp).

Combine grape skins and pulp, sugar, cornstarch, butter, lemon peel and juice, salt, cinnamon and nutmeg; set aside.

Unroll piecrusts. Ease 1 piecrust into a 9-inch pie plate. Transfer filling to pastry-lined pie plate. Trim bottom crust even with rim of pie plate. Cut slits in remaining piecrust; place on filling. Fold top crust under bottom pastry. Crimp edge.

To prevent overbrowning, cover edge of pie with foil. Place pie in oven; position baking sheet on oven rack below pie. Bake in a 375° oven for 25 minutes. Remove foil. Bake about 20 minutes more or until filling is bubbly. Carefully remove pie from oven.

Cool on a wire rack for at least 4 hours before serving. If you like, serve with scoops of vanilla ice cream. *Makes 8 servings.*

The day's final stop is just seven miles southwest of Mapleton (population 1,300) in Monona County to visit, of all things, a Loess Hills vineyard, planted by Richard Bumann. He's the owner of Timber Ridge, a private, 3,000-acre "recreation ranch" getaway. At sunset, I wander through some of the nine acres of Concord, Niagara, Elvira and Fontanelle grapes and sample Richard's grape and other fruit wines (chokecherry, cherry, wild plum, wild raspberry and apple). Timber Ridge and seven other wineries have revived a long-forgotten tradition here, prevalent before agricultural use of the potent pesticide 2,4-D in the 1950s and '60s killed the existing grapevines.

Where the Hawks Soar

The creation of Pottawattamie County's Hitchcock Nature Center, six miles off I-29 near Honey Creek, is one of those rescued-from-ecological-ruin stories I love hearing in the Loess Hills. In 1991, this land was slated to become a rail destination for New Jersey garbage! (In fact, 22 acres already were a junkyard.) Fortunately, a substantial part of the present nature center was somewhat protected as a YMCA camp; other sections were used for farming and grazing. Begun with 500 acres, the preserve has now doubled in size (the public has access to 700 acres) and ultimately will encompass more than 2,100 acres of the Loess Hills.

Today, visitors enjoy 10 miles of hiking trails along with primitive campsites and picnic shelters. Popular pastimes include bird-watching, hunting (deer and turkey) and archery. Chad Graeve, the center's natural resource specialist, grew up just 11 miles south of here in Council Bluffs. Like me, he did not know much about the natural treasure at his doorstep. "I had to go away to college to learn what the Loess Hills are and why we need to save them," Chad says.

Named for the founder of the *Omaha World-Herald* newspaper, whose legacy has helped fund the nature center, Hitchcock is the Loess Hills park closest to the Omaha area. "We're eight years into a 50-year restoration plan that will restore biodiversity to the prairies, savannas and woodlands you see here," Chad explains, as he shows me where trees have been removed to open the ground to sunlight so grasses and plants can thrive once again. At one point, a lizardlike prairie race runner darts across our path; at another, an ornate box turtle creeps along. Trees here include bur oak, ash, elm, hackberry, walnut, ironwood, honey locust and red oak—so many that they all but obscure the configuration of the hills.

Few people realize that the Loess Hills is one of the nation's top hawk-watching areas (highly appropriate, since Iowa is the Hawkeye State). More than 20 species have been sighted here by staff members and volunteers, primarily during the peak migration period from September 1 to December 20, when the raptors wing on updrafts from the hills. During their incredible journeys, the hawks can range as far north as the Arctic and as far south as Argentina. The 45-foot Hawk Tower beside the interpretive center perches atop a 300-foot bluff, providing quite a view.

"We've counted as many as 800 hawks here in one hour, 2,000 in one day—including Cooper's, Swainson's and broad-wing hawks," says Mark Orsag, a college instructor who volunteers here. "In all, we tallied 16,000 raptors here last year—including bald and golden eagles, turkey vultures and kestrel falcons. They don't have to work as hard when they fly on the thermals."

Soon, I'm tracking several of the regal birds in my binocular sights. I wonder if they're as happy as I am to be here, surveying Iowa's unexpected and underappreciated natural treasure, the Loess Hills.

CLOCKWISE, FROM TOP: Chad Graeve and Dan at Hitchcock Nature Center. Hoary vervain, a Loess Hills wildflower. Grape vineyard at Timber Ridge near Mapleton. Prairie coneflower.

TOP TO BOTTOM:
Sheer Loess Hills road cut. Blufftop Sioux City obelisk honoring Sergeant Floyd of the Lewis and Clark Expedition.

Dan's Travel Journal

FEATURED STOPS

Hitchcock Nature Center Honey Creek. This 1,000-acre preserve boasts outstanding Loess Hills overlooks and hiking trails, plus large prairie remnants. Facilities include campgrounds, modern cabins and an interpretive center (712/545-3283).

Loess Hills National Scenic Byway. The 220-mile byway parallels I-29, following paved roads south from Akron to Hamburg. View the hills from the overlook deck in Loess Hills State Forest near Preparation Canyon State Park (five miles southwest of Moorhead), which features hiking trails leading to primitive camping sites. Scenic Waubonsie State Park, at the southern end of the byway (six miles south of Sidney), offers modern camping and hiking and equestrian trails. Free maps and information available at visitors centers along the byway (712/255-4698).

Sioux City Lewis & Clark Interpretive Center Sioux City. Learn what it was like to serve with Lewis and Clark at this Missouri Riverfront attraction (712/224-5242).

Stone State Park and **Dorothy Pecaut Nature Center** Sioux City. At this 1,130-acre park, view vistas Lewis and Clark might have seen (712/255-4698). The nature center features dioramas, live native fish and reptiles and a "walk-under" prairie (712/258-0838).

Lodging, Dining and More

Country Homestead Bed and Breakfast Turin. Stay in an 1800s farmhouse or a cottage or bunkhouse. $$ (712/353-6772, www.country-homestead.com).

Feedbunk Cafe Moorhead. Line up for breaded pork tenderloin sandwiches and hot roast beef dinners (712/886-5111).

Hampton Inn Council Bluffs. On I-29 along the Missouri River, with 98 rooms and suites, pool, hot tub, fitness center and Continental breakfast. $$ (712/328-2500).

Historic 4th Street Sioux City. Visit Luciano's for Italian specialties (712/258-5174) and Sweet Fanny's Pub and Dining Room for prime rib, burgers and chicken-fried steak (712/258-3434).

Holiday Inn Downtown Sioux City. Remodeled 114-room hotel with indoor pool, sauna, restaurant and easy access to the hills. $$ (712/277-9400).

Mama Keri's Diner Mondamin. Feast on fried chicken, half-pound burgers, fresh-cut curly fries, rhubarb cobbler and other from-scratch cooking (712/646-2244).

River of Glory Country Retreat Council Bluffs. Loess Hills and valleys, landscaped gardens and wildflowers surround this restored 1890 Victorian-style farmhouse. $$$$ (712/366-4678).

Timber Ridge Ranch and Winery Mapleton. Its wines all come from Loess Hills-grown fruits. The 3,000-acre recreation ranch is open to ATVs, fishing, camping, hiking and bicycling (712/353-6600).

More Information

Council Bluffs Convention & Visitors Bureau (800/228-6878, www.councilbluffsiowa.com).

Iowa Tourism Office (800/345-4692, traveliowa.com).

Loess Hills Hospitality Association (800/886-5441, www.loesshillstours.com).

Loess Hills National Scenic Byway (712/482-5590, www.loesshillsnationalscenicbyway.com).

Sioux City Convention Center & Tourism Bureau (800/593-2228, siouxcitytourism.com).

DAN'S OTHER STOPS

(See also More Parks section that follows.)
Neal Smith National Wildlife Refuge Prairie City (515/994-3400), **Yellow River State Forest** Harpers Ferry (563/586-2254).

More Iowa Parks

Cedar Valley Nature Trail

Forested bottomlands, pristine farmsteads and friendly small towns await cyclists on this 52-mile route between the eastern Iowa towns of Hiawatha and Evansdale. Connecting trails lead to Waterloo, Cedar Falls and Cedar Rapids. Built on the abandoned Illinois Central Gulf Railroad right-of-way, the route is relatively flat, making it easygoing for bicyclists, plus hikers, joggers, in-line skaters and cross-country skiers (also wheelchair accessible). Asphalt covers the 15 miles from Evansdale to McFarlane Park just south of La Porte City, with camping beside the trail at the park. At Hiawatha, the trail turns to crushed limestone.

Riders pedal across rivers and streams, through wetlands for bird-watching, amid open stretches of prairie and beneath canopies of trees. Restaurants and shops along the way make tempting stops. Restored train stations in Gilbertville and Center Point recall the trail's heritage.

Contact: Cedar Valley Nature Trail (319/892-6450, cedarvalleytrail.com). Nearest lodgings: in Cedar Falls (800/845-1955, cedarfallstourism.org), Cedar Rapids (800/735-5557, cedar-rapids.com) and Waterloo (319/233-8350, waterloocvb.org).

Dolliver State Park

Amid the rich farmlands that dominate north-central Iowa, this park, with its shady green glens, seems like a mirage near the little town of Lehigh (10 miles south of Fort Dodge). At the 500-acre enclave, creeks burble through verdant ravines, and aspens quake in the breeze. You'll hear songbirds and see shorebirds galore.

Visitors can picnic, splash in Prairie Creek, fish in the Des Moines River and hike six miles of trails. The paths lead to Indian burial mounds on the park's bluffs. Along one trail beside Prairie Creek, you'll see the Copperas Beds, towering sandstone that provides a cross-section of a riverbed more than 150 million years old. You can tent at campsites or stay in family cabins.

Contact: Dolliver State Park (515/359-2539, iowadnr.com). Nearest lodgings: in Fort Dodge (515/955-5500, fortdodge chamber.com).

Grant Wood National Scenic Byway

Countryside that inspired the paintings of Iowa-born Grant Wood unfurls serenely on this 68-mile drive west from the Mississippi River through a central section of the state. Driving west from historic Bellevue, with its four-block-long riverside main street, you'll see the scenes and hamlets that inspired the 1930s artist. Visit Bellevue State Park just south of town for lofty Mississippi overlooks and a tour of the butterfly garden.

In the county seat of Maquoketa to the southwest, Banowetz Antique Mall stocks an assortment of vintage finds. You also can shop for works of art at Costello's Old Mill Gallery. Just beyond town, more-adventurous hikers follow trails linking the caves at Maquoketa Caves State Park. The drive ends at the Grant Wood Tourism Center & Gallery in Anamosa, where you can buy prints of the artist's works.

Contact: National Scenic Byways (800/429-9297, byways.org). Anamosa Area Chamber of Commerce (319/462-4879, anamosachamber.com). Bellevue Area Chamber of Commerce (563/872-5830, bellevueia.com). Jackson County Tourism (800/342-1837, jacksoncountyiowa.com). Maquoketa Chamber of Commerce (800/989-4602, maquoketa.com). Nearest

LEFT TO RIGHT: The Mississippi from a Great River Road overlook in northeast Iowa. Vintage caboose at Walnut Grove Pioneer Village, Scott County Park. Buffalo at Neal Smith National Wildlife Refuge.

lodgings: in Anamosa, Bellevue and Maquoketa (see previous contacts).

Great River Road National Scenic Byway

On Iowa's 326 miles of this scenic byway, you'll experience the topographic diversity of the state and the Mississippi River. Steep bluffs cut by melting glaciers in the north give way to floodplains in the south. Travelers pass through small towns and bustling cities, as well as state parks with far-reaching overlooks and up close river views.

To the north, brick buildings in the small towns of McGregor and Marquette recall days when these communities served as gateways to settling the region. From Pikes Peak State Park, Iowa's highest point above the Mississippi, you can see for miles. The city of Dubuque climbs the hills. A new waterfront complex includes a museum detailing the river's history.

Farther south, plan to watch barges ply the Mississippi from Davenport's Le Claire Park. Then, continue to the city of Fort Madison and tour a reconstruction of the Upper Mississippi's first military fort.

Contact: National Scenic Byways (800/429-9297, byways.org). For Davenport, Quad Cities Convention & Visitors Bureau (800/747-7800, visitquadcities .com). Dubuque Area Chamber of Commerce (800/798-4748, dubuquechamber .com). Fort Madison Chamber of Commerce (319/372-5472, fortmadison .com). McGregor-Marquette Area Chamber of Commerce (800/896-0910, mcgreg marq.org). Nearest lodgings: in Davenport, Dubuque, Fort Madison, McGregor and Marquette (contacts above).

Lacey-Keosauqua State Park

This 1,600-plus-acre southeastern Iowa park is one of the state's largest and most picturesque. Its bluffs and forested valleys wind along the Des Moines River (45 miles west of Burlington). You might spot deer and red foxes along hiking trails that follow the river. A series of 19 Indian burial mounds overlook the water. Swimmers and anglers head for the 22-acre lake (boat rentals). You also can try your luck at landing catfish. Shady campgrounds dot the park, and trees shade six rustic cabins.

Many park visitors browse the Villages of Van Buren County (Bentonsport, Bonaparte, Farmington and the largest, Keosauqua, with 1,000 residents). A few miles apart along the Des Moines River, they're charming reminders of paddle-wheel days.

Contact: Lacey-Keosauqua State Park (319/293-3502, iowadnr.com). Villages of Van Buren County (800/868-7822, villages ofvanburen.com). Nearest lodgings: in Keosauqua and Bentonsport (contact above).

The Loess Hills
(See previous section of this chapter.)

Neal Smith National Wildlife Refuge

Buffalo and elk are at home again on the Iowa range, where they flourished some 150 years ago when tallgrass prairie covered 85 per cent of the state. Only a smidgen of prairie remains, but you can return to those times at this 8,600-plus-acre refuge near Prairie City (25 miles east of Des Moines).

The best place to begin your visit is the Prairie Learning Center, with hands-on exhibits. A music box shows how insects,

birds and plants fit into the ecosystem. You'll also learn about the prairie's ongoing reconstruction. On a drive through the refuge, visitors see buffalo and elk. Nature trails lead through tallgrass prairie and oak savannas. Watch for nesting birds such as rare Henslow's sparrows. Special events include Migratory Bird Day in April and Buffalo Day in June, plus prairie-restoration programs the second Saturday each month.

Contact: Neal Smith National Wildlife Refuge (515/994-3400, tallgrass.org). Nearest lodgings: seven miles north in Colfax (515/674-4096, colfaxiowachamber.com), in Des Moines (800/451-2625, desmoinesia .com) and 16 miles northeast in Newton (800/798-0299, visitnewton.com).

Scott County Park

When work began in the 1960s at the site for Scott County's largest park (nine miles north of Davenport), a country lane that led through the shady grove was preserved. Visitors still walk it today at this 1,300-acre haven near the little town of Long Grove.

Though the eastern Iowa park has mushroomed in size and activities, it retains its wilderness atmosphere along 10 miles of hiking trails through deep forests and open fields, where you might spot coyotes or deer. In the park's northwestern corner, visitors get a glimpse of days gone by at the Dan Nagle Walnut Grove Pioneer Village. Among the 18 refurbished early-1800s buildngs, you can tour log cabins and a bank, barbershop and vintage train depot.

The park also includes an Olympic-size pool, an 18-hole golf course, basketball and volleyball courts, picnic areas and five campgrounds. Two new cabins recently opened. Just four miles east, plan to tour the 1847 Buffalo Bill Cody Homestead, where the famous Wild West showman grew up. Buffalo graze there.

Contact: Scott County Park (563/328-3282, scottcountyiowa.com). Nearest lodgings: in Davenport (800/747-7800, visitquad cities.com).

Yellow River State Forest

Rocky outcroppings, bluffs and steep slopes distinguish this rugged 8,500-acre forest west of the Mississippi River town of Harper's Ferry (60 miles east of Decorah). It offers a haven for outdoor enthusiasts.

This northeastern Iowa forest consists of hardwoods and pines near the confluence of the Yellow and Mississippi rivers. The extensive system of fire lanes that helped protect the timberlands figures into the trail network for hiking, horseback riding, cross-country skiing and snowmobiling.

Most visitors head for the forest's Paint Creek Unit, cut by Big Paint and Little Paint creeks. You can camp, hike 25 miles of trails and cast for trout on six miles of stocked stream. Some anglers also try their luck for bass and panfish in marshy areas. Deer and other wild creatures rustle in the woods. You'll see waterfowl and wading birds in marshes and beaver ponds on Little Paint Creek. South of the forest at Iowa's only national monument, Effigy Mounds, Native Americans created 31 burial mounds in the shapes of birds and bears.

Contact: Yellow River State Forest (563/586-2256, iowadnr.com). Effigy Mounds National Monument (563/873-3491, nps.gov). Nearest lodgings: in Harpers Ferry and 10 miles north in Lansing (800/824-1424, allamakeecounty.com).

KANSAS

A renowned bird-watching paradise

SPRAWLING, WIDE-OPEN KANSAS is better known for its signature commodities of wheat, cattle and oil than for its parks, but my foray here turns up several natural gems that defy the stereotypes about this Great Plains state.

Upon departing Kansas City's handsome, tree-canopied suburbs, I feel like a modern-day version of an early-Santa Fe Trail traveler—albeit one driving an air-conditioned four-wheel-drive vehicle rather than a lumbering Conestoga wagon. With my wireless e-mail device taking an extended hiatus (no service in the area), I watch for signs of agoraphobia in my gung ho helper, Eager Assistant Rob, a recent communications graduate from New York and a real East Coast city guy. But the flat, unfettered Kansas landscape seems to beguile him just as it always does me.

During most of my Kansas interlude, I'll explore Quivira National Wildlife Refuge and Cheyenne Bottoms Wildlife Area, two world-renowned bird and wildlife habitats in the Great Bend area, near the center of the state. Before and after, I'll stop briefly at several other parklands along the way.

Grasslands and Prairie Dogs

At the Tallgrass Prairie National Preserve north of tiny Strong City along east-central Kansas' Flint Hills National Scenic Byway, I grab my trusty walking stick, and

Gangly pelicans, among the many bird species that stop to feast at Cheyenne Bottoms.

Photography by Per Breiehagen

LEFT TO RIGHT: Vigilant white-tailed deer grazing at Quivira. Fiery sunset at Cheyenne Bottoms. Mallard ducks in splashy takeoff mode. Bird-watcher at Quivira National Wildlife Refuge observation tower at Little Salt Marsh.

Rob and I tramp a gently sloping, 1.3-mile segment of the Southwind Nature Trail, accompanied only by gentle breezes, buzzing insects and chirping birds. Like a brilliantly colored impressionistic canvas, the sun-washed prairie is dappled with native flowers—orange butterfly milkweed, purple wild alfalfa and cream and blue wild indigo. It's a perfect introduction to a state carpeted by these splendid, seemingly endless grasslands.

In the northwest corner of the Sunflower State, I pull over just west of Norton at Prairie Dog State Park. Here, approximately 1,000 busy, barking prairie dogs scamper above their extensive network of 30-foot-deep tunnels, which at one time extended up to hundreds of miles beneath the prairies.

It's my first of many encounters on the plains with these cartoon-cute rodents (oft-maligned by ranchers and farmers) and their curious companion, the burrowing owl, which makes its home in abandoned prairie dog holes (a great recycling idea, with few trees available hereabouts). The adjoining man-made Keith Sebelius Reservoir is an uncrowded 2,500-acre fishing, camping and boating oasis in this semiarid region.

Nearer my destination, within the gentle arc formed by the Arkansas River (aptly pronounced ArKANsas in this state), I prowl about the meticulously restored, white-trimmed sandstone barracks and other buildings at lonesome, windswept Fort Larned, an 1860s Santa Fe Trail cavalry outpost. Nearby, the locally run Santa Fe Trail Center, complete with a sod house on the grounds, gives me yet more glimpses of life along this once-vital frontier thoroughfare through Kansas.

Just up US-56, on the way to Great Bend, an observation platform offers an awesome 15-mile view from atop Pawnee Rock, a 240-foot-circumference red-sandstone outcrop once utilized by vigilant Plains Indians on the lookout for buffalo and unwelcome wagon trains passing along the trail through their home turf. Now reduced some 20 feet from its original 100-foot elevation by erosion and quarrying, it's still the tallest citadel in these parts.

After fortifying myself with multiple cups of strong black coffee and a superhearty breakfast of biscuits and sausage gravy plus a fittingly named Twister omelet at Granny's Kitchen in Great Bend, I move on to keep a date with a few thousand birds.

Quivira Wildlife Refuge

Few people would expect landlocked Kansas to harbor saltwater marshes, but here they are, at this glistening refuge about 20 miles southeast of Great Bend, welcoming thousands of shorebirds, waders and waterfowl. It's as if this area were some kind of avian airport packed with feathered travelers of myriad species and sizes stopping to refuel en route to their final destinations during their spring and fall migrations.

Great Bend is a county-seat community of about 16,000 whose fortunes rise and fall with those of the oil-and-gas industry. Back in the 1800s, the old Santa Fe Trail passed right across the present-day lawn of the stately white 1917 Barton County Courthouse along what's now Main Street downtown. These days, the city's civic leaders are trying to diversify the local economy by welcoming more tourists, especially bird-watchers.

It's a growing economic-development theme throughout the region, and, thanks largely to baby boomers like me, one of the fastest growing outdoor-recreation activities in the United States, with more than 50 million of us bird-watching. Before the introduction of modern binoculars,

bird-watchers literally shot their specimens first and examined them later. These days, thanks to binoculars, telescopic sights and cameras, the pastime is much more pleasant, especially for the birds. There are thought to be about 10,000 bird species globally and about a tenth that number in the United States alone.

Both Quivira and Cheyenne Bottoms Wildlife Area have been designated Wetlands of International Importance by a global environmental group. Part of their prominence derives from the fact that this is a very salty part of Kansas; Hutchinson, about a half hour southeast of Quivira, is a salt-mining center and just opened a new museum devoted to the subject. Such underground salt deposits, left behind by long-vanished oceans, help create the salt-water marshes that attract birds to the area from all over the hemisphere.

The name Quivira comes from a Native American tribe (whose fashion-conscious members liked to tattoo their eyes so they resembled raccoons) encountered by the Spanish explorer Francisco Vásquez de Coronado. The refuge starts on Great Bend's newly designated, 77-mile Wetlands and Wildlife National Scenic Byway and

is anchored at the north end by Cheyenne Bottoms. The byway wends primarily on country roads through three counties and seven area communities. Quivira is one of 530 such refuges managed by the U.S. Fish and Wildlife Service and encompasses almost 22,000 acres of prairie, with grass-covered sand dunes crisscrossed by 21 miles of canals and 25 miles of dikes. The two features that draw most visitors are dubbed Little Salt Marsh and Big Salt Marsh.

Ornithologists call it the "hourglass effect": Each spring and fall, migratory birds funnel into these nutrient-rich marshes seeking sustenance, rest and, sometimes, nesting opportunities on their way to and from destinations as far north as the Arctic and as far south as Patagonia in South America. Many are species not often seen elsewhere in Kansas, or the rest of the Midwest for that matter: long-necked waders, such as great and snowy egrets and great blue herons; large shorebirds, including the American avocet, black-necked stilt and godwit; small shorebirds, such as the white-rumped sandpiper, long-billed dowitcher and snowy plover; and waterfowl, including snow and white-fronted geese, blue-winged teal and mallards.

During my brief tour, I also run across a menagerie of other migratory and resident species, including the western grebe, least bittern, white-faced ibis, common moorhen, black rail, bobolink, Baird's sandpiper and Forster's tern. For most of Quivira's assorted winged dining patrons, the primary culinary attraction is millions of mud-loving invertebrate larvae called bloodworms, which the birds greedily consume to fatten up for the remainder of their epic journeys.

As I drive past bobbing oil derricks and golden fields of harvested winter wheat, Quivira's marshes suddenly shimmer like silvery mirages behind ancient stands of cottonwood and box elder. Turning onto Big Salt Marsh Wildlife Drive, I note some of the wingless critters that seem to like it here as much as the birds do: White-tailed and mule deer graze, then leap away when they spy me; clumsy box turtles cross the roadway before me at their own glacial pace. Soon several small shorebirds fearlessly dart in front of my car, and I spot a line of geese flapping overhead. I pull off the road for a closer look through my binoculars.

Amiable Robert Penner has volunteered to be my birding guide, both here at Quivira and at Cheyenne Bottoms, where he's a project director for The Nature Conservancy. Among his other credentials, Robert has a doctorate in ornithology from the University of Nebraska. Even though my June visit doesn't coincide with the peak spring and fall migrations, I'm plenty impressed by what I see and hear. In short order, Robert identifies more than 20 bird species from this one vantage point. In addition to the varieties I've already seen, I add an ever-more-disparate collection: mourning dove, brown thrasher, Baltimore oriole and a huge conclave of pelicans. Then come the western and eastern meadowlark,

as the "dawn chorus." The chitchat begins daily with the first light at about 4:30 a.m. and ends at about 7:30 a.m. "The birds are telling the world they made it through the night without getting eaten by predators—raccoons, skunks, snakes and, sometimes, human hunters. They're still in their territory, and they're ravenous," Robert says. I jot more notes for the birding life list I've vowed to start. Robert tells me his list now runs to more than 400 species, which is about how many kinds of birds you'll find in Kansas, including the western meadowlark, the state bird.

the underground salt deposits. I swing by the observation tower for a bird's-eye view of several of Quivira's 32 wetland areas, then head to the nearby visitors center for an informative self-guided tour of the exhibits. Before leaving, I stop at a stocked pond crowded with kids and their parents here for a fishing clinic—obviously a success, based on the catfish and largemouth bass I see them reeling in.

Cheyenne Bottoms

Despite the long-term drought plaguing this area at the time of my visit, Quivira has plenty of water to greet the birds refueling at its marshes, thanks to abundant natural springs; the healthy flow of its primary tributary, Rattlesnake Creek (I didn't encounter any of the namesake massasauga rattlers, which is fine with me); and the winning of a meteorological lottery when it came to spotty snows and rains over the past year.

All around me, a million chirps, screeches, cackles and shrieks seem to combine into one unforgettable symphony.

redheaded woodpecker, eastern kingbird and double-crested cormorant. I can hardly keep up as I scribble down their names, juggling my notebook and binoculars!

I'm most intrigued by the big, long-necked and long-legged waders that Robert calls his reliable "boys of summer" because they always hang around through the hottest months of the year. The various egret, crane and ibis species proudly strut at water's edge, feasting on a banquet of crayfish, snails and minnows. Their smaller counterparts content themselves with insects, larvae and those tiny bloodworms. If I were here in spring, Robert tells me, I might see more than 125 bird species in one day alone. I'm amazed to learn that nearly 40 percent of America's shorebirds stop at Quivira, and 90 percent of some species, such as Baird's and white-rumped sandpipers.

All around me, a million chirps, screeches, cackles and shrieks seem to combine into one unforgettable symphony playing in stereo surround. Robert says it's known

Robert gives me some expert advice: "Birds are secretive. They like to hide out in trees or grasses. Learn to recognize them by their distinctive calls [which you can study by visiting websites and listening to CDs]. Then track them down visually," he says. "Hear that meadowlark? It sounds like he's saying 'Hey, look at me!' The dickcissel seems to be saying exactly that: 'Dic, dic, cissel, cissel.'" Robert says several other species, such as the killdeer, are named for the sounds they make. He encourages me to read up on birds' habits (early-morning feeding times usually are best for viewing) and habitats (robins and cardinals hang out in trees; shorebirds, waders and waterfowl at water's edge). "Keep several guides with good illustrations handy for cross-referencing, and acquire a good pair of binoculars."

Quivira's flora fascinates me as well. The refuge is packed with salt-tolerant plants and grasses, such as butterfly milkweed, inland saltgrass and dozens of other species that have adapted to the salinity created by

That's not the case, however, at state-managed Cheyenne Bottoms Wildlife Area, 30 miles north of Quivira on the other side of Great Bend and the barely-there Arkansas River. Periodic droughts are a grim fact of life on these semiarid plains (ever heard of the 1930s dust bowl?). Normal precipitation for the area is about 25 inches, most of it in the first half of the year. As of June this year, there's been only 14 inches.

Usually, the bottoms can be replenished with water diverted from the Arkansas River, but even that major Mississippi tributary is almost dry because of drought, agricultural irrigation and urban water demands (even by Denver, 400 miles away). The three intermittently flowing creeks that feed the basin—Deception, Blood and Shopp—are bone-dry. Still, I learn much during my visit to this temporarily underoccupied bird haven, and I'll come back when the rains return.

Cheyenne Bottoms is a flat, 41,000-acre natural basin some 10 miles long and eight miles across, held partly by the state of Kansas (20,000 acres) and The Nature Conservancy (7,300 acres), with the rest in private hands. Its topography is fascinating—like a huge oval meat platter with a thin lip at the edges. Named for a Native American tribe that once hunted here, the unique depression is thought to have been formed when an undergirding salt dome collapsed because of subterranean erosion about 100,000 years ago. Over the aeons, Cheyenne Bottoms has been the floor of a huge ocean as well as an aspen forest complete with black bears. Explorer Zebulon Pike poked around here in 1806, and during World War II the area served as a practice range for bomber-pilots-in-training (I bet nobody consulted the birds).

Robert and I chat with Cheyenne Bottoms Field Supervisor Karl Grover as we view the wetlands in their current dry state. Karl explains that this is the perfect time to groom the marshes: "This lets us disk troublesome plants like cattails and bulrushes that can choke the marshes when they're wet." Karl also tells me he's working with Robert and The Nature Conservancy to rid the area of unwanted native and invasive trees, such as the constantly proliferating eastern red cedar, locust, Russian olive, Siberian elm, hackberry and mulberry.

I thought birds liked trees! Not most of the species that stop here, Karl explains: "We want to maintain an open prairie and wetland environment. That's important to attracting the waterfowl, shorebirds and grassland birds we want to see here. Trees also soak up a lot of our water supply." Before Europeans settled here, Native Americans (deliberately setting fires to attract buffalo) and unchecked lightning-caused blazes regularly handled the tree-removal job.

When times are good, Cheyenne Bottoms

Red-winged blackbirds in the marshes at Cheyenne Bottoms.

Birdseed Trail Mix

This honey-sweetened trail mix makes a sensational snack for bird-watchers, hikers or most anyone exploring central Kansas, a birding mecca with Cheyenne Bottoms Wildlife Area to the north and Quivira National Wildlife Refuge to the south.

Nonstick cooking spray
3 cups regular rolled oats
1 cup unsalted sunflower kernels
1 cup unsalted cashews, almonds and/or peanuts
½ cup toasted wheat germ
½ cup shredded coconut
⅔ cup honey
⅓ cup light-colored corn syrup
¼ cup orange or tangerine juice
3 tablespoons cooking oil
1 teaspoon vanilla
1 teaspoon ground cinnamon
1 7-ounce package mixed tropical blend dried-fruit bits
½ cup raisins, dried cranberries and/or dried cherries

Lightly coat a 15x10x1-inch baking pan with cooking spray; set aside. In a large bowl, stir together oats, sunflower kernels, cashews, wheat germ and coconut.

In a small bowl, stir together honey, corn syrup, orange juice, cooking oil, vanilla and cinnamon. Pour honey mixture over oat mixture; toss to coat. Spread evenly in prepared pan.

Bake in a 325° oven for 45 to 50 minutes or until oats are lightly browned, stirring three times. Remove from oven. Stir in fruit bits and raisins. Immediately turn out onto a large piece of foil. Cool completely. (To store, seal in storage bags and keep at room temperature for up to 1 week.) *Makes about 9 (1-cup) servings.*

welcomes two principal classes of visitors: nature enthusiasts such as bird-watchers, photographers and hikers (all primarily in springtime), and waterfowl hunters (in fall when, incidentally, the photos on these pages were taken to showcase the golden autumnal beauty of the landscape). Duck- and goose-hunting was the primary motivation for creating the preserve back in the 1940s, but these days a growing contingent of visitors shoots with cameras.

The wildlife area offers rare opportunities to bag (on film) such threatened and endangered bird species as the whooping crane, peregrine falcon, bald eagle, piping plover and pintail, as well as hundreds of others; more than 325 have been sighted here. There also are 31 endangered or threatened mammal species, including coyote, red fox, raccoon, white-tailed and mule deer, opossum, bobcat, beaver, jackrabbit, gopher, muskrat, mink, badger and skunk.

Of course, wetlands attract reptiles, and Cheyenne Bottoms doesn't disappoint, with 19 species of slithering critters, including various frogs, toads, turtles and snakes, such as the diamondback water snake we spot from the road and (thankfully) bashful massasauga rattlesnakes. On a one-mile solo hike, I encounter a 30-pound snapping turtle suffering in the heat as he tries to cross a gravel road. Later, Karl will give him a lift in the pickup to new life in one of Cheyenne's few remaining water holes.

There are more than 200-plus species of grassland plants here in the normally wet upland meadows and marshes. Karl and Robert point out the spike rush, winged loosestrife, aster and western wheat, inland salt, buffalo and prairie cordgrasses, which seem the most unaffected by drought. Unlike Quivira's saltwater ecosystem, the marshes at Cheyenne Bottoms are freshwater for the most part (although the saline content can be quite high here as well).

I spot occasional depressions that look like big potholes in the parched meadows. Robert explains they've been created for migratory birds—they're sort of like mini fast-food stops for the waterfowl he hopes will fill the skies come fall, to the tune of up to 400,000 geese and 200,000 ducks alone. Spring shorebirds number in the millions.

As we continue our drive, Karl further informs me about the concept of natural succession, which is helping me see this, and all the ecosystems I'll encounter on my parklands journey, in a broader context: "All ecosystems are constantly in flux in terms of nature's timetable, which is obviously much longer than ours. Every landscape is changing. Here, we're trying to slow down a natural process, the filling in of these bottomlands with silt, by disking and employing a form of dredging to eliminate troublesome perennials, such as cattail."

It's been several years since Cheyenne Bottoms had plentiful rains. But wet or dry, it's clear this habitat is worth preserving (in fact, I note a new $3.5 million interpretive center is planned just east of the wildlife refuge). Karl explains that, from 1780 to 1980, Kansas lost an estimated half of its wetlands to the march of human development. "This is a great opportunity to conserve these vanishing wetlands," he says. "When the water returns, we'll be ready to welcome all the birds back again. The dry weather is all part of nature's grand plan."

Postscript: Karl is right. Our camera crew returns in October to find Cheyenne Bottoms golden-hued and temporarily replenished by several late-summer rains. In contrast to the scene we first encountered, its marshes now teem with tens of thousands of migrating waterfowl and shorebirds. "Things can change abruptly on the Great Plains," Karl says. "That's how it's always been here at Cheyenne Bottoms."

Dan's Travel Journal

FEATURED STOPS

Cheyenne Bottoms Wildlife Area Six miles northeast of Great Bend. This 27,000-acre wildlife haven, considered the largest marsh in the interior of the United States, attracts 325 bird species, among them whooping cranes, snowy plovers, bald eagles and peregrine falcons. Visit in fall for waterfowl and spring for shorebirds. Coming in late 2007: a new wetlands interpretive center (620/793-7730).

Quivira National Wildlife Refuge Twenty miles southeast of Great Bend. A major stopover for thousands of migrating waterfowl—as many as 260,000 sandhill cranes and a million geese during fall migration—on 22,000 acres of salt marshes, prairie grasses and sand dunes. Explore the visitors center and walking trails. For the best viewing, take the designated Wildlife Drive (620/486-2393).

Lodging, Dining and More

Brit Spaugh Zoo Great Bend. At this free zoo, hawks, vultures, owls, alligators and snakes star at daily summer Wings of Wonder bird shows, alligator feedings and reptile programs. Also at the zoo: bird education programs at the new Central Kansas Raptor Rehab facility, set to open in late 2007 (620/793-4160).

Classic Inn Great Bend. American and Asian favorites, featuring prime rib on Saturday nights and a daily Oriental lunch buffet (620/792-3100).

Delgado's Great Bend. Authentic Mexican fare, including secret-recipe pork chili and from-scratch tamales (620/793-3786).

Eazy Street Great Bend. North of town on the way to Cheyenne Bottoms, stop for a burger basket with a heap of hand-cut French fries or a family-style chicken dinner Sundays at noon (620/793-6966).

Granny's Kitchen Great Bend. Order break-fast anytime in this cozy kitchen, known for the Wheat Belt Skillet (with marinated steak), Granny's Barn Burner omelet (the works) and other favorites (620/793-7441).

Highland Hotel & Convention Center Great Bend. Easy access to the wetlands from the town's largest full-service hotel, with a restaurant, lounge and recreational FunDome under one roof. $ (866/212-7122).

The Page Great Bend. American bistro with a full menu including steaks, seafood and pasta (620/792-8700).

Related Area Event

Wings and Wetlands Weekend Great Bend, during odd-numbered years in late April. Birders flock to Cheyenne Bottoms Wildlife Area and Quivira National Wildlife Refuge for guided field trips and educational seminars (877/427-9299).

More Information

Great Bend Convention & Visitors Bureau (877/427-9299, www.visitgreatbend.com). Kansas Travel & Tourism (800/252-6727, www.travelks.com). National Audubon Society (212/979-3000, www.audubon.org). The Nature Conservancy (800/628-6860, www.nature.org). The Nature Conservancy of Kansas (785/233-4400, www.nature.org/kansas).

DAN'S OTHER STOPS

(See also More Parks section that follows.) Fort Larned National Historic Site Larned (620/285-6911), Keith Sebelius Reservoir Norton (785/877-2953), Pawnee Rock State Historic Site Pawnee Rock (785/272-8681), Prairie Dog State Park Norton (785/877-2953), Santa Fe Trail Center, Larned (620/285-2054), Tallgrass Prairie National Preserve Strong City (620/273-8494).

TOP TO BOTTOM: Great egrets in flight, Cheyenne Bottoms. Phragmites, or common reed, Quivira.

More Kansas Parks

Keith Sebelius Reservoir,
Prairie Dog State Park
and Norton Wildlife Area

NE

CO

KANSAS

MO

Lake Scott
State Park

Mushroom Rock
State Park

Cheyenne Bottoms
Wildlife Area

Tallgrass Prairie
National Preserve

Prairie Spirit
Trail

Kanopolis
State Park

Wetlands and Wildlife
National Scenic Byway

Quivira
National Wildlife
Refuge

Flint
Hills

Arkansas River

Flint Hills
National Scenic Byway

Cimarron
National Grassland

Gypsum Hills

Gypsum Hills State Scenic Byway

OK

Cheyenne Bottoms Wildlife Area
(See previous section of this chapter.)

Cimarron National Grassland
Beneath the bluest sky you've ever seen, golden grasses and yucca spikes roll toward the horizon. Antelope, deer and elk nose buffalograss where bison once grazed. Except for an occasional gas well, nothing mars Kansas' largest expanse of public land—some 108,000 acres. Signs of civilization are rare hereabouts, but gravel roads access the Cimarron National Grassland here and there. In the 1820s, the first Santa Fe Trail wagon trains creaked along near the normally dry Cimarron River. Limestone pillars mark 23 miles of that trail, where wagon ruts still furrow the sandy southwest-Kansas soil.

Visitors can hike, bicycle, ride horses and camp along trails, including the 19-mile Santa Fe Companion Trail paralleling the original wagon route. A 30-mile gravel road travels to overlooks and historical markers. More than 360 types of birds have been spotted in this remote region. You can view prairie chickens' colorful courting rituals March–May from a blind maintained by the U.S. Forest Service, which administers the grassland from its ranger's office in the gateway town of Elkhart.

Contact: Cimarron National Grassland (620/697-4621,fs.fed.us/r2/psicc/cim).Kansas Travel & Tourism (800/252-6727, travelks.com). Nearest lodgings: in Elkhart (620/697-4600, ci.elkhart.ks.us) and 35 miles northeast in Hugoton (620/544-4440, hugotonchamber.com).

Flint Hills
North America's largest untouched tract of tallgrass prairie challenges the notion that prairies are flat. In this nearly treeless domain of ranchers, cowboys and cattle, you can soar and dive between east-central Kansas hilltops and valleys along lonesome country highways.

To sample this untamed 4,500 million acres, visit its core west of Emporia. The Flint Hills National Scenic Byway (State-177) extends 48 miles from Council Grove, once a Santa Fe Trail staging area, south through the communities of Strong City and Cottonwood Falls, ending in the little ranch town of Cassoday. Limestone homes and barns, most from the 1800s, peer through cottonwood groves. Winding lanes lead through carpets of wildflowers. In spring, flames dance across the hills as fires renew prairie grasses.

Between Council Grove and Cottonwood Falls at the Spring Hill Ranch complex, you can't miss the French Second Empire home, completed in 1881, within the 11,000-acre Tallgrass Prairie National Preserve. Visitors can hike 20 miles of trails and take guided van and house tours.

Contact: Kansas Department of Transportation (800/684-6966, ksbyways.org). Kansas Travel & Tourism (800/252-6727, travelks.com). Tallgrass Prairie National Preserve (620/273-8494, nps.gov/tapr). Nearest lodgings: limited in Cottonwood Falls (800/431-6344, chasecountychamber .org) and Council Grove (800/732-9211, councilgrove.com); more motels in Emporia (800/279-3730, emporiakschamber.org).

Gypsum Hills
Like the setting for your favorite Western movie, the Gypsum Hills make a rugged 20-mile-wide swipe west of the prairie town of Medicine Lodge (80 miles southwest of

Wichita) south into Oklahoma. Startling scenery awaits around nearly every turn in this fractured land of buttes and bluffs, rocky spires, mesas, ravines and canyons thick with cedars.

The Gypsum Hills State Scenic Byway (US-160) winds through the rumpled red-rock hills of this ranch country for about 42 miles west from Medicine Lodge to Coldwater. Along some sections of the route, you're more likely to see an armadillo or a Hereford than another car. Hard-packed dirt roads and trails—great for mountain biking and horseback riding—angle off the blacktop. Twin Peaks, a pair of nearly identical cone-shaped buttes, towers on the horizon.

In Medicine Lodge, plan to tour the home of crusader Carry Nation, who started her ax-wielding temperance movement here, and visit the Stockade Museum, a replica of a frontier outpost.

Contact: Kansas Department of Transportation (800/684-6966, ksbyways.org). Kansas Travel & Tourism (800/252-6727, travelks.com). Nearest lodgings: limited in Medicine Lodge (620/886-3417, cyberlodg.com/mlcity) and Coldwater (620/582-2859, coldwaterkansas.com); others 30 miles north of Medicine Lodge in Pratt (888/886-1164, prattkan.com).

Kanopolis State Park

Pitch your tent or park your RV at Kansas' oldest and among its most popular state parks (35 miles southwest of Salina). The 6,600-acre preserve, excellent for camping thanks to abundant mature trees, frames man-made Kanopolis Reservoir.

Riders on horseback amble along park trails, where signs point to Horsethief Canyon and Bison Creek, from the Goverland

CLOCKWISE, FROM TOP: Tallgrass Prairie National Preserve. Cholla in bloom along the Gypsum Hills State Scenic Byway. Surveying Cimarron National Grassland.

LEFT TO RIGHT: Sandstone formation, Mushroom Rock State Park. Scenic overlook, Lake Scott State Park. Towering limestone monoliths at Monument Rocks near Lake Scott State Park.

Stage Stop, which also provides stagecoach rides. Visitors might encounter deer, wild turkeys and even beavers along the nearly 25 miles of trails, also used for mountain biking and hiking. Keep an eye out and you'll even discover a prairie dog town. Water recreation—from swimming to boating and fishing—occupies other vacationers on the 3,500-acre lake. Sunbathers love the sandy beach.

You can make a side trip just north to hip-pocket-size Mushroom Rock State Park (only five acres). Since frontier times, the mushroom-shaped sandstone formations that reach toward the sky have been landmarks for travelers journeying west.

Contact: Kanopolis and Mushroom Rock state parks (785/546-2565, kdwp.state .ks.us). Kansas Travel & Tourism (800/252-6727, travelks.com). Nearest lodgings: in Salina (877/725-4525, salinakansas.org); more-limited options in Ellsworth (785/472-4071, ellsworthks.net/chamber.htm) and Lindsborg (888/227-2227, lindsborg .org), about 25 miles northwest and southeast, respectively.

Keith Sebelius Reservoir

As Prairie Dog Creek flows through the High Plains near the Nebraska state line, Norton Dam creates this 900-acre lake, bordered by Prairie Dog State Park and Norton Wildlife Area. You can take advantage of all three when visiting this area (four miles southwest of the Kansas county seat town of Norton).

At the lake, boating, swimming and beach fun complement excellent fishing for a variety of catches. But the lake is perhaps best known for its trophy wipers, a white-bass/striped-bass hybrid that anglers say puts up a ferocious fight.

You can camp at the state park, hike a nature trail and visit an 1880s school and adobe house. South of the park office, busy little black-tailed creatures race among the mounds of a thriving prairie dog colony. Listen for the sentries' jubilant "barks," sounding the all-clear from prairie dog predators such as coyotes and eagles.

For more nature watching, venture into the 5,500-acre Norton Wildlife Area, which pheasants, deer and wild turkeys call home. Lake roads also provide views of waterfowl and shorebirds during migrating season.

Contact: Keith Sebelius Reservoir, Prairie Dog State Park and Norton Wildlife Area (785/877-2953, kdwp.state.ks.us). Kansas Travel & Tourism (800/252-6727, travelks.com). Nearest lodgings: in Norton (785/877-2501, discovernorton.com).

Lake Scott State Park

Amid a buff-colored ocean of grass, this 1,120-acre state park is so perfectly hidden you'd never stumble upon it without signs

helping to point the way. The park's lake, natural springs, meadows and cottonwood groves tuck into a secluded High Plains valley protected by sandstone walls. Travelers spanning the centuries—Native Americans to Spanish troops, French traders and the cavalry—have journeyed to this appealing western-Kansas recreational oasis just west of US-83 between Oakley and Scott City (about 30 miles south of I-70).

Today, vacationers camp in shady groves—rare in this region where windmills outnumber trees—and fish, swim and boat in the spring-fed lake. From the campground, it's a short walk to the beach. Hiking and horse trails fan out past cattail marshes and up yucca-studded slopes. Other paths lead to interesting historic sites, including the reconstructed foundation of El Quartelejo Pueblo, a National Historic Landmark that dates back to 1680. You'll find more exhibits on display at the El Quartelejo Museum in Scott City. A gravel road eight miles northeast of the park wends among the sandstone monoliths of Monument Rocks.

Contact: Lake Scott State Park (620/872-2061, kdwp.state.ks.us). Kansas Travel & Tourism (800/252-6727, travelks.com). Nearest lodgings: in Scott City (620/872-3525, scottcitycofc.com) and Oakley (785/672-4862, discoveroakley.com).

Prairie Spirit Trail

Get set for easy pedaling through some of the state's prettiest countryside on Kansas' first rail-trail. The 33-mile-long bicycling and hiking route follows the converted right-of-way of the Atchison, Topeka and Santa Fe Railway from the eastern-Kansas county seat town of Ottawa (30 miles south of Lawrence) south to tiny Welda. Blooming prairies, woodlands and farms line the crushed-limestone path most of the way, though some in-town sections are paved. You'll cross bridges overlooking ponds, creeks and the Marais Des Cygnes River as you pedal your way through pleasant little communities. A restored prairie flourishes south of Garnett.

Bicyclists, as well as hikers, can access the trail, along with rest and picnic areas, in Ottawa, Princeton, Richmond, Garnett and Welda. Planning is under way for the third phase of the trail, another 17 miles continuing south to Iola.

Contact: Kansas Travel & Tourism (800/252-6727, travelks.com). Nearest lodgings: in Ottawa (785/242-1411, visit ottawakansas.com); more-limited lodging options in Garnett (785/448-6767, garnett chamber.org).

Quivira National Wildlife Refuge

(See previous section of this chapter.)

MICHIGAN

Secrets of the towering dunes

OUTDOOR MICHIGAN offers so much to choose from: beaches, from sandy and serene to rocky and wild; forests—coniferous, deciduous and mixed—that grip the landscape with ever-more astonishing tenacity the farther north you travel; hundreds of islands, both familiar and barely noted; isolated peninsulas lashed by crashing seas. Plopped amid four of the five Great Lakes, the state is set apart on all sorts of terms.

I'll spotlight the Great Lakes at Sleeping Bear Dunes, a national lakeshore anchored in one of the Upper Midwest's premier playgrounds, northwest lower Michigan. My two secondary stops are on the remote Upper Peninsula (UP), where the elements rule: One is a mini mountain range packed with trees and wildlife; the other, an enchanted, once-forgotten spring I've yearned for decades to see firsthand.

Porcupine Mountains

Although it has the longest park name I'll encounter on this journey, Porcupine Mountains Wilderness State Park also has the shortest nickname; it's simply referred to as "the Porkies" by most of its devoted fans. The prickly name comes from the Ojibwa, who knew the area as the Place of the Crouching Porcupine, based on the rocky silhouette they viewed from their encampment beside the nearby Ontonagon River here on the far-western UP.

Photography by Jason Lindsey

Frothy waves lapping at Sleeping Bear Dunes National Lakeshore.

LEFT TO RIGHT: Lake of the Clouds, Porcupine Mountains Wilderness State Park. Denizens of Kitch-iti-kipi, Palms Book State Park. Dan surveying a sunset at Empire Bluffs, Sleeping Bear Dunes National Lakeshore.

This is the state's largest pristine wilderness—25 miles long and 10 miles wide—a remote (Detroit is 12 hours away) 60,000-acre domain that hugs the south shore of Lake Superior and draws 280,000 visitors annually. Its rhyolite, basalt and sandstone rocks were formed as many as a billion years ago, and some of the park's signature eastern hemlocks predate the founding of the Jamestown Colony in Virginia almost 400 years ago. I'm awed by the history!

The park offers hiking and backpacking on 90 miles of interconnected trails; climbing on age-old escarpments; canoeing on streams and rivers completely within the park; kayaking along 21 miles of Lake Superior shoreline; wildlife- and bird-watching; hunting animals from white-tailed deer to black bears; and fishing for brook trout, smallmouth bass and steelhead salmon. Typically, each year by January, an awesome 230 inches of lake-effect snow guarantees a fantasy world for downhill and cross-country skiing and snowshoeing, as well as winter camping. If you're not into tenting at

one of the park's 200 primitive and modern campsites, you can choose from 19 cabins that sleep up to eight or stay snug inside one of the three yurts (circular domed tents) scattered throughout the park.

Famed naturalist Aldo Leopold once called the Porkies the Great Uncut. "The main reason this park was founded in 1945 was our huge eastern hemlocks and the other old-growth trees," says my host, Sandy Richardson, park communications assistant. "They've never seen an ax or a saw—the largest undisturbed tract between the Adirondacks and the Rockies."

Sandy camped here with her family as a child and is thrilled to be living and working on the UP (she even has a coveted bear-hunting license). She tells me the arboreal smorgasbord here also includes sugar maple, red oak, white pine, ironwood, aspen, balsam and spruce—free of signs of human habitation. She explains that these trees are survivors: Soil is thin to nonexistent atop the rocks, winters can be brutal and the existing canopy blocks much sunlight from

reaching seedlings. As a result, it can take a century for one of these eastern hemlocks to reach just 20 feet (eventually, they can attain a height of 80 feet).

Our tour begins at lofty Lake of the Clouds overlook. Two rivers begin and end within the park: Big Carp and Little Carp. The first feeds the Lake of the Clouds, which was called Carp Lake until the 1930s (the new label definitely fits today's cotton-white and brilliant-blue skies).

At Summit Peak, Sandy and I hike a trail and then several long flights of stairs to a 40-foot observation tower. At 1,958 feet above sea level, we're atop the highest peak in the Porkies. What a panorama! I hike a short stretch of trail on my own. Hiding from me are a population of about 35 rarely seen black bears (they're shy); transient gray wolves and moose; bobcats, fishers and beavers; warblers, least bitterns and owls; raptors, including bald eagles, red-shouldered hawks and peregrine falcons (nature's fastest predators, dive-bombing their prey at 175 miles per hour).

Near the mouth of the Presque Isle (PreskIL) River, we follow a boardwalk trail and cross a suspension bridge to the crashing Lake Superior shore. Of the more than 150 waterfalls on the UP, 90 of them are in the Porkies, including Manabezho Falls, the UP's second largest, and stair-step Manido Falls. The streams are filled with clear yet brown-tinted water (from tannins released by tamarack trees), with thin layers of shale and water-sculpted bowls. Beautiful.

My drive across the UP includes a stop in Ishpeming (population 6,700), the home of Da Yoopers Tourist Trap, for an armload of gag gifts. Beyond the rugged scenery and the hearty pastie meat pies, the natives' local brand of self-deprecating humor is a key reason I love the isolated UP.

Palms Book State Park
My next stop is an obscure Midwest gem that almost got buried in a pile of garbage. I'm here fulfilling a dream, visiting Kitch-iti-kipi, or Big Spring, 11 miles north of Manistique. The spring is tucked into 388-acre Palms Book State Park at the northwest corner of Indian Lake, home to two units of Michigan State Park of the same name. Lee Vaughn, a Manistique native who supervises all three parks, answers my first question—how the spring got its name: "It's not really certain, but some say the name is Chippewa for 'the great water' or 'the big sky I see' or 'the roaring, bubbling spring.' Take your pick."

A short walk later, I could concur with any of the translations, based on what I'm seeing: an oval pool that measures about 300 feet wide and 45 feet deep, almost hidden behind a veil of tamarack, cedar, spruce and balsam. I step onto a raft that visitors self-propel by slowly turning a wheel attached to a 100-yard cable. Soon I'm out in the middle of the spring.

Below is a "lava lamp" of bubbling sand, fed by 45-degree water (the spring never freezes, even here) spurting at the rate of 10,000 gallons per minute from fissures in a pressurized underground limestone river. The crystal-clear water has a greenish tinge caused by sulfur content (I detect no odor). Fat brown and brook trout from nearby Indian Lake weave around naturally fallen tree trunks—some half buried in the ever-moving sand—as ducks compete in a frenzy for the vending machine food pellets I toss. No fishing or swimming is permitted at Kitch-iti-kipi.

The spring was a lumber-camp rubbish dump when John I. Bellaire, who owned a five-and-dime in Manistique, rediscovered and rescued it. With the support of the wealthy Detroit Palms and Book families, who owned land in the area, the spring and the land around it were sold to the state for the grand sum of $10 to become a state park in 1926. Next door, 847-acre Indian Lake State Park draws campers and anglers to the fourth-largest inland lake on the UP. Its waters teem with trout, perch, walleye, muskie, bass and bluegill. Wildlife includes white-tailed deer, black bears, porcupines, raccoon, wild turkeys, geese and ducks, plus an occasional moose. A mixed forest of hardwoods and evergreens rings the lake.

Sleeping Bear Dunes Lakeshore

The five Great Lakes account for 20 percent of the world's freshwater and almost 10,000 miles of shoreline. They define a region that's home to 107 million Americans and Canadians, which would make it the world's 12th most populous nation. Michigan alone is rimmed by 3,200 miles of Great Lakes beaches—more than the entire West Coast. An amazing 35,000 islands—some large and popular, some small and rarely visited—spangle Great Lakes waters.

Even at its top 307-mile length and 118-mile width (and at an average depth of almost 280 feet), Lake Michigan isn't the largest of the Great Lakes—that crown goes to Lake Superior; however, it's the

the edge of town is named for the late U.S. senator from Michigan who helped create this National Lakeshore in 1970. Inside, I gravitate to a big relief map of this 71,000-acre park that hugs a narrow swath of scalloped northwest Michigan coastline, as well as two nearly uninhabited offshore islands, the larger North and the smaller South Manitou. The star here is a combined total of 65 miles of pristine Lake Michigan beaches and lumpy dunes—31 miles along the mainland and 24 miles around those two islands about six miles from shore.

I'm greeted by Public Information Officer Bruce Huffman and Chief of Natural Resources Steve Yancho. Bruce, about a year into his job here, proves an able and eager guide—his newbie enthusiasm is

swim across Lake Michigan to escape a Wisconsin forest fire. From the Michigan shore, the mother bear saw that her cubs had drowned. Today, those lost cubs are North and South Manitou islands; Sleeping Bear is the resting place of the heartbroken mother bear.

Steve explains another of the lakeshore's hallmarks—a succession of ecosystems that quickly progresses inland from the crystal-clear lake. First come the pebble and sand beaches, then dunes, swamps, meadows, forests, streams and valleys and inland lakes. Each environment sustains its own discrete community of plant and animal life. Occasional "ghost forests," groves of trees that cling to the dunes, completely buried by shifting sands only to be exposed like specters when the restless dunes rearrange themselves, serve as reminders of how fickle the shifting dunes can be.

There are more than 900 plant species and 250 bird types here, including 20 pairs of piping plovers, almost half the Great Lakes population of this endangered species. The lake harbors an assortment of fish: trout, whitefish, perch, chinook or king salmon, coho and sturgeon, plus the problematic sea lamprey and alewife and zebra and quagga mussel.

The five Great Lakes account for 20 percent of the world's freshwater and almost 10,000 miles of shoreline.

only one entirely within the United States. Michigan, Wisconsin, Indiana and Illinois claim stretches of its mesmerizing aquamarine waters.

Eager Assistant Rob is at the wheel on our pastoral 24-mile drive west from thriving Traverse City (population 14,500) to Sleeping Bear Dunes. So far it's been quite a day: introducing Rob to the slender, five-mile Mackinac Bridge linking the UP to the rest of Michigan and inhaling fresh-cherry malts and juicy burgers at Don's Drive-in, a personal favorite in Traverse City.

Sleeping Bear sprawls just outside tiny Empire (population 380), one of two lakeside towns "bookended" by the national lakeshore proper (the other is Glen Arbor, eight miles north, with 790 year-round residents and thousands more summer visitors). The Philip A. Hart Visitor Center at

contagious. Steve is a friendly and extremely knowledgeable 28-year Sleeping Bear veteran who obviously loves his posting. We head for the nearest beach, at Empire.

About 11,000 years ago, the last retreating glacier gouged out Lake Michigan. Aeons of slow-motion glacial action had helped form Sleeping Bear's ivory-colored, jumbo-size dunes, soaring up to 400 feet above the lake. Steve explains that the monoliths in the distance actually are called "perched" dunes—gravelly glacial rubble topped with sand, like fluffy frosting on a loaf cake.

Sleeping Bear entices 1.1 million visitors annually to enjoy beach activities, hiking, backpacking, camping, sailing, canoeing, hunting, fishing, climbing, paragliding, historic sites and nature watching. Legend suggests the origin of the park's name: A mother bear and two cubs attempted to

Several of the latter species hitched a ride here in the ballast of oceangoing vessels on Lake Michigan via the St. Lawrence Seaway, a system of canals and locks opened in 1959 linking the Atlantic Ocean and the Great Lakes. "Dealing with the nonnative species is one of our biggest challenges these days," Steve laments, explaining that they're blamed for everything from decimating native fish to causing the excessive algae growth apparent on some Sleeping Bear beaches.

Steve shows me one of the area's signature Petoskey stones (named for an Ottawa term meaning "rays of dawn"). Split one

CLOCKWISE, FROM TOP: (All taken at Sleeping Bear Dunes) Viewing Lake Michigan at Overlook No. 9. Polished Petoskey stone. Beachgoers. Glen Lake from Pierce Stocking Drive.

WARNING : STEEP BLUFF
450 Foot Drop To Lake Michigan
Return climb is extremely exhausting.
DO NOT RUN
DO NOT THROW ROCKS

open and you'll see a tan-and-brown honeycomb design left by living coral when this area was submerged under an ocean aeons ago. Steve reminds me, "Twenty years ago, the lake was high. Now it's low. That's how it works." There is a benefit of the current water level: The sugar-fine sand beaches are wider than ever before.

Also of interest are the historic farm sites once owned by fisher-farmers, like the properties preservationists are trying to rescue in the Port Oneida Rural Historic District. This corner of Michigan still is famed for bumper crops of fruits such as tart cherries, blueberries, apricots, peaches and grapes, as well as asparagus and sweet corn—and maple syrup.

In 1970, more than 1,500 privately held properties within the national lakeshore boundary—those historic farmsteads, as well as year-round residences and vacation homes—were acquired to create the National Lakeshore. Some hard feelings still exist on the part of former residents. But the bottom line is that far more visitors now enjoy Sleeping Bear's charms, and future generations will benefit from public stewardship of the environment.

Near unincorporated Leland, seven miles north of Empire, is the 7.5-mile Pierce Stocking Scenic Drive, one of the Midwest's shortest byways. The path burrows through dense woods and coasts along ridges that reveal awesome overlooks of Lake Michigan beaches and dunes, as well as inland Glen Lake. I'm on my way to the 230-foot Dune Climb.

Random climbing can harm the fragile dune ecosystem, so the park has "sacrificed" one dune (a perched dune) for that purpose. From the large, packed parking lot, I begin my ascent along with dozens of other Sir Edmund Hillary wannabes. In a few minutes, I'm rewarded with a grand panorama of Glen Lake. (A view of Lake

Michigan is still a mile hike behind me.)

My next vista, christened overlook No. 9, is a short hike from the road. A path and boardwalk lead to a large wooden platform that seems to balance precariously on huge stilts jabbed into the sand. I'm 1,024 feet above sea level and 450 feet above the lake. The water shimmers and glistens with ever-swirling shadows and highlights. At the top of the dune, a sign advises: "Warning: steep bluff, 450-foot drop to Lake Michigan. Return climb is extremely exhausting. Do not run. Do not throw rocks."

Despite the warnings, climbers long ago blazed a swath down the middle of the bare dune. I chuckle as I watch initially energetic adventurers of nearly all ages walking and scooting on their fannies down the colossus, gradually transformed into antlike specks by the time they reach the water. Their return trip appears far less exuberant, punctuated by frequent rest stops. I pass.

The day's last stop beckons: Empire Bluffs, just south of Empire. Another short hike up the back side of a dune leads to a boardwalk and a tiny platform with a view of the Sleeping Bear, a wooded hump atop a nearby dune. The sun gradually becomes a huge orange orb that finally goes "kerplunk" behind the rippling horizon in a showstopping sunset finale I'll never forget.

Discoveries among the Dunes

Good Harbor Bay at the far northeast end of the national lakeshore is aptly named. The gentle crescent resembles a curved sofa with cushy, tree-covered armrests at either end. On this weekday morning, there's nobody to be seen, just footprints left by previous visitors. Emerald green North Manitou Island and a passing freighter draw my eye to the lake. A turkey vulture feeding on the carrion of a salmon reminds me that nature's law rules here. I turn away from the lake and note one of the ecological progressions

Steve explained to me earlier: beach, grassy ridge, shrubs, forest.

Nearby Shell Lake is my next destination. It's a small inland jewel hidden in the fat camel's hump that juts between Good Harbor Bay and the main channel of the Manitou Passage (the tip of the peninsula, Pyramid Point, is another great overlook and paragliding hangout). On the way, we see an occasional abandoned cabin half hidden in the trees; one is being demolished as we pass, evidence of the ongoing effort to restore this area to its wild state.

Soon, the rutted road dead-ends at Shell Lake, where a St. Louis-area family is kayaking and sunning on the beach. At first, I sense poorly concealed disappointment at having intruders in "their" hideaway. But that soon passes (they're Midwesterners, after all). "Want to give it a try?" a young woman asks, handing me a kayak paddle. I get my first, self-instructed kayaking lesson as a black-and-white loon mocks me from the other side of the lake with its eerie call.

Time to explore the historical secrets hidden in these dunes. We head back south on State-22 to Glen Haven, just west of Glen Arbor. Founded in 1856 as a steamboat fueling stop, the once-busy Manitou Passage village is a windswept collection of historic buildings on Sleeping Bear Bay. I poke my head inside an 1870 blacksmith shop and stroll past the 1863 Sleeping Bear Inn, which is no longer open to the public. Near the lake, tucked behind a low dune, is the former D.H. Day Cannery, now a boathouse museum.

D.H. Day (1853–1928) was the leading citizen and entrepreneur hereabouts, the owner of a large farm, a lumber mill and this former fruit-processing facility. I'm eager to check out the Great Lakes' largest collection of small inland boats, but first I'm distracted by what's going on outside. Bill Love, a jack-of-all-trades carpenter, is

Salmon with Chipotle Sauce

You can't beat Lake Michigan salmon cooked to succulent perfection. To give it even more pizzazz, Chef Tim Weiss at Western Avenue Grill in Glen Arbor adds chipotle pepper and Gorgonzola cheese.

4   5- to 6-ounce fresh or frozen skinless salmon fillets, about ¾ to 1 inch thick
4   teaspoons olive oil
    Kosher salt and ground black pepper
½   to 1 teaspoon ground chipotle pepper
⅓   cup barbecue sauce (Chef Tim uses Sweet Baby Ray's Original Barbecue Sauce)
¼   to ½ teaspoon ground chipotle pepper
    Dash ground white pepper
    Dash cayenne pepper
¼   cup crumbled Gorgonzola cheese

Thaw fish, if frozen. Rinse fish and pat dry with paper towels; set aside. Set a heavy roasting pan into a cold oven. Heat pan and oven to 450°. Tear off an 18×18-inch piece of heavy foil; cut into four 9×9-inch pieces. Place fish in center of each foil piece. Tuck thin salmon edges under to make pieces of even thickness, if needed. Drizzle 1 teaspoon oil over each fish piece and sprinkle lightly with salt and black pepper. Rub ⅛ to ¼ teaspoon chipotle pepper on each fish piece. Use foil to lift fish and carefully set into hot roasting pan. Bake fish for 8 minutes in preheated oven.

For sauce: In a bowl, combine barbecue sauce, 2 tablespoons water, the ¼ to ½ teaspoon chipotle pepper, white pepper, cayenne pepper and 2 tablespoons water.

Remove roasting pan from oven. Spoon sauce over fish. Return to oven. Bake about 4 minutes more or until fish flakes easily when tested with a fork. Use foil to lift fish from pan. Use a wide spatula to transfer fish to a serving platter. Sprinkle with Gorgonzola. *Makes 4 main-dish servings.*

stabilizing the *Grace,* a 41-foot Great Lakes fishing tug formerly based in nearby Frankfort, the largest exhibit in this dry-docked collection. Bill explains that hundreds of tugs like this once dropped several miles of gill nets each to haul in tremendous catches of whitefish, perch and chub.

Economics, overfishing and those nasty invasive species have drastically curtailed the once-thriving industry. "Most of the fishing on Lake Michigan is done by charters these days—salmon, trout, whitefish and perch," Bill tells me. I ask him about his other projects. "Well, last summer I helped tuck-point and whitewash the lighthouse over on South Manitou Island. We just started at the top and worked our way down in a rig attached to a cable—100 feet from top to bottom. That was an interesting job, especially when it was windy."

Inside the low-rise, red-and-white former cannery, I view craft that plied Lake Michigan over the centuries: a long-submerged prehistoric pine dugout canoe made with stone tools; a lifeboat carried on a Great Lakes shipping vessel; a trader's Mackinaw boat, a type of sailing boat once found all over the Great Lakes; a U.S. Coast Guard boat that traveled between the mainland and remote lighthouses; a motorized, "unsinkable" lifeboat with a cork-filled hull; and a simple fishing rowboat. Back outside, I gaze at the remaining pilings of the dock used for 80 years by ships loading and unloading things from cordwood to vacationers to immigrants beginning anew here.

Just a half mile away, at the Sleeping Bear Point Coast Guard Station Maritime Museum, I visit the former lifesaving station, staffed until 1942. Within the eight-mile-wide Manitou Passage, the one-mile-wide channel was the Great Lakes' busiest traffic lane because of its depth and somewhat sheltered location between the Manitou and the mainland. At the beginning of the

20th century, 50–100 ships could be seen traveling through at once. Navigational equipment was rudimentary by today's standards, so fog, storms and shoals often spelled disaster.

I tour the exhibits in the tidy white house where the keeper and his family lived on one side, the crew on the other. It was built in 1901 at Sleeping Bear Point and moved to this site in 1931 when sand threatened to bury it in its original location. I'm awed by the courageous story of the U.S. Life-Saving Service, instituted by Congress to replace haphazardly organized local efforts following disastrous winter storms on the Atlantic Coast. From 1871 to 1915, when it was integrated into the newly created U.S. Coast Guard, the service saved 178,000 lives.

Here on the Manitou Passage, the brave men who staffed this station rescued 178 people from 1902 to 1915. In the pre-Coast Guard era, these heroes were paid just 25 cents per day. They accomplished their mission either by rowing surfboats out into the roiling waters or by firing a Lyle gun, which I learn about a few steps away in the large boathouse, where a volunteer demonstrates the invention.

Devised in 1878 by U.S. Army Lt. (later Col.) David Lyle (1845–1937), the cannonlike mechanism fired a rope that was painstakingly stored on pegs, tightly wound, in a wooden box. That rope, a lifeline if there ever was one, made it possible to reel in passengers and crew. "David Lyle was very proud of saying he invented the only gun ever created for the purpose of saving lives," our docent explains.

Good Eating—and Adventure!

We head for a late lunch at Art's Tavern in Glen Arbor, a local landmark with vintage Michigan college pennants covering the walls and ceiling. My burger is great, but my favorite courses are a delectable

CLOCKWISE, FROM TOP LEFT:
(All taken at Sleeping Bear Dunes)
Lake Michigan horizon. Dan on
Shell Lake. The *Francisco Morazon*.
Boathouse museum, Glen Arbor.

smoked-whitefish dip and a dish of locally renowned Moomer's ice cream topped with real maple syrup. I'm not too stuffed to amble a couple blocks to greet my old friends at Cherry Republic, the famous all-things-cherry retailer featured in my book *Taste of the Midwest,* for one of their huge Boomchunka chocolate chip cookies.

Before long I'm aboard Steve Nowicki's 26-foot fishing-charter boat, the *Finicky Fish.* Several miles into the outing, skies turn foreboding and the lake choppy atop about 80 feet of water. After several minutes of being slapped by 6- to 8-foot waves, we head back to the mainland.

Of course, every cloud has a silver lining! At Sleeping Bear, mine turns out to be a whopping, silvery 15-pound king salmon I reel in with Steve's capable coaching. I proudly parade my catch down the main street of Glen Arbor en route to the Western Avenue Grill, where manager/head chef/all-round good sport Tim Weiss agrees to prepare my trophy for our evening meal.

I'm awed when Tim serves up that salmon not one, but six delectable ways. I vote for the barbecue (see recipe, page 64) and the parmesan-encrusted versions, but all are superb. Tim shares his secret: Cook the fish really fast in a 450-degree oven.

A Lighthouse Island

United States lighthouses date back to 1716 in Boston. More than 1,200 of the sentinels exist nationally, with 445 still in service; Michigan boasts 123, more than any other state. These days, sophisticated navigation and communications devices have largely supplanted the structures, whose main benefits are history, tourism and romance. Preservationists have gone on a crusade to save many of them.

Lighthouses on South Manitou date back to 1839, when a light was mounted to the top of the first keeper's house. As the island's pride comes into view, I feel I've stepped into a painting: This structure, built in 1871 and decommissioned in 1958, is 100 feet tall with walls 6 feet thick at the base, narrowing to 2 feet at the top. Inside, a spiral iron staircase (freestanding, to avoid destabilizing the main structure) leads to a 360-degree view of the lake, mainland and a nine-mile-long stretch of limestone bluffs, rocky beaches and forests (including a virgin stand of 500-year-old cedar).

My guide is Kim McCrary, a National Park Service ranger who lives and works on the island during the tourist season and returns to her hometown of San Diego in winter. She explains that the sentinel's big Fresnel glass lens, now gone, once shined faithfully 17 miles in all directions—24 hours a day, 365 days a year. That light was fueled by kerosene the keepers carried in 5-gallon containers up the 117 steps.

From the walkway on top, Kim also points out a small building where wood-burning boilers produced steam to sound a foghorn when the light wasn't visible. Three families (the keeper's and two assistants') lived in the walkway-connected house next door. We see a family hiking and divers probing the submerged *Three Brothers,* a 1911 shipwreck, intermittently visible when it's not buried under shifting sands. At the south end of the island rests the rusting hulk of the *Francisco Morazon,* a 1922 freighter already on its last legs when it ran aground during a fierce snowstorm on November 29, 1960. No lives were lost, just cargo.

Everywhere I look, the colors are intense: every shade of blue water and sky and green trees and grass imaginable, muted only by the subtle beiges and grays of sand and rocks. Minutes later, after we've safely crossed the passage to the mainland, we pause for one last bottom-up look at the biggest of Sleeping Bear's dunes—haunting and unforgettable in its looming enormity.

Dan's Travel Journal

FEATURED STOP

Sleeping Bear Dunes National Lakeshore. In the Lower Peninsula's northwestern corner (about 25 miles west of Traverse City), this 71,000-acre national park spans a 35-mile strip of Lake Michigan shore, plus the undeveloped North and South Manitou islands. Climb to the top of the half-mile-wide wall of sand at the designated Dune Climb for a great overview of North America's largest freshwater dunes and a panorama of Glen Lake and Lake Michigan. You can hike about 100 miles of trails, including Empire Bluff Trail, which takes you to high vistas, and Bayview Trail, which goes through fields of wildflowers. Camping options range from spots with electrical hookups and modern bathrooms to some of the state's best backcountry camping on the islands (ride the ferry from Leland). Also at this immense sandbox: historic sites, scenic drives, forests and excellent fishing. Park information and maps at the Philip A. Hart Visitor Center in Empire (231/326-5134, ext. 328).

Lodging, Dining and More

Area accommodations range from first-class **Homestead Resort** on the Lake Michigan shore (231/334-5000) to the cozy 1890s farmhouse at Sleeping Bear Bed and Breakfast near Empire (231/326-5375). For more lodging information, contact the Benzie Area Convention & Visitors Bureau (800/882-5801), the Glen Lake Chamber of Commerce (231/334-3238) or the Leelanau Peninsula Chamber of Commerce (231/271-9895).
Art's Tavern Glen Arbor. A local legend since before prohibition, this no-frills, one-room burger joint (hamburger ground fresh daily) offers a surprising menu of breakfast, lunch, appetizer and dinner choices (231/334-3754).
Cannery Boathouse Museum Glen Haven. A 1920s cherry cannery now boasts the Great Lakes' largest exhibit of small boats, within the national lakeshore's Historic Village (231/326-5134).
Cherry Republic Glen Arbor. In the heart of the world's largest tart-cherry-growing region, choose from a bumper crop of 150 cherry products in the main store, bakery/cafe and winery or by mail order (800/206-6949).
Don's Drive-In Traverse City. At this classic burger-and-malt drive-in, opened in 1958, pull in—or dine inside the retro pink building—for quarter-pounders, fries and real-fruit shakes (231/938-1860).
Finicky Fishing Charters Glen Arbor. Reel in salmon and lake trout around the Manitou Islands on half- or full-day fishing trips aboard a 26-foot charter boat (231/645-0020).
Joe's Friendly Tavern Empire. A 1940s landmark a short walk from the beach, open for hearty breakfasts (until 11 a.m.), fresh-ground cheeseburgers and whitefish dinners (231/326-5506).
Manitou Island Transit Leland. Board the passenger ferry *Mishe-Mokwa* for day trips to South Manitou Island or sunset shoreline cruises. Also ride a ferry to North and South Manitou for overnight camping (231/256-9061).
Sleeping Bear Point Coast Guard Station Maritime Museum Glen Haven. Original 1901 Life-Saving Station, with exhibits about the U.S. Coast Guard, the U.S. Life-Saving Service and Great Lakes shipping history. Rescue reenactments daily in summer by National Park Service rangers (231/326-5134).
Western Avenue Grill Glen Arbor. Downtown, dine on the brick patio out front or inside the cottagelike restaurant with birch-bark walls, where fresh Lake Michigan whitefish and filet mignon star on the menu (231/334-3362).

Related Area Events

Asparagus Festival Empire, third weekend in May—Empire salutes its shoots with an asparagus garden walk, parade, asparagus cook-off and "Ode to Asparagus" poetry reading (231/326-5922).
Manitou Music Festival Glen Arbor, July–August—Classical, jazz and folk concerts in idyllic settings, starting with a free concert at the foot of Sleeping Bear Dunes (231/334-6112).

More Information

Benzie Area Convention & Visitors Bureau (800/882-5801, www.visitbenzie.com).
Empire Chamber of Commerce (www.empirechamber.com).
Glen Lake Chamber of Commerce (231/334-3238, www.visitglenarbor.com).
Leelanau Peninsula Chamber of Commerce (231/271-9895, www.leelanauchamber.com).
Travel Michigan (888/784-7328, www.michigan.org).

DAN'S OTHER STOPS

(See also More Parks section that follows.)
Palms Book State Park Manistique (906/341-2355), Porcupine Mountains Wilderness State Park Ontonagon (906/885-5275).

Lodging, Dining and More

Da Yoopers Tourist Trap Ishpeming. Roadside attraction championing Michigan Upper Peninsula innovations with quirky outdoor displays (such as "Gus," the world's largest working chain saw) and a gift store (800/628-9978).
Holiday Inn Express Manistique. Along Lake Michigan, a short drive from Palms Book State Park. $$ (906/341-3777).
Porcupine Mountains AmericInn Lodge & Suites Silver City. Full-service hotel on Lake Superior shores near Porcupine Mountains Wilderness State Park. $$ (906/885-5311).
Three Mile Supper Club Manistique. Fresh Lake Michigan whitefish (broiled or deep-fried) in knotty-pine surroundings (906/341-8048).

More Michigan Parks

state and national forest sites or stay at cabins and motels in Grayling. While you're in the area, venture just north of Grayling to nearly 10,000-acre Hartwick Pines State Park for a glimpse of the "big woods" that once covered most of Michigan. One trail leads through giant 300-year-old trees to a re-created 19th-century logging camp.

Contact: Au Sable State Forest (989/732-3541, michigan.gov/dnr). Grayling Visitors Bureau (800/937-8837, grayling-mi.com). Hartwick Pines State Park (989/348-7068, michigan.gov/dnr). Huron-Manistee National Forest (800/821-6263, fs.fed.us). Nearest lodgings: in Grayling (contact above).

Copper Country Trail National Scenic Byway

History and natural wonders combine along this 47-mile byway through the rugged Keweenaw Peninsula, cradled by Lake Superior as far north on Michigan's Upper Peninsula as you can get. Sites tracing the region's heritage, history-rich towns and North Woods scenery highlight the drive.

The route follows US-41 from the Portage Lake Lift Bridge, linking Houghton and Hancock across a channel carved through the Keweenaw's center for ore ships to pass through (the peninsula once supplied most of the nation's copper). In Hancock, visitors can ride a tram into century-old tunnels of the Quincy Mining Company, one of several attractions included in the multisite Keweenaw National Historical Park along the byway.

Heading north through the woods, plan stops in towns such as Calumet and Laurium. Make a short detour to tiny Eagle Harbor, with its crescent of beach and venerable lighthouse. Lake Superior stretches beyond Copper Harbor at the Keweenaw's tip, where you can mingle with costumed "soldiers" at Fort Wilkins (May–October), a 19th-century post that helped keep peace during the copper boom.

Contact: Keweenaw Peninsula Chamber of Commerce (866/304-5722, keweenaw.org). Keweenaw Tourism Council (906/337-4579, keweenaw.info). Nearest lodgings: in Hancock, Houghton, Copper Harbor and a few other towns along the byway.

Grand Island National Recreation Area

Though it's only a five-minute ferry ride from Munising along the Upper Peninsula's northern shore, this eight-mile-long island looks much as it did when the Ojibwas roamed the forests. Hemlocks, birches and hardwoods create a verdant backdrop for Lake Superior's chilly waters.

On the short ferry trip to the 13,000-acre island, part of Hiawatha National Forest, you'll see Native American sites and the 1863 North Channel Lighthouse, along with a shipwreck through the boat's well. Once on land, recreational options include hiking and biking some 30 miles of primitive trails. One trail leads to Trout Bay overlook, where you can spot the colorful cliffs of Pictured Rocks National Lakeshore four miles across the water. Pristine beaches fringe the island's scenic western shore.

An interpretive bus tour takes visitors to lake overlooks along rugged interior roads (no cars permitted on the island). You can camp at 19 primitive campsites.

Au Sable River and State Forest

For scenic floats on the Au Sable River, surrounded by forests of majestic hardwoods and pines, canoeists converge on Grayling (55 miles east of Traverse City). The sparkling-clear river runs through 400,000-acre Au Sable State Forest and 500,000-acre Huron National Forest. Outfitters arrange trips from two hours to seven days on this 120-mile twisting waterway, which eventually spills into Lake Huron. Paddling is relatively easy and popular with families. You might spot ospreys and herons on the shore or overhead.

Canoeists can camp along the river at

PHOTOGRAPHS: (CLOCKWISE, FROM TOP LEFT) JOHN ROBERT WILLIAMS; GREG RYAN; LAYNE KENNEDY

Contact: Alger County Chamber of Commerce (906/387-2138, algercounty .org). Hiawatha National Forest (906/387-0700, fs.fed.us). Upper Peninsula Travel & Recreation Association (800/562-7134, uptravel.com). Nearest lodgings: in Munising (see Alger County above).

Isle Royale National Park

Often shrouded in fog and mist, this rocky sliver (45 miles long and nine miles wide) anchors a Lake Superior archipelago of some 400 smaller islands. It's Michigan's only national park. Ferries carry backpackers, canoeists, kayakers, campers, hikers and wildlife watchers to the island settlement of Rock Harbor from the Upper Peninsula towns of Houghton and Copper Harbor and from Grand Portage, Minnesota. Though you're only 50 miles offshore, the woods and coves make you feel like you're a million miles from anywhere.

Paddlers navigate inlets, bays and channels beyond the island's craggy shore. Anglers go for pike, trout and walleye in some 30 inland lakes and in Lake Superior. Moose may amble by as you hike some 165 miles of trails to rocky overlooks. Visitors also explore historic Edisen Fishery, operating near the 1855 Rock Harbor Lighthouse. A 60-room lodge, restaurant and 20 housekeeping cabins overlook Rock Harbor and Tobin Harbor. Guests also settle into 36 campgrounds. The park stays open mid-April through late October.

Contact: Isle Royale National Park (906/482-0984, nps.gov/isro). Upper Peninsula Travel & Recreation Association (800/562-7134, uptravel.com). Lodgings: in Rock Harbor Lodge on the island (park contact above) or in Copper Harbor and Houghton (contact above).

CLOCKWISE, FROM TOP LEFT: Canoeists on the Au Sable River. Quincy Mine tour, Copper Country Trail National Scenic Byway. Dockside at Isle Royale National Park.

Kal-Haven Trail State Park

Last year, some 100,000 outdoor enthusiasts traveled this 34-mile southwestern-Michigan trail, built on the abandoned bed of the Kalamazoo & South Haven Railroad. The rail-trail links the resort town of South Haven with the city of Kalamazoo.

On the wide crushed-limestone path, you pedal through a marsh, tunnels of trees and flat stretches of open farmland. The route is easy pedaling, from a stretch that resembles a shady boulevard to sunny, open sections where gentle hills dive into wooded areas. Most bicyclists can't resist stopping along the way at restaurants and shops in the small towns of Grand Junction, Bloomingdale and Kendall.

Just east of Kalamazoo, cyclists pedal across seven bridges, once railroad trestles, including a covered bridge. In season, wildflowers abound along this hilly part of the ride. Hikers also travel the trail in warm weather, cross-country skiers and snowmobilers in winter.

Contact: Kal-Haven Trail State Park (269/637-2788, michigan.gov/dnr). Kalama-

zoo County Convention & Visitors Bureau (800/530-9192, discoverkalamazoo.com). South Haven Visitors Bureau (800/764-2836, southhaven.org). Lodgings: in Kalamazoo and South Haven (contacts above).

Ludington State Park

This breezy 5,300-acre park embraces the best of two watery worlds. It stretches for nearly six miles along the Lake Michigan shore and surrounds placid Hamlin Lake inland eight miles north of Ludington.

Beaches and dunes along a swath of undeveloped Lake Michigan that bounds the state park to the west complement 18 miles of hiking trails. They wind past Hamlin Lake, along the Big Sable River and on boardwalks that scale tall dunes for grand views. The 1867 Big Sable Point Light Station rises from the beach. You can trek out to the beacon to climb the light tower. Campers pitch their tents beneath shade trees in the park. Visitors also rent canoes to paddle a marked trail that traces the shore of Hamlin Lake, weaving through marshes and ponds.

You'll probably have trouble deciding where to go for beach and water fun: Lake Michigan, Hamlin Lake or—as a bonus—Stearns Park in the community of Ludington. At this city park, a protected point of land along Lake Michigan, not even the tiniest pebble rolls onto the soft sand.

Contact: Ludington State Park (231/843-2423, michigan.gov/dnr). Ludington Area Convention & Visitors Bureau (800/542-4600, ludingtoncvb.com). Nearest lodgings: in Ludington (contact above).

Manistee River and National Forest

Dancing through Manistee National Forest, the glistening Manistee River supplies some of Michigan's best canoeing. Along the way, just enough currents streak through the river to make your paddling trip an adventure.

From the old lumbering town of Deward, the 198-mile river cuts through the forest's half-million acres of hardwoods and pines, eventually spilling into Lake Michigan at the shore community of Manistee (40

miles west of Cadillac). You might see beavers, deer and otters along the banks as you paddle. Sometimes eagles and herons glide and swoop through the sky. With the help of outfitters, vacationers can set out on excursions of a few hours or several days, camping at some of the forest's 20 campgrounds. Fly-fishing for trout also is popular.

The Manistee National Forest, which includes a portion of the North Country National Scenic Trail, is a hiker's paradise. Memorable vistas lace the trail near Manistee. Hiking the route through miles of dense woodlands, you'll crest sandy hilltops with sweeping views.

Contact: Huron-Manistee National Forests (800/821-6263, fs.fd.us). For outfitters, Manistee County Convention & Visitors Bureau (877/626-4783, manistee-cvb.com). Nearest lodgings: in Manistee (contact above).

Palms Book State Park (Kitch-iti-Kipi Spring)

Peering into crystal-clear Kitch-iti-kipi Spring, you'll see waters swirling and bubbling around sand formations 40 feet below. This crystalline pool, Michigan's largest freshwater spring, stars as the main attraction at nearly 400-acre Palms Book State Park (adjoining Indian Lake State Park just northwest of Manistique near the Upper Peninsula's southern shore). Visitors can float across the 300-foot-wide spring on a self-propelled observation raft.

The more than 10,000 gallons of water that gush every minute from fissures in underwater limestone create clouds of sand that shift shapes and forms. You'll also see ancient limestone-encrusted branches resembling haphazard sculptures on the bottom, plus fish swimming through the eerie underwater fantasyland.

The spring-fed pool, with a water temperature that hovers around 45 degrees year-round, empties into a stream that flows into neighboring Indian Lake. Visitors can picnic nearby. Though there's no camping or fishing at Palms Book, you'll find both just south at Indian Lake State Park, which also includes sandy swimming beaches.

Contact: Palms Book and Indian Lake state parks (906/341-2355, michigan.gov/dnr). Nearest lodgings: in Manistique (800/342-4282, visitmanistique.com).

P.H. Hoeft State Park

A mile-long stretch of sand eases down to Lake Huron from a broad band of dunes at this peaceful Lower Peninsula park (40 miles southeast of Mackinaw City). The 300-acre enclave is the perfect spot to tickle your toes in the surf and laze on the beach, which you may have all to yourself.

The clear lake is shallow enough to wade out several yards. You also can hike more than four miles of trails that follow the shore and lead into gently rolling woods. Bicyclists hit the park's pathways, which connect with the Lake Huron Sunrise Trail that runs five miles north to Rogers City.

Picnickers love the park's shelter, built by the Civilian Conservation Corps (CCC) of native cut stone and huge logs, with its striking lake view. Visitors can pitch their tents at more than 140 sites in the shady campground, which spreads behind the dunes along the shore.

Contact: P.H. Hoeft State Park (989/734-2543, michigan.gov/dnr). Lodgings: in Rogers City (989/734-2535, rogerscity.com).

Pictured Rocks National Lakeshore

Extending 42 miles along the Upper Peninsula's Lake Superior shore, Pictured Rocks defies every stereotype of Midwest scenery. Seeping minerals have painted the dunes, solitary beaches and hulking cliffs in a rainbow of colors. Cliffs at this 73,000-acre preserve loom as high as 200 feet above the lake, forming arches and caves for 15 miles at the western end of the preserve near Munising. To the east, the Grand Sable Dunes well up from the shore.

You can take narrated boat tours from Munising. Kayakers glide along the base of the cliffs for even better views. Vacationers, who can stay at one of three campgrounds, also drive or hike to some of the most scenic locations, including Miners Castle. Paths lead up to dune-top overlooks and down to remote beaches along the shore. Mosquito Falls, which spills over ledges into the lake, is a favorite stop. Pick up maps west of the lakeshore at visitors centers in Munising and in Grand Marais, the national lakeshore's eastern gateway.

Contact: Pictured Rocks National Lakeshore Visitors Center (906/387-3700, nps.gov). Lodgings: in Grand Marais (906/494-2447, grandmaraismichigan.com) and Munising (906/387-2138, algercounty.org).

Porcupine Mountains Wilderness State Park

Before the rising sun colors Lake Superior pink and gold, pull up a driftwood log along the shore. With the Porcupine Mountains over your shoulder, there's no better seat for nature's show in this rugged Upper Peninsula park (50 miles northeast of Ironwood).

Beyond the beach, pristine woods blanket the timeworn peaks known as the "Porkies" in Michigan's largest state park (92 square miles in all). Most visitors head first to the Lake of the Clouds overlook on the eastern side of the park. The deep-blue lake gleams like a gem far below. The wilderness also harbors Summit Peak, among the Midwest's highest points (1,958 feet).

Hikers and backpackers might glimpse black bears on the 90 miles of trails. For more adventure, backpack into one of the rustic cabins or primitive campsites for the night. You also can explore the park by car, making stops to walk the short paths to overlooks, swift-running rivers and waterfalls. At the visitors center, a film details the history of the Porkies, including its Ojibwa legacy and early copper-mining days.

Contact: Porcupine Mountains Wilderness State Park (906/885-5275, michigan.gov/dnr). Nearest lodgings: just northeast of the park in Ontonagon and Silver City (906/884-4735, ontonagonmi.com).

Seney National Wildlife Refuge

A family of raccoons lopes across a gravel road, returning from an early-morning fishing expedition in one of 21 placid pools at this Upper Peninsula refuge (85 miles west of Sault Ste. Marie). As you round the next bend, regal trumpeter swans glide across a lake. But amid the refuge's 95,000 acres of second-growth forests, bogs, pools, marshes and meadows, that's just a preview of the wildlife pageant you'll see. More than 200 types of birds, including eagles, loons and grouse, have been spotted. Deer, bears and a host of other woodland creatures also call the refuge home.

Originally part of a vast natural marsh, Seney was burned, drained and left for wasteland until the CCC began restoration in the 1930s. Though the drive through the refuge is only seven miles, plan at least an hour for stops at observation decks along the way. Telescopes provide close-up views of wildlife. Plan to see the slide show at the visitors center, too. Just east of the refuge in tiny Germfask, you can rent canoes, kayaks and mountain bikes to explore the refuge's backcountry.

Contact: Seney National Wildlife Refuge (906/586-9851, fws.gov). Lodgings: in Germfask and about five miles north in Seney (800/562-7134, uptravel.com).

Sleeping Bear Dunes National Lakeshore

(See previous section of this chapter.)

Tawas Point State Park

Wind and waves have washed almost two miles of sand snowy white at this Lower Peninsula state park (75 miles northeast of Bay City), which curves around a breezy point between Lake Huron and Tawas Bay. None of the more than 190 campsites at the nearly 200-acre park are far from the water (five border the lake). As shadows lengthen, visitors head for the beach to watch the sun set across Tawas Bay.

On the park's Lake Huron shore, you can wade into the waves and stroll walkways that circle marshes where songbirds serenade. The Sandy Hook Nature Trail meanders past meadows of wildflowers and through rolling dunes to Tawas Point Lighthouse, which has been guiding freighters and other craft for 130 years. Windsurfers scud across the waves, and anglers cast from boats just off shore. A bicycle path connects the beach with the nearby town of East Tawas. There and in neighboring Tawas City, shops, restaurants and motels cater to vacationers.

Contact: Tawas Point State Park (989/362-5041, michigan.gov/dnr). Nearest lodgings: in East Tawas and Tawas City (800/

CLOCKWISE, FROM TOP LEFT: Pictured Rocks National Lakeshore. Trumpeter swans, Seney National Wildlife Refuge. Manido Falls, Porcupine Mountains Wilderness State Park. Tawas Point State Park.

MINNESOTA

Houseboat docked at a quiet cove in Voyageurs National Park

Wondrous North Woods lake country

MY FORAY INTO WATERY, woodsy Minnesota, the recreational boating and fishing capital of the Midwest, begins at an urban parkland that encircles the state's largest city, Minneapolis. Then, along with thousands of campers, anglers and resort patrons, I'll trek north to the spot where America's greatest waterway makes its diminutive debut. Finally, I'll invest the biggest share of my North Star State sojourn along the Canadian border at Voyageurs National Park, reveling in a paradise of lakes, forests and islands.

Grand Rounds Scenic Byway

In several respects, this is one of the more unusual parklands I'll visit—entirely urban and more of an attraction-studded drive than a single park. My host is sailing enthusiast Nick Eoloff, Grand Rounds National Scenic Byway director for the Minneapolis Park and Recreation Board. We'll drive about 25 miles, or almost half, of this circular loop around the perimeter of the Upper Midwest's Emerald City, Minneapolis (population 383,000), which has more acres of parkland per capita than any other major U.S. metropolis. Here, every resident lives within six blocks of a park!

Nick tells me the history of the Grand Rounds: "This ring of parks was created in the 1880s, when the City Beautiful Movement resulted in a lot of new parks

Photography by John Noltner

in rapidly developing, overcrowded cities." The coveted National Scenic Byway designation? "That came along in 1998, because of all the attractions and scenery located in such an urban setting."

We begin at the colossal granite-and-limestone Stone Arch Bridge over the Mississippi, built by railroad tycoon James J. Hill in 1883 and, since 1991, an elevated recreational thoroughfare for Twin Cities walkers, skaters and bicyclists. The bridge and surrounding area recall the days when the St. Anthony Falls, now largely eroded and camouflaged by dams, fostered the city's huge flour mills. The burned-out limestone ruins of the Washburn "A" Mill became the Mill City Museum, where Nick accompanies me on a whirlwind tour of exhibits that explain the city's once largely flour-powered economy. Soon I'm teetering on a Segway, the gyroscope-balanced conveyance of choice for visitors on a 5½-mile "Magical History Tour" along this stretch of the Grand Rounds.

Later, Nick claims us a shady table just outside the Old Pavilion at Minnehaha Park for a light seafood lunch from a restaurant inside the open-air structure. This almost-200-acre park, one of the city's oldest, boasts trails, Mississippi River overlooks, a pergola garden, and a quaint, restored 1875 train depot. But the star attraction sits in a rocky gorge just yards away: Minnehaha Falls, made famous by Henry Wadsworth Longfellow's 1855 epic poem, *Song of Hiawatha*. It's fitting that a two-thirds-size replica of Longfellow's home, built in 1907, was moved to the park in 1994 and opened as a hospitality center in 2001.

The last leg of our Grand Rounds drive leads us to the west side of the city and lakes strung like pearls on a necklace: Nokomis, Hiawatha, Calhoun, Lake of the Isles, Cedar, Wirth and our destination, Harriet. Minneapolis residents of all ages are walking, running, bicycling, in-line skating, beach-going, sailing and windsurfing here—within yet another appealing neighborhood of attractive homes.

Itasca State Park

About 4½ hours northwest of Minneapolis, Minnesota's rolling, glacier-smoothed landscape grows increasingly wooded. Here, Itasca, the state's oldest and most iconic state park, claims 32,000 acres of lakes and forests. A half-million visitors come here to motorboat, canoe, kayak, camp, fish, hike, bicycle and simply relish the scenery around the park's 100 lakes. The 10-mile Wilderness Drive and an area known as Preacher's Grove boast some of Minnesota's biggest and oldest white and red (Norway) pines—a main reason the park was created. Oak, maple, basswood and birch enliven the mix.

Itasca's wildlife denizens include black bears, timber wolves, bobcats, fishers, otters, mink, weasels, beavers and porcupines, plus winged creatures from hummingbirds to herons, including bald eagles and some of Minnesota's emblematic loons. Visitors stay or dine at the refurbished 1905 Douglas Lodge (the park also offers dozens of campsites and rustic cabins). But the chief attraction here is shallow, six-mile-long Lake Itasca, whose three spring- and stream-fed arms are the source of the Mississippi River.

The lake's name derives from a contraction of the Latin words *veritas* and *caput*, which means "true head." Nobody was quite certain where the Mississippi began its journey to the Gulf of Mexico until 1832, when explorer and all-round Renaissance man Henry Schoolcraft, with the help of an Ojibwe guide named Ozawindib, declared this the origin. Schoolcraft's assertion was confirmed by a later explorer, Jacob Brower, who campaigned for the creation of the state park and became its first commissioner.

Brower was succeeded by 24-year-old Mary Gibbs, who in 1903 refused to yield, even when she was threatened at gunpoint by greedy logging interests who wanted to fell the park's towering pines. Brower and Gibbs each is honored with a visitor center. With Lead Interpretive Naturalist Connie Cox as my guide, I view the big topographical relief map of the entire Mississippi River system at the new Mary Gibbs Visitor Center at the park's north end.

What the Ojibwe christened "The Great River" is the world's fourth-longest, discharging 650,000 cubic feet of water per second at its mouth. It rolls in and past 10 states, with a length of 2,318 miles, 600 in Minnesota. Connie explains: "The river actually flows 66 miles north from here before heading south, which is why it was difficult for some early explorers to accept that this was the head of the river."

At the spot where the Mississippi riffles out of Itasca and begins its incredible journey, the river is 18 feet wide and 18 inches deep; by the time it reaches New Orleans, it is 1,000 feet wide and 200 feet deep! The Mississippi never freezes here, even during Itasca's bone-numbing winters. "It's always 46 degrees at the headwaters, thanks to the natural springs," Connie tells me. "There's a legend here that if you make a wish, it will come true in 90 days; that's how long it takes this water to make its way to the Gulf of Mexico." My wish: to return someday.

Voyageurs National Park

Time to forge northward yet again. Eager Assistant Rob and I pass through Bemidji (population 11,900), a thriving state-university community and the nexus of 400 fishing lakes within a 25-mile radius. We cross a continental divide about 12 miles north of town. It runs primarily east and west in Minnesota, dipping down from Canada to

A Sunny Outing on Rainy Lake

Kate waves as I motor off with Mike Williams, who's just retired as owner of the Thunderbird. Five generations of Williamses have made their homes here, and Mike has been a fishing guide since he was 11. Our tour will take us from this western end of Rainy Lake to the historic Kettle Falls Hotel at the far eastern end—32 miles one way, six hours all told, with lots of poking around en route. I have another excellent host, Kathleen Przybylski, the park's chief of visitor education and planning. She's a native of Michigan's Lower Peninsula and has been at Voyageurs eight years.

I wonder how the voyageurs managed to navigate this daunting maze of woodlands and lakes. "They'd watch for unusual rock formations, or they'd create a 'lob stick': They'd send a man up to remove the lower branches from a prominent tree so it could easily be identified," Mike explains.

Those trees are predominately towering white, red and jack pine; spruce; balsam fir; and quaking aspen. I ask Kathleen about wildlife. "We have it all: black bears, timber wolves, moose, beavers, otters, white-tailed deer, bald eagles, ospreys, loons, pelicans, blue herons, mergansers, cormorants, gulls and kingfishers," she says. "In spring and fall, we have up to 200 species of migratory birds. And people love to come here to fish for walleye, northern, smallmouth bass, sauger, whitefish and perch."

Our first stop recalls a surprising mini gold rush that began in 1893. On Little American Island, I hike a short interpretive trail starring two abandoned mine shafts, 100 and 210 feet deep respectively. During the brief boom, several dozen mines operated in the area of now-forgotten Rainy Lake City, Minnesota's answer to rowdy Deadwood. On nearby Bushyhead Island, we view another mine shaft, this one ingeniously burrowed horizontally into rock and angled vertically downward.

I love the homey names of the islands my guides point out as I continue my Voyageurs visit: Dryweed, Cranberry, Blueberry, Duckfoot, Rabbit, Blind Pig, Rottenwood, My and Your (the latter two resulting from a long-ago ownership dispute). On one island, we get a glimpse of an old-timer's 1950s-vintage fishing camp, a vestige of the once-thriving commercial fishing industry (walleye, sturgeon and whitefish) that peaked around 1910.

Beavers reveal their presence with lodges that extend out from the shores of several small islands. As we skim along in open water, Mike watches for submerged rocks, which are well-marked on maps and by buoys. He suggests another way to avoid trouble ahead: "If there's a colony of shorebirds that seem to be clustered on the water, you'll usually find rocks." Soon, he points out a big boulder in the lake, hosting just such a bird colony.

Despite today's sunshine, much of Rainy Lake appears mysteriously moody and dark—not because of pollution, but because of tannins released by spruce and balsam trees. That dark-colored water can be a plus, because it heats up faster than clear water, Mike tells me. As with

Voyageurs' other lakes, Rainy's waters ultimately flow north into Hudson Bay. Is the lake's name a comment about the weather? "No," Mike explains. "At one time, the falls in what's now International Falls created a lot of mist. The word translated to English as 'rainy,' and it stuck." (Those falls are now hidden by a dam and reservoir.)

Short hiking trails on several islands reveal remote, little-visited inland lakes rimmed with sedgegrasses, wild rice, cattails and reeds. At the Rainy Lake Group campsite on the Kabetogama Peninsula, we break out sack lunches at a campsite and I listen with rapt attention as Mike and Kathleen trade bear stories (these hulking creatures—up to 500 pounds and five feet tall—rarely cause serious problems, but locals love to share their yarns). "If you don't see a bearproof locker, hang your food up high from a tree," Kathleen says. "If you do have a run-in, scream at the top of your lungs or bang together some pots and pans. And remember, bears swim between islands, so one could show up anywhere."

Soon we're idling above a submerged reef in 42-foot-deep water to try our luck fishing. After about 10 minutes of casting, I proudly display a 25-inch walleye, which Mike gently returns to the water. I ask him what's the biggest fish he's ever hooked here. "A 35-pound sturgeon, years ago. These days, the big ones usually are northerns."

At Anderson Bay, we join some houseboaters clambering up the back side of a huge mound of granite for a view of the lake. Next, we stop at the white-frame, red-roofed Kettle Falls Hotel, fondly known as the "Tiltin' Hilton," which Mike's family operated for 25 years. It's setting was once part of a busy portage route, then a steamboat landing linking Rainy and Namakan lakes; tourists can reach it only by boat or floatplane.

One side of the original hotel, completed in 1913, gradually sank on its foundation over the years. When the National Park Service restored the structure in 1986, they wisely left the lopsided Lumberjack Saloon intact and simply leveled the pool table. The 12-room, two-story hotel, the only lodging within the park, is well-maintained but nothing fancy—sort of a big, old-fashioned summer place with a few antiques and lots of memorabilia and photos.

The 12-foot-high dam that now conceals the original Kettle Falls is half in Canada and half in the United States. This is one of those quirky spots where I'm looking south into Canada! Today, the dam maintains a consistent water level on Rainy Lake.

Tranquillity on the Angry Water

Next morning, I'm ready to roam Kab Lake, accompanied again by Kathleen, along with two new guides: Larry Warrington and his daughter, Sally McRoberts, plus their spouses and the McRobertses' two young sons. The family moved here from the Chicago area five years ago when they purchased Arrowhead Lodge. As we stand on the screened porch of the rustic log-style main lodge, Sally tells me they offer 10 cabins, six lodge rooms and three RV sites in the enclave flanked by Voyageurs. Wooden

Frog State Campground is just behind the lodge, which was built as a resort back in the 1920s and '30s.

Larry explains that Kabetogama reportedly means "lake of the angry water" in the Ojibwe language. Twenty-six miles long and six miles wide, the lake runs roughly parallel to much larger Rainy Lake. We pass some of Kab's 200 one-acre-plus, rocky, pine-covered islands.

Soon we're on dry land again, hiking a short, stony trail along a stretch of frothy green rapids. The Gold Portage Route—once a primary crossing for the Ojibwe, voyageurs and those hapless gold seekers—links Kab Lake with Rainy Lake.

We also stop at the Ellsworth Rock Gardens on the peninsula, a restoration in progress. Jack Ellsworth was a Chicago contractor and carpenter who vacationed here from the mid-1940s to the mid-'60s. Apparently the type who couldn't sit still, he created an impressive hillside grotto dotted by daylilies and primitive rock sculptures.

Next we're off to probe more islands with names such as Pine and Wolf (I happily note that even in this wilderness, a few campsites are wheelchair-accessible). Our final hike is on the peninsula to Lake Agnes, a hushed interior lake ringed with pine, spruce and aspen. Road-sign cairns (heaps of stones piled as landmarks) guide our bumpy hike over rocks and gnarly tree roots, and moose scat indicates we aren't the only ones who find the area appealing. A proud bald eagle presides above us from a tall white pine tree.

More Voyageurs Adventures

Greeting us later at the Crane Lake area at the park's southern tip is a huge statue of a voyageur. I head for the parklike grounds of Nelson's Resort and my rendezvous with Jim Janssen, owner of Voyagaire Houseboats, the largest of the four houseboat-rental concessionaires here at Voyageurs. Jim was a vacationer from northwest Indiana who decided to try to make a living here and succeeded in spades.

Soon, we're in a motorboat heading to Crane Lake's Northwest Bay. I knew I would be spending the night on a houseboat, but I envisioned something more spartan. Ours has four bedrooms that together sleep up to twelve, two bathrooms, a living room/sunroom, two refrigerators, a microwave, a gas grill, a TV, a sound system, a full radio setup, a twisty slide in back and a hot tub on the roof—the price tag a mere $300,000 (renting for about $1,000 per day)!

"We give you all the instruction you need beforehand, then come out to check on you and deliver supplies daily. We're always in radio contact as well," Jim says. "With this boat you get live Maine lobster delivered, too. Fancy or basic, houseboating is very popular on these lakes. You get all the amenities you want right in the wilderness."

Back on land, we're at rustic Nelson's Resort, founded by Swedish immigrant John Nelson and his wife Milly in 1931. Its brown-painted log cabins with their red roofs cluster like a small Scandinavian village at the south end of Crane Lake (only the north shore of the lake officially is part of Voyageurs). Here, I meet Lennart Ostberg, a distant cousin of the Nelson family who grew up in Sweden, attended college and served in the Swedish Army. He came here for a visit in 1972 and wound up as an airline attendant based in Minneapolis, a commercial fisherman in Alaska, and a carpenter and a fishing guide here. "I stayed because I love it here," he says. "It's a lot like northern Sweden, you know."

We pass through Sand Point Lake and then Namakan Narrows, which connects Crane Lake with Namakan Lake to the north. Lennart points out Old Man Rock, which resembles an old man's face. "You're supposed to salute him for good luck fishing," he advises. I ask Lennart about his clientele. "I get a lot of people from Chicago and the Twin Cities. We fish and then I do a shore lunch of battered walleye and fried potatoes." As we skim along on Namakan Lake, Lennart tells me at one point that he's in Canada and I'm in the United States! Again, I'm awed by the unspoiled solitude.

How does the terrain change in the park and beyond, I ask? "The farther west you go, the more it flattens out in general, like farm country," Lennart says. "Here, we have more rocks and cliffs. All of these islands were logged off at least once. Some of those original trees were so big it took three people with their arms extended to encircle them!" We stop at a few islands to hike and sightsee. Along the way, we pass another rock with a famous face: Winston Churchill. Lennart also points out the foundations of bygone resorts.

We pull our boat beside a cliff decorated with faint pictographs created untold years ago by the Ojibwe, who first settled here in the early 1700s. With Lennart's help, I barely discern the artists' outlines of sturgeon bones and canoes and a moose. So much of the Voyageurs' story is related in various ways via the park's primordial rocks. I ask Lennart one of my stock questions: What's your favorite time of year here? "August through October, when it's good weather yet quiet like today. Winter is fun, too. I'm planning to take people on winter camping and fishing trips. We'll snowshoe, cross-country ski and ice-fish."

As we pass a sheer rock face that plunges into the lake, I'm reminded of a framed print by Minnesota wildlife artist Francis Lee Jaques (1887–1969), hanging on the wall of my home. It depicts voyageurs canoeing past just such a scene. When I return, I'll appreciate its intense colors and stunning scenery all the more.

Dan's Travel Journal

FEATURED STOP

Voyageurs National Park Along 55 miles of the Canadian border in Northeast Minnesota. More than 30 lakes and hundreds of rocky-shored islands distinguish this 218,000-acre paradise. Four large lakes—Rainy, Kabetogama, Namakan and Sand Point—cover much of Voyageurs, best explored by houseboat, motorboat, canoe and kayak (access to nearly all the shoreline is by boat). Visitors can dock at more than 150 boat-in campsites or overnight at the park's Kettle Falls Hotel or at North Woods lodges and resorts outside the park. Area lodgings and outfitters offer boat rental, plus fishing excursions and guides for some of the best walleye fishing anywhere. Visitors can start at the communities of International Falls, Kabetogama, Crane Lake and Ash River, all gateways to the park. Three visitor centers offer maps, introductory films, interpretive exhibits, hiking trails and, at Rainy Lake and Kabetogama, guided trips aboard 26-foot-long Voyageur-like canoes. Call ahead for updated park information (Rainy Lake Visitor Center, the only one open year-round: 218/286-5258; Ash River Visitor Center: 218/374-3221; and Kabetogama Lake Visitor Center: 218/875-2111).

Lodging, Dining and More

Arrowhead Lodge Kabetogama. On Lake Kabetogama, rooms in a historic log lodge, built 80 years ago as a logging camp, and 10 cabins. Other amenities: a dining room (ask about meal plans), boat rentals, canoe and kayak rentals, RV sites and fishing and sightseeing guides. $ rooms; $$$$ cabins (218/875-2141).

Kettle Falls Hotel Voyageurs National Park. In the heart of the park, this 1913 historic landmark and its 12 guest rooms and dining room are open mid-May–early October and accessible only by air or water. (Shortest water route is 12 miles from the Ash River Visitor Center, but guests can boat here from any of the park's visitor centers, or hotel staff will shuttle overnight guests by boat from Ash River.) Another lodging option: villas in the woods, popular with anglers. $ (218/240-1726).

Nelson's Resort Crane Lake. Near Voyageurs National Park and the entrance to Boundary Waters Canoe Area Wilderness, 27 log cabins along the Crane Lake shore, dining in the lodge (meal plans available), hiking trails, sauna and beach (open May–September). $$$$ (800/433-0743).

Thunderbird Lodge International Falls. Just ½ mile from the park's Rainy Lake Visitor Center, a full-service resort on Rainy Lake with 15 lodge rooms, 10 cabins and fine dining. Also: complete marina facilities, fishing guide service and boat rental. $–$$ rooms; $$$$ cabins (800/351-5133).

Voyagaire Houseboats Crane Lake. Explore the watery wilderness aboard floating homes ranging from a basic 36-footer to a 57-footer. Optional meal packages and canoe, kayak and boat rental available (800/882-6287).

More Information

Ash River Tourism Association (800/950-2061, www.ashriver.com).

Crane Lake Visitor & Tourism Bureau (800/362-7405, visitcranelake.com).

Explore Minnesota Tourism (888/868-7476, www.exploreminnesota.com).

International Falls, Ranier and Rainy Lake Convention & Visitors Bureau (800/325-5766, www.rainylake.org).

Kabetogama Lake Association & Tourism Bureau (800/524-9085, kabetogama.com).

DAN'S OTHER STOPS

(See also More Parks section that follows.)

Grand Rounds National Scenic Byway (612/230-6400), Itasca State Park (218/266-2100).

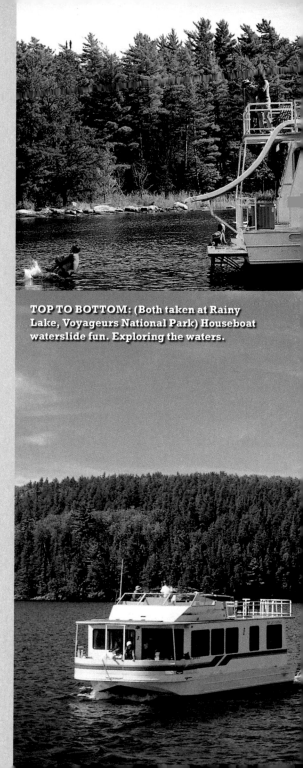

TOP TO BOTTOM: (Both taken at Rainy Lake, Voyageurs National Park) Houseboat waterslide fun. Exploring the waters.

More Minnesota Parks

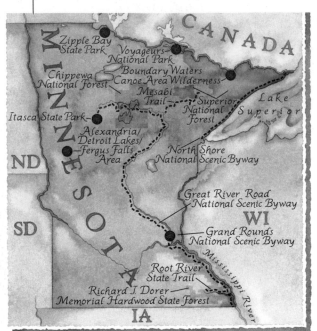

pond beside 1889 Phelps Mill in its namesake county park. Inspiration Peak rises above a postcard-like scene. The byway connects to the paved 55-mile Central Lakes State Bike Trail. Tamarac National Wildlife Refuge, known for abundant waterfowl, is located 20 miles northeast of Detroit Lakes.

Contact: Otter Trail State Scenic Byway (800/726-8959, visitfergus falls.com). Tamarac National Wildlife Refuge (218/847-2641, fws.gov/ refuges). Nearest lodgings: throughout the region, including in Alexandria (800/235-9441, alexandriamn .org), Detroit Lakes (800/542-3992, visitdetroitlakes.com) and Fergus Falls (800/726-8959, visitfergus falls.com).

from lake to lake, portaging your gear and canoe in between. At night, a crackling fire warms your soul and your dinner. You can bring your own gear or hire an outfitter (with or without a guide) to plan your route and provide everything you'll need.

Contact: Boundary Waters Canoe Area Wilderness (218/626-4300, fs.fed.us/r9/ superior). Ely Chamber of Commerce (800/ 777-7281, ely.org). Lodgings: at cabins and lodges on inholdings within the canoe area; also in entry-point communities (888/868-7476, exploreminnesota.com).

Chippewa National Forest

Leave US-2, which bisects this north-central Minnesota forest, and you venture into a million-acre mosaic of lakes, streams and wetlands. Chippewa claims more water per mile than any other national forest. Nine canoe trails, some with campgrounds, beckon paddlers. Leech Lake, the forest's largest, yields some of the state's biggest fish. It stretches north from Walker, a vacation hub at the forest's southwestern corner (about 65 miles north of Brainerd).

Some 300 miles of hiking trails weave through the woods, known for bald eagles. Nearly 70 miles of the North Country National Scenic Trail climb through the southern reaches. Cyclists love the paved 18-mile Mi-gi-zi Trail, which loops around Cass Lake. Mountain bikers also can pedal a section of the North Country Trail, with sites for camp-to-camp rides.

Three national scenic byways cross or border the forest: a segment of the Great River Road; the 47-mile Edge of the Wilderness route (State-38) between Grand Rapids and Effie; and the 46-mile Avenue of the Pines byway (State-46) between Deer River and Northhome, with one of

Alexandria, Detroit Lakes and Fergus Falls

Between wooded hills and farms, thousands of lakes etch this three-county region (150 miles northwest of the Twin Cities). They range from Otter Tail, among the largest, to tiny nameless gems along gravel roads that snake from highways. Main streets in many communities are steps from the water.

Besides visiting Alexandria and Detroit Lakes, set out from the county seat of Fergus Falls on the 150-mile Otter Trail State Scenic Byway. It loops past parks and little towns. Lakes for fishing and water fun are the prime attraction at Glendalough State Park and larger, more developed Maplewood (some 9,000 acres). On many lakes, there's often nobody else in sight (canoes and kayaks for rent). Both parks include hiking trails and campgrounds.

The Otter Tail River cascades into the

Boundary Waters Canoe Area Wilderness

Dipping your paddle into the water, it's easy to imagine how the Ojibwas and French voyageurs felt 200 years ago. The silence and immensity of northeastern minnesota's North Woods enfolds you as fish ripple the lake's glassy surface. Sounds of wildlife and the swoosh of your paddle are all you hear.

Interrupted by few roads, even fewer people and very limited motorized watercraft, there's no place like the pristine million-acre Boundary Waters, surrounded by Superior National Forest beside the Canadian border. The U.S. Forest Service reinforces the magnificent isolation with permits limiting the people who enter. You also can camp only at designated sites spaced for privacy.

Most visitors begin their trips near Ely and Crane Lake on the west or Grand Marais and Tofte on the east. You paddle two forest visitors centers located nearby.

Contact: Chippewa National Forest (218/335-8600, fs.fed.us/r9/chippewa). Nearest lodgings: in small towns throughout the forest, plus Walker (800/833-1118, leechlake.com) and Grand Rapids (800/355-9740, visitgrandrapids.com).

Grand Rounds National Scenic Byway

The only national scenic byway entirely within a city makes a 53-mile loop through Minneapolis' tree-lined neighborhoods. You can travel the two-lane route in an afternoon or turn it into a weekend jaunt with stops along the way.

The byway extends from northeast of the heart of downtown at the Mississippi River near Nicollet Island southeast along the river's west bank. You'll pass the landmark Stone Arch Bridge above the St. Anthony Falls dam and the historic West Side Milling District. Pull off at Minnehaha Park, which surrounds Minnehaha Falls, gleaming among limestone bluffs and tall oaks. The Longfellow House near the falls serves as an information center.

The byway links lakes and ponds known as the Chain of Lakes. Many border parks with gardens and recreational facilities. Near the fashionable Uptown area, joggers, bicyclists and windsurfers converge around Lake Calhoun. You'll discover woods, wilderness, even a bog at Theodore Wirth Park. To the northwest, trees along Victory Memorial Parkway honor area soldiers who died in World War I. The byway returns east toward the Mississippi at the parkway's northern end, connecting two golf courses.

Contact: Minneapolis Park & Recreation Board (612/230-6400 or 612/370-4969 for the information center, minneapolisparks

CLOCKWISE, FROM TOP: Aerial View of western Minnesota lakes region, a vacation mecca. Autumn scene, Chippewa National Forest. Paddling the pristine Boundary Waters Canoe Area Wilderness.

LEFT TO RIGHT: Stone Arch Bridge and St. Anthony Falls, Grand Rounds National Scenic Byway. Apple orchard, Great River Road National Scenic Byway. Superior Hiking Trail.

.org). Nearest lodgings: throughout the city (800/620-1958, minneapolis.org).

Great River Road National Scenic Byway

From a humble North Woods stream, the Mississippi flows through the Twin Cities, becoming a mighty waterway that forms Minnesota's southeastern border. The 575-mile Great River Road National Scenic Byway traces the beginnings of the nation's greatest river.

From an ankle-deep trickle (see Itasca State Park, right), the Mississippi shows itself reluctantly flowing northeast through Lake Bemidji, past little towns camouflaged in the woods. It hides in big lakes such as Cass and Winnibigoshish, then loops southeast through Grand Rapids, once a lumbering hub, before arrowing south through the Brainerd lakes region to the bustling city of St. Cloud. The mature Mississippi starts to show its mettle, separating Minneapolis and St. Paul. Continuing south, barges and boats ease through locks as the river flows toward Lake Pepin, a boaters' paradise.

Towns such as Red Wing, Lake City and Wabasha, which grew on 19th-century river commerce, flourish contentedly amid forested bluffs that become steeper the farther south you go. Countless islands, including the island community of Winona, speckle the river. You can stop at Great Bluffs State Park before reaching La Crescent, where apple orchards stripe the hills.

Contact: America's Byways (800/429-9297, byways.org). Minnesota Office of Tourism (888/868-7476, exploreminnesota.com). Nearest lodgings: all along the river (contact Minnesota Tourism above).

Itasca State Park

Amid a basin of sky-blue lakes, towering trees and tales of Paul Bunyan, the Mississippi begins as a fickle northern Minnesota stream, dribbling from Lake Itasca. But the significance of this site, where you can tip-toe across the river's headwaters on a handful of stones, was realized long ago, when the lake became part of Minnesota's first state park (25 miles southwest of Bemidji).

Today, 32,000-acre Itasca State Park,

much of it a wildlife sanctuary, provides the setting for outdoor recreation, including five lakes excellent for fishing. A scenic drive, also popular with cyclists, loops through the park (bicycles, boats and canoes for rent). Some 27 miles of trails with hike-in campsites lead into the woods. Visitors also can backpack into Itasca's boonies.

One of two campgrounds edges the water; the other is in the woods. Some vacationers stay at historic Douglas Lodge. Flanked by cabins, it peeks through the trees near modern motel-style accommodations. Lodge restaurant specialties include fresh walleye and wild rice.

Contact: Itasca State Park (218/266-2100, www.dnr.state.mn.us/state_parks. Nearest lodgings: Outside the park in Bemidji (800/458-2223, visitbemidji.com) and 20 miles southeast in Park Rapids (800/247-0054, parkrapids.com).

Mesabi Trail

To pedal one of the nation's longest rail-trails, head for the Mesabi Iron Range. Bicycles hum along the route ore trains

once traveled, through an area known as the "great canyons of the north," rich with Native American and immigrant history, forests, rivers and former iron mines .

Some 90 paved miles of the 130-mile northeastern Minnesota trail are complete. The longest uninterrupted stretch—more than 50 miles—extends from Nashwauk (20 miles east of Grand Rapids) east to Eveleth and McKinley. A lodge-to-lodge cycling program provides accommodations.

Pedaling isn't always easy along the trail. Heaps of earth from mining operations resemble man-made mountains. The path cuts through outcroppings and ancient stands of pines. Most of the former mines have been transformed into lakes, often stocked for fishing.

The trail links some two-dozen towns, where attractions include historic buildings, museums and mine overlooks. In Hibbing, the biggest community, you'll discover the world's largest open-pit mine. In Chisholm, costumed interpreters and exhibits re-create life in the miners' immigrant home-lands at the Ironworld Discovery Center.

Contact: Iron Trail Convention & Visitors Bureau (800/777-8497, irontrail.org). Lodge-to-lodge bicycling (800/322-8327, mesabitrail.com). Nearest lodgings: in communities all along the trail (see Iron Trail contact above).

North Shore National Scenic Byway

Few places compare to the land of woods, waterfalls and engaging harbor towns along this byway (State-61), which trails ocean-like Lake Superior from the lively port city of Duluth north to Canada. Savor this 154-mile route in short spurts, with plenty of stops. The byway ventures between forested bluffs and the lakeshore, where cliffs rise like castles, battered by waves. Rivers rush from the rolling Sawtooth Mountains, transforming the shore with waterfalls. Trails lead to overlooks and feed into the 220-mile Superior Hiking Trail.

Seven state parks provide fishing, hiking, mountain-biking, kayaking and camping options. At Gooseberry Falls State Park, trails lead to five waterfalls. Visitors tour a

shore icon, the 1910 Split Rock Lighthouse, atop a cliff at a state park by the same name. Plan to view Minnesota's highest waterfall at Grand Portage State Park, near a re-created 1700s fur-trading post at Grand Portage National Monument. Lakeshore towns also tempt you to linger: Two Harbors claims the shore's first lighthouse. The artists' colony of Grand Marais, once a fishing village, bustles with galleries and shops.

Contact: America's Byways (800/429-9297, byways.org). Minnesota Office of Tourism (888/868-7476 exploreminnesota .com). Nearest lodgings: all along the shore (contact Minnesota Tourism above).

Richard J. Dorer Memorial Hardwood State Forest

With spring's first wildflowers, hardy hikers and backpackers head for this 43,000-acre state forest, extending from Hastings (15 miles southeast of the Twin Cities) south along Mississippi backwaters to the state line. With 10 units, it's the largest of Minnesota's 56 state forests.

Challenging trails and remote rivers

attract adventurous mountain bikers, canoeists and horseback riders. The Kruger Unit is a favorite of hikers (five miles southwest of Wabasha). Views of the Zumbro River Valley unfold as trails weave among bluffs overlooking forests and fields.

First-timers need maps to navigate the seven miles of well-maintained trails. Less-traveled paths deeper in the woods can be tougher going. Shorter jaunts loop through flat woodlands; longer treks on narrow trails include challenging climbs. At dusk, pitch your tent at one of 19 primitive campsites on a river bluff as breezes whisper in the trees and whippoorwills trill serenades. You'll also find campsites in the Reno North and Vinegar Ridge units (horse camping is popular in several units).

Contact: Richard J. Dorer Memorial Hardwood State Forest, Kruger Unit (651/345-3401, www.dnr.state.mn.us/state_forests); Reno North and Vinegar Ridge units (507/724-2107, same website). Lodgings: in Wabasha (800/565-4158, wabashamn.org).

Root River State Trail
Glaciers that flattened most of central Minnesota missed the state's southeastern corner, leaving hills and deep valleys (100 miles southeast of the Twin Cities). Through the Root River Valley, you can bicycle a 43-mile paved trail on a converted rail bed across creaky trestles, through limestone corridors and into serene villages along the lazy river.

Families and serious cyclists share the easy route from Houston west to tiny Fountain, roughly paralleling State-16, the Historic Bluff Country National Scenic Byway. Plan to stop in Rushford and Peterson, with restored 1800s depots. In tiny Whalen, the Aroma Pie Shoppe is known for its homemade creations.

The National Register of Historic Places lists the entire business district in Lanesboro (bicycle rentals available). Brick storefronts from the 1880s, inns, and bed and breakfasts line the main street. About five miles west of Lanesboro, the trail joins the Harmony-Preston Valley State Trail, with some steep hills along the 18-mile route. In Harmony, the center for the area's Amish community, shops stock handmade furniture and crafts.

Contact: Root River and Harmony-Preston Valley state trails (507/285-7176 www.dnr.state.mn.us/state_trails). Southeastern Minnesota Historic Bluff Country (800/428-2030, bluffcountry.com). Nearest lodgings: in trail towns, with the most options in Lanesboro (contact Bluff Country above).

Superior National Forest
There's no greater Midwest wild kingdom than this 3-million acres of lakes, rivers and woods from the Canadian border east of International Falls southeast to Lake Superior's shore. Moose splash in the shallows, while beavers trail shimmering wakes. Occasionally, even black bears panhandle motorists on the paved 57-mile Gunflint Trail, which angles up to the forest's northern reaches.

Though it's wild, the forest isn't deserted. Some roads veer off to nowhere, but others lead to campgrounds, cabins and lodges. The 61-mile Superior National Forest Scenic Byway between Lake Superior's shore at Silver Bay and the inland town of Aurora previews this labyrinth of water and pines.

Backpackers spend weeks trekking the 220-mile Lake Superior Hiking Trail, girdling the region's steep slopes, crossing streams and twisting through the woods. But with dozens of trailheads, you can hike almost any distance. Some dozen accommodations participate in a lodge-to-lodge hiking program.

Other trails also lead through the forest, where visitors can fish and canoe down gentle waterways (see the Boundary Waters Canoe Area Wilderness, page 84).

Contact: Superior Hiking Trail Association (218/834-2700, shta.org). Superior National Forest (218/626-4300, fs.fed.us/r9/superior/). For lodge-to-lodge hiking (800/322-8327, boundarycountry.com). Lodgings: in many sections of the forest (888/868-7476, exploreminnesota.com).

Voyageurs National Park
(See previous section of this chapter.)

Zipple Bay State Park
You can't get much farther north in the lower 48 states than this 3,000-acre northwestern Minnesota state park (90 miles northwest of International Falls). Among jack pines and birches, it borders a bay beside 80-mile-long Lake of the Woods from Baudette, Minnesota, to Kenora, Canada.

Zipple Bay is Minnesota's northernmost state park and remains one of the wildest, drawing adventurers who comb miles of sandy shore, hike trails, fish among the rushes and bird-watch. The park's namesake, Wilhelm Zipple, was among the area's first European settlers. Before him, fur trappers, traders, the Ojibwas and other tribes ruled the area.

From the park's marina, you can canoe, kayak and powerboat into Lake of the Woods. More than 14,000 islands rise from its waters. Thanks to a sandbar, the lake is only about 3 feet deep up to an eighth of a mile out. Swimming and splashing are fine—for those who can brave the chilly waters. The park also includes horse trails and four campgrounds in the woods.

Contact: Zipple Bay State Park (218/783-6252, www.dnr.state.mn.us/state_parks). Nearest lodgings: at small resorts around Lake of the Woods and about 15 miles southeast in Baudette (800/382-3474, lakeofthewoodsmn.com).

CLOCKWISE, FROM TOP LEFT: Richard J. Dorer Memorial Hardwood State Forest. Near the Root River State Trail. Majestic High Falls, Grand Portage State Park. Bicycling the Mesabi Trail.

MISSOURI

A great cross-state biking trail

MISSOURIANS ARE PROUD of their state parks—and justifiably so. Three times since 1984 they've enthusiastically approved a one-tenth percent sales tax for the Missouri Department of Natural Resources, with half the revenue supporting 83 state parks and historic sites and half funding soil conservation efforts. They also steadfastly adhere to a tradition of keeping their parks fee-free or as affordable as possible.

On this trip, I'll check out several Missouri state parklands. Three are rocky, forested wonders clustered around the Arcadia Valley in rugged southeast Missouri's age-old St. Francois Mountains: Elephant Rocks, Taum Sauk Mountain and Johnson's Shut-Ins. About an hour from the suburbs of St. Louis, I'll canoe a serene river and "spelunk" for a spell in a huge subterranean cavern at Meramec State Park. Finally, I'll be off to the star attraction of my Missouri sojourn: a self-powered bicycle tour along the Katy Trail State Park.

Three Arcadia Valley Parks

It's early morning, and I'm clambering up a pinkish granite monolith dotted with gargantuan boulders. The improbable scene here at Elephant Rocks State Park resembles pebbles clinging to a monstrous glob of Silly Putty. The four-mile-long Arcadia Valley cuts through Missouri's highest outcrops, the St. Francois Mountains (many

Dan pedaling past a wildflower meadow on the Katy Trail near Defiance.

Photography by Bob Stefko

Missourians say "Sant Francis"). At 1.4 billion years old, the region's rhyolite and red, rose, pink and purple granite rocks are some of the world's oldest. By way of comparison, the Appalachians are 460 million years old and the upstart Rocky Mountains a mere 70 million years "young."

Minerals abound—especially iron (it's still being mined here), lead, barite, zinc, silver, manganese, cobalt and nickel ores. During the Civil War, when Missouri was a halfhearted Union state, future President Ulysses S. Grant held a command here early on. The state's coveted iron ore was the reason for a major 1864 battle in the Arcadia Valley, in which 1,000 Confederates lost their lives trying to overtake a Union earthwork fortification—Fort Davidson, now on the National Register of Historic Places. In the late 1800s, tourism became the big draw that it remains today.

My host at Elephant Rocks, Natural Resource Manager Kimberly Burfield, explains that this pint-size park—just 129 acres, including a laudable one-mile Braille Trail—takes its name from the way one string of the partially lichen- and moss-covered monoliths resembles a line of lumbering circus elephants, complete with surface fissures that resemble a pachyderm's wrinkles. Kimberly manages two area parks, Taum Sauk Mountain and Johnson's Shut-Ins, as well as a 61,000-acre, privately held conservation area known as Roger Pryor Pioneer Backcountry. As a geologist, she was drawn to the St. Francois Mountain region. "I always liked rocks, so I love it here," she says.

I'm intrigued by the names and dates I see chiseled here and there. Early masons who quarried this granite for buildings, streets and tombstones were granted rights to cleave their marks for future generations. Having ascended to the brow of the outcrop, I survey wave after wave of New England-like ridges carpeted with oak, hickory and maple.

Next is Taum Sauk Mountain State Park, 7,500 forested acres starring Missouri's highest peak (elevation 1,772 feet above sea level). These timeworn mountains don't have raw, jagged peaks, but the view is nonetheless impressive: fifteen miles of incredibly dense hardwoods occasionally interspersed with open, grassy glades. The park also includes Missouri's tallest waterfall, 132-foot Mina Sauk Falls. And these names? Nobody seems to have the story quite straight, but it has something to do with a lovesick Native American princess and her dreamboat warrior who ended their ill-fated romance by jumping off the waterfall—a familiar legend in these parts.

Last stop: the 8,549-acre Johnson's Shut-Ins State Park, named for the Johnson family who once owned the land and for the stair-step rhyolite formations that constrict or "shut in" the East Fork of the Black River. Kimberly explains that almost 900 plant species thrive in this general area—close to a third of the plant types found in all of Missouri, along with the animals that go with them. Wildflowers such as the rare marsh blue violet, meadow phlox and yellow lady's slipper. Insects such as the striped scorpion. Amphibians such as the collared toad and wood frog. Fish such as the small darter and shiner. Birds such as the Cooper's hawk. Mammals such as the white-tailed deer, black bear, mountain lion and raccoon.

Here, work crews are busy on a long-term project to repair the devastation caused by a December 2005 breach in a power-company-owned impoundment. That nightmare sent 1.3 billion gallons of water savagely churning down Proffit Mountain and funneling into the Johnson's Shut-Ins. The deluge destroyed the former park manager's home (he and his family miraculously survived). Kimberly shows me an area where all vegetation and trees were scoured away to a height of about 30 feet. Before the disaster, Johnson's Shut-Ins was one of Missouri's prime watery playgrounds, a sentimental getaway favorite of many families; residents look forward to children splashing once again amid its uniquely weird rocks and chutes. The park is closed for restoration with a goal of reopening in 2008.

Meramec State Park

As I move northward from the rugged Arcadia Valley region, the terrain relaxes into the gentle rural mix of farm fields and woodlands so characteristic of Missouri. I'm going canoeing and caving at Meramec State Park, a secluded, 6,900-acre recreational area in a shady, spring-fed river valley 400 feet below the surrounding uplands, just an hour from St. Louis, near Sullivan (population 6,400).

Founded in 1927, the park, whose name comes from a Native American word for "catfish," boasts a wide range of attractions: well-groomed campsites, cabins, a rustic dining lodge, a general store, canoe rentals, hiking trails and an interpretive center, where I'm meeting Park Superintendent Dan Wedemayer and Park Naturalist Brian Wilcox, who are orchestrating my visit.

Because Missouri sits atop a honeycomb of underground tunnels, caverns and streams, one of its nicknames is the Cave State. Well over 6,000 of the spooky labyrinths—40 of them within this park alone—delight spelunkers. Claustrophobic, I'm rather hesitant as Dan unlocks the big metal gate to Fisher Cave, the park's most popular cave, open to the public for naturalist-led tours.

Immediately, the temperature drops to about 57 degrees, a welcome blast of natural air-conditioning on this broiling day. We don caving hard hats with battery-operated lights in front and venture in single-file. The narrow passage soon opens into a series of spectacular rooms resembling a *Phantom of the Opera* set complete with 50-foot ceilings and those peculiar, iciclelike stalactite and stalagmite deposits. It's hard to believe anything lives in this dark world, but along the way Brian shines his flashlight onto a cave frog, a salamander and a tan-colored pipistrelle bat (the cave is closed to the public during winter, when hundreds of little bats hibernate here). Soon I'm back in the sunny, wide-open outdoors, hiking twisting Walking Fern Trail on a bluff about 100 feet above the cave.

With 50 canoeable rivers, including the popular Current, Jacks Fork, Black and North Fork, Missouri is a paddler's paradise. Depending on the time of year, you can test your white-water skills in a churning springtime torrent or lazily float along shallow streams in summer. We canoe a two-mile stretch of the gentle 230-mile Meramec, which feeds into the Mississippi just 15 miles south of downtown St. Louis.

Occasional campers, swimmers and anglers wave as we pass during this serene interlude, gliding by banks crowded with burr oak, shellbark hickory, silver maple and basswood, among other species. Dan and Brian tell me this valley also is home to bobcats, several endangered species of bats (in those caves) and white-tailed deer. Feathered residents include wild turkeys, great blue herons, bald eagles, osprey and warblers. In the river itself are some 75 types of fish, including smallmouth bass, catfish, sunfish and the relatively common goggle-eye. You'll find crayfish, turtles and nonvenomous snakes such as the speckled king snake here as well, but the Meramec's real celebrities are recluses who live in shells at the bottom of the river—the park's 45 freshwater mussel species, many of them endangered.

Katy Trail State Park

In the early 1960s the late Chicago naturalist May Theilgaard Watts had a great idea. With so many miles of railroad track being abandoned, why not create a network of bicycling trails on the usually flat right-of-ways? May's bright idea caught on. The Illinois Prairie Path Trail was completed in 1965 in suburban Chicago, followed by Wisconsin's Elroy-Sparta State Trail in 1967, initiating the national rails-to-trails movement.

Fast-forward about 20 years. The Missouri Department of Natural Resources, assisted by contributors and volunteers led by the late St. Louis financier Edward "Ted" Jones and his wife, Pat; Missouri Governor and U.S. Attorney General John Ashcroft; and Columbia Mayor Darwin Hindman, spearheaded the Katy Trail ("Katy" was the nickname for the Missouri-Kansas-Texas Railroad, or the M-K-T, which was absorbed by the Union Pacific in 1988). Their campaign resulted in the nation's longest rail-trail—at least until Nebraska connects the remaining dots on its projected 321-mile Cowboy Trail.

Today, the Katy Trail extends 238 miles from St. Charles to Clinton (225 miles are developed) and attracts 350,000 bicyclists and hikers each year, plus a few horseback riders on a 25-mile stretch near Sedalia. During most of its flat, winding route, the well-maintained crushed-limestone trail skirts the broad valley of America's second-longest river, the Big Muddy, or "Muddy Mo," which courses 2,341 miles from southwest Montana to St. Louis.

The path is all well-marked and punctuated approximately every 10 miles by trailheads (26 in all) with maps, local information, parking and restrooms. And true to the Katy's railroad roots, you can opt to cycle and train-ride your way across the state, thanks to Amtrak stations in St.

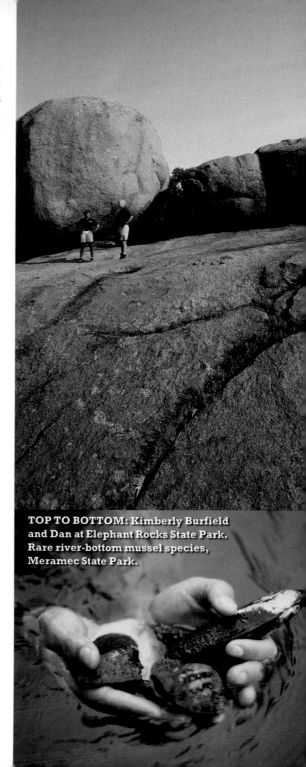

TOP TO BOTTOM: Kimberly Burfield and Dan at Elephant Rocks State Park. Rare river-bottom mussel species, Meramec State Park.

Louis, Washington, Hermann, Jefferson City and Sedalia.

I'm starting in tiny Defiance near St. Charles with my shuttle driver and host, Tracey Berry of the state tourism office. I'll focus on several areas that represent various aspects of the Katy Trail experience and limit sightseeing to within about five miles of the trail. Tracey has been kind enough to pick up a rented hybrid bicycle at a shop in Sedalia, which will be my final stop several days hence in west-central Missouri.

I also visit with Larry Larson, Katy Trail State Park coordinator since 1995 (he's retired several months after my visit). Larry likes to say he manages "arguably, America's longest, skinniest state park." Although his parkland domain extends across most of the state and totals 3,000 acres, it's just 100 feet wide; the trail itself is 10–12 feet wide. That presents some challenges for this good-humored supervisor and his staff of 20: "There's a lot of vegetation to keep under control," he says. "And when a storm system crosses the state, there's a good chance we'll have to clean up the mess somewhere along the trail."

Larry proffers some valuable advice: "On the Katy, you almost always want what's known as a hybrid or comfort style of bicycle—a combination between a fat-tire mountain bike and a skinny-tire racing model. Be sure you take along plenty of drinking water. Don't forget your helmet, and bring an emergency-bike-repair kit. Train ahead of time if you'll be riding any distance; the trail is flat, but that doesn't mean you don't have to pedal. And plan ahead! That way you can see the sights, enjoy some good food and wine, and stay where you want, whether it's a campground, a hotel or a bed and breakfast."

A Frontiersman's Home

Most historians trace the modern bicycle to Great Britain in the late 1800s, when those early versions with a huge front wheel and tiny back wheel first appeared. By the early 1900s, American manufacturers were turning out a million bicycles a year; then automobiles and motorcycles spoiled the party temporarily. Now, it's estimated there are 1 billion bicycles worldwide.

Bicycles weren't around at all when Ken-

tucky frontiersman (as well as legislator, surveyor and gunsmith, among other vocations) Daniel Boone arrived in Missouri in 1799. He came here at the invitation of the Spanish government, which controlled the area and wanted to encourage orderly settlement. Boone spent the final two decades of his life hunting, trapping and helping keep the peace, until his death at age 85 in 1820. His large family flourished here, and Boone descendants still live in the area.

I'm just five miles from the Katy Trail (an hour from downtown St. Louis), visiting the Daniel Boone Home and Boonesfield Village National Historic Site, owned by Lindenwood University of St. Charles. My tour guide, Site Manager Pam Jensen, is garbed in a period costume. She tells me Daniel Boone was highly regarded in his day. "He was considered very honest. He came here partly because of debts and clouded land titles, a common problem in Kentucky in that day. By the time of his death, he'd repaid all of those debts."

Pam leads me through Boone's blue-tinged four-story limestone home, built in 1810 and furnished with tasteful period

antiques and detailed with original black-walnut woodwork. I ask about several tiny holes in the 2½-foot-thick walls. "They're gun ports, just in case of attack," Pam says. Outside, I explore several of the dozen or so historical buildings, including a woodworking shop, a chapel and a schoolhouse—all moved here to re-create a village setting at this living-history gem.

Daniel Boone is buried with his wife Rebecca in a family plot just 13 miles from here in Marthasville—at least that's what most people hereabouts think. Residents of Frankfort, in Boone's home state of Kentucky, also claim his burial site. As I leave, I pay my respects at an important reminder of Boone's legacy: a tree stump on the lawn beside his home, the remains of a once-majestic American elm known as the Judgment Tree, which marked the spot where Daniel Boone, an honest man, adjudicated frontier disputes.

Not far down the trail, I brake for wine. Prior to Prohibition, Missouri boasted 60 wineries and ranked behind only New York in wine production. Wine making was a tradition in the Missouri River Valley dating to the arrival of German immigrants in the 1830s. I've written before about the charming old-world towns of Missouri's *Weinstrasse,* or wine road, particularly my favorite, Hermann. Today, 58 wineries and 1,200 acres of vineyards flourish in the state, most of them near the Katy Trail. Just up a hillside from the trail near Defiance, I make my way to the Miller family's Sugar Creek Winery. Its 10.5-acre vineyards have been worthy representatives of Missouri's resurgent wine industry since 1994. "Visiting a winery is a chance to unwind and enjoy the local flavors," Becky Miller says. "Come back sometime and see the sunset from up here—it's fantastic."

Next I'm at the parking area for Klondike Park, a St. Charles county park. I pedal through a small restored prairie loaded with big bluestem grass and purple coneflower and black-eyed Susan all abloom. Occasionally, limestone bluffs peek out from under their dense veil of foliage. A turkey vulture glides overhead, and I glimpse a deer before it darts into the woods. I see many interpretive signs about local flora and fauna and the Lewis and Clark Expedition, which passed by here on the river in 1804 and 1806.

Elsewhere, I cross some of the Katy's more than 1,000 bridges and culverts and half-dozen tunnels. I find myself spinning along under craggy limestone bluffs; orderly vineyards and lush farm fields; woodlands filled with oak and hickory; river and creek bottoms crowded with quaking eastern cottonwoods, cattails and rushes; and patches of prairie alive with native grasses and wildflowers. At a moderate bicycling speed of only 10 miles per hour, I find I'm savoring sights I normally overlook.

Cycling a Capital City

About 90 miles from the Defiance area, I approach the gray-steel twin arches of the State-54/63 bridge that spans the Missouri and leads into the laid-back capital city, Jefferson City (population 39,262). I have a lot to see here! First, there's the regal 1918 Missouri Capitol itself, situated like a temple on a hillside high above the river traffic below. Both the grandly domed Missouri limestone-marble edifice and its grounds are classically designed and well-maintained. I pay my respects at a statue of Thomas Jefferson signing the Declaration of Independence, then park my bicycle and head inside.

Looking upward inside the dome, which soars 262 feet above the lower level, I'm engaged by colorful decorative paintings depicting Missouri's history, created by London artist Frank Brangwyn. On the first floor, my historian's nose leads me to the Missouri State Museum, especially the gallery honoring "Missourians Worth Remembering," such as Dred Scott, Joseph Pulitzer, Josephine Baker and the late Governor Mel Carnahan, who died tragically in a 2000 plane crash.

But what really takes my breath away awaits in the House Lounge on the second floor: a four-wall mural, *A Social History of Missouri,* painted in 1936 by Missouri's most famous artist, regionalist Thomas Hart Benton. A Neosho native who lived many years in New York, Benton returned to spend his final years in Kansas City. The mural tells the state's history through depictions of famous and ordinary Missourians in Benton's unmistakably vibrant, powerful and sometimes-raw style.

On to more stops in the downtown district: the 1871 Renaissance Revival governor's mansion and Jefferson Landing State Historic Site, a three-building legacy of the city's original river wharf area (which also includes Jefferson City's train station, where bicyclists can hop on and off the Amtrak line during their Katy Trail adventure). A dish of some of the most amazing ice cream awaits at the often-packed Central Dairy.

If any theme has inspired my parklands adventure, it's been nature. So my next stop is six miles to the west side of town, the Runge Conservation Nature Center, one of the best such facilities I've seen (cyclists can make shuttle arrangements with their hotel or ride a city bus). Here, the Missouri Department of Conservation spotlights the plants and critters found in the state's wetlands, prairies, savannas and woodlands and the riparian corridors of its many rivers. In the 3,500-gallon freshwater fish aquarium, a giant alligator snapping turtle chomps on a small fish.

Elsewhere, a huge plastic frog croaks at the push of a button. Mounted specimens include a 130-pound paddlefish caught in the Osage River and a 5½-foot mountain lion accidentally struck by a car. A pygmy rattlesnake and a Missouri tarantula star in the glade-ecosystem exhibit. Outside, the 97-acre site offers two miles of trails and a panoramic view of "Jeff City."

Bikers' R & R in Rocheport

Along the Katy, there are so many places—hotels and motels, inns, bed and breakfasts and campgrounds—that cater to bicyclists; many of their staffs are happy to pick up cyclists along the trail and shuttle them back again. A stellar example is my overnight base in the historic village and Katy trailhead town of Rocheport (population 200; the name means "rock port" in French, the language of the first Europeans in the area). Rocheport is about 35 trail miles from Jefferson City and just 17 interstate miles west of Columbia (population 92,000).

The pleasantly disheveled town is an antebellum gem, its streets lined with little Southern-style cottages, a reminder that Confederates dominated the area during most of the Civil War. Shops in the tiny downtown offer a chance to browse for antiques, gifts, art and books. Rocheport also has several bed and breakfasts, including the 10-room, circa-1914 School House Inn. The innkeepers are busy yet attentive Lisa and Mike Friedemann, both CPAs from Tulsa, Oklahoma, who decided to fulfill their dream here. Every room at the School House has a name recalling its past life. I'm in the spacious Teacher's Pet suite.

Another Rocheport attraction is the acclaimed Les Bourgeois Vineyards, founded by the family of the same name in 1985; it's along the trail a little more than one mile from town. I'm having a sunset dinner at the winery's popular bluff-top bistro. On the terrace, I sip a glass of the signature Riverboat Red and feast on a gourmet view of the valley below (the Katy Trail runs at the foot of the bluff). Affectionately known as The Bistro to fans, the modern timber-frame restaurant captures more of that view inside with its huge window wall. The cuisine is impressive as well. I order lobster ravioli, Caesar salad, beef tenderloin and a sinful slice of flourless chocolate cake for dessert (see recipe, page 98). Part of the fun at the busy bistro is the range of attire: Everybody is welcome, whether they're bicyclists in spandex and helmets or gussied-up couples from nearby Columbia.

The next morning, my dawn warm-up ride from the trailhead in town takes me across Moniteau Creek on one of the Katy's old iron bridges, retrofitted for bicyclists and hikers. I love the sound of the muted clatter of my tires on the bridge's wooden floor. I kid some fellow cyclists as we meet in a dark, smoke-stained tunnel that burrows 240 feet through a tall limestone bluff. "Watch out for the bear!" I mockingly caution. "We just saw him!" they fire back (there are none in this area).

Next stop: Prosperous Boonville (population 8,200), 13 trail miles from Rocheport. (No, "Boonville" isn't a typo: The origin of the town's name is uncertain, but it doesn't stem from a corrupted spelling of Daniel Boone's surname, as one might suspect.) The 1912 Spanish Mission-style brick-and-stucco station houses the main Katy Trail State Park offices. Nearby is a vintage M-K-T green caboose: No. 134 was on its way to a new home in Mexico when Boonville

CLOCKWISE, FROM TOP LEFT: (All taken along the Katy Trail) Les Bourgeois Vineyards bluff-top bistro. Onetime M-K-T railroad tunnel near Rocheport. Dan bicycling outside Sedalia's restored depot. Rocheport's downtown shops.

SEDALIA, MO

Katy Trail Chocolate Flourless Cake

Diners at Les Bourgeois Vineyards winery and bluff-top bistro near Rocheport rave about this elegant dessert, listed on the menu as Nemesis. Warm and creamy, the irresistible indulgence is very rich.

1½ cup sugar
12 ounces unsweetened chocolate, chopped
¾ cup unsalted butter, melted
6 eggs, room temperature
   Sweetened whipped cream

In a heavy 2-quart saucepan, combine 1 cup of sugar and ½ cup water. Cook and stir over medium-high heat until mixture boils, stirring constantly to dissolve sugar. Reduce heat to medium; continue boiling at a moderate, steady rate for 4 minutes, stirring occasionally. (Adjust heat as necessary to maintain a steady boil.) Remove saucepan from heat. Immediately add chocolate; stir until chocolate melts and mixture is smooth. Gradually add melted butter, stirring until combined. Transfer chocolate mixture to a very large bowl; set aside.

In an 8-cup glass measure, combine eggs and remaining ½ cup sugar. Beat on high speed about 10 minutes or until mixture rises to about 7 cups in glass measure. Fold one-fourth of egg mixture into chocolate mixture. Gently fold in remaining egg mixture. Transfer batter to a 9-inch springform pan; spread to an even layer.

Bake in a 300° oven for 30 to 35 minutes or until top springs back when touched. Cool in pan for 20 minutes. Run a metal spatula around edges. Loosen pan but do not remove sides. Cool for 45 minutes more. Remove sides of pan.

Serve cake warm or at room temperature. Top with sweetened whipped cream. *Makes 12 servings.*

preservationists rescued it. Now it gives visitors a glimpse of railroad workers' quarters and showcases photos and memorabilia.

Sedalia, My Trail's End

The 35-mile route from Boonville southwest to Sedalia (population 20,000) veers away from the Missouri River through the gently rolling hills of the Lamine River Valley—past hedgerows, copses, pastures, fields and several Civil War-era farmhouses, at least one with slave quarters still out back. Soon I'm at Sedalia, home to Missouri's state fair each August. It's a sedate, family-oriented community, but that wasn't always the case.

Remember the 1950s TV series *Rawhide*? Sedalia was the end of the trail for Rowdy Yates, Boss Favor, Cookie and the rest of the drovers. It was also a hub of the M-K-T line, which shipped Texas cattle east. Ladies of the evening and wide-open saloons were so plentiful in the city that a St. Louis newspaper of the day once termed it "the Midwest's Sodom and Gomorrah." These days, the meat-processing and health-care industries are this agricultural center's major employers, and Sedalia is a Katy Trail hub.

Katy Trail bicyclists like to camp and cool off in the pool at shady Liberty Park, less than a mile from the trail. But I'm headed to the 1947-vintage Wheel Inn, an old-fashioned red-and-white drive-in complete with carhops. I order the locally renowned "guber burger." It's a hamburger patty with runny peanut butter drizzled on top and served with mayo, lettuce and tomato.

At the historic 1896 brick-and-limestone depot near the heart of town, I explore the extensive exhibits, including reminders that women and men once had separate waiting rooms and, sadly, blacks were required to use a separate ticket window. From here I pedal west down the tree-lined trail past the state fairgrounds to the unexpected Daum

Museum of Contemporary Art. Founded by a local radiologist and housed in a striking building completed in 2001, it showcases a major collection of abstract paintings, drawings, prints, ceramics and sculptures. Included are works by 20th-century American masters such as Andy Warhol, Helen Frankenthaler and Robert Motherwell. A glasswork by Dale Chihuly charms me with its shimmering purple hues.

Sedalia's other cultural claim to fame is musical. Ragtime composer and self-taught pianist Scott Joplin (1868–1917) came here on the Katy line from his childhood home in Texarkana in 1893. Despite an itinerant lifestyle (he also lived in St. Louis, Chicago and New York), Joplin spent about 10 years in Sedalia all told, composing his signature "Maple Leaf Rag" here. Today the town is host to the Scott Joplin International Ragtime Foundation and a June festival.

My last night in Missouri, I lodge at the venerable 1927 Hotel Bothwell, across the street from Sedalia's handsome Pettis County Courthouse, and dine in its Ivory Keys restaurant, which honors Joplin. The hotel was partly financed by local legend John Bothwell (1848–1928), an eccentric lawyer, politician, banker and philanthropist. You can visit his rambling 31-room hilltop home, Bothwell Lodge State Historic Site, near State-65 four miles north of the trail.

I dutifully return my rented bicycle to Ebby Norman at his Pro-Velo Cycle Sport Shop. Cyclists can rent wheels here for something like $25 per day or $100 per week. I ask about Sam Baugh, the Clinton, Missouri, "ultracyclist" I've heard has cycled the entire length of the Katy Trail in one day. I don't think I'm quite up to that feat.

"How did it go for you on the trail?" Eddy asks. "Fine," I reply. "Just wish I'd had more time."

Dan's Travel Journal

FEATURED STOP

Katy Trail State Park From near St. Charles (just outside of St. Louis) west to Clinton (southeast of Kansas City). Hikers and cyclists chug along the former rail route, now the 238-mile-long Katy Trail State Park, the nation's longest rail-trail run. The Missouri River and towering bluffs flank much of the smooth crushed-limestone trail, dotted with mile markers and 26 well-spaced trailheads. The western third of the trail abandons the river at Boonville and passes through pastoral farmlands en route to Clinton. Horses are allowed on a 25-mile section from Sedalia to Calhoun (660/882-8196).

Lodging, Dining and More

Daniel Boone Home & Boonesfield Village Defiance. Tour the four-story limestone home hand-built by the Boone family and the re-created 19th-century village (636/798-2005).
Hotel Bothwell Sedalia. At this downtown 48-room, seven-story landmark, an Art Deco atrium lobby, crystal chandeliers and a grand ballroom recall the hotel's elegance when it opened in 1927. $$–$$$$ (660/826-5588).
Katy Depot Boonville. Find visitor information at the Boonville Chamber of Commerce (660/882-2721) and Katy Trail State Park area offices (660/882-8196) in this 1912 depot.
Katy Depot Sedalia. The historic 1896 depot houses the Railroad Heritage Museum and Visitors Center (800/827-5295).
Les Bourgeois Vineyards Rocheport. Tour this family-owned winery just off I-70; three-fourths mile away, indulge at its bluff-top restaurant and outdoor wine garden (800/690-1830).
Missouri State Capitol Jefferson City. Free guided tours of this 1918 architectural gem (573/751-2854).
Runge Conservation Nature Center Jefferson City. A 97-acre menagerie of Missouri wildlife and habitats, with indoor interactive exhibits and aquarium, plus outdoor hiking trails through prairie, wetlands and forest (573-526-5544).
School House Bed and Breakfast Inn Rocheport. This historic three-story brick school is now a 10-room inn, with full breakfast included. $$$–$$$$ (573/698-2022).
Sugar Creek Winery Defiance. A favorite Katy Trail stop for dry Cynthiana, fruity Raspberry Patch and other wines (636/987-2400).

Related Area Events

Katy Trail Ride St. Charles to Clinton, third week in June—Five-day, 225-mile bicycle ride (660/882-8196).
Missouri State Fair Sedalia, 11 days, beginning the second Thursday in August—Since 1901 (800/422-3247).
Scott Joplin Ragtime Festival Sedalia, first full weekend in June—Ragtime concerts in the town where Joplin wrote "Maple Leaf Rag" (866/218-6258).

More Information

Amtrak Cyclists and their bikes can ride Am-trak to stations near the Katy Trail (Washington, Hermann, Jefferson City and Sedalia), then pedal back (for train schedule and reservations, 800/872-7245, www.amtrak.com).
Jefferson City Convention & Visitors Bureau (800/769-4183, visitjeffersoncity.com).
Missouri Division of Tourism (800/877-1234, www.visitmo.com).
Missouri Wine & Grape Board for information about Missouri's 50 wineries (800/392-9463, www.missouriwine.org).
Rocheport Area Merchants Association (573/698-2022, www.rocheport.com).
Sedalia Convention & Visitors Bureau (800/827-5295, www.visit sedaliamo.com).

DAN'S OTHER STOPS

(See also More Parks section that follows.)
Arcadia Valley state parks: Elephant Rocks (573/546-3454), Johnson's Shut-Ins and Taum Sauk Mountain (573/546-2450); Meramec State Park Sullivan (573/468-6072).

TOP TO BOTTOM: (Both taken along the Katy Trail) A former railroad bridge outside Rocheport. Vintage downtown buildings in Sedalia.

More Missouri Parks

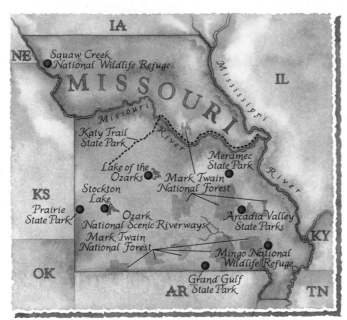

Arcadia Valley State Parks

A trio of southeastern Missouri state parks—Taum Sauk Mountain, Elephant Rocks and Johnson's Shut-Ins—neighbors one another in the rugged St. Francois Mountains' Arcadia Valley (60 miles west of Cape Girardeau). Most of Taum Sauk Mountain State Park's nearly 7,500 acres remains wilderness. Woodlands scatter among domelike mountains and rocky knobs. A commanding view rewards visitors from the state's highest point. Or you can hike the 3.5-mile Mina Sauk Falls Trail to the state's highest waterfall.

Bring a picnic when you venture 10 miles northwest of Taum Sauk Mountain to small Elephant Rocks State Park. Visitors scramble around house-size humps of granite. Trails lead into the woods, and a little lake attracts anglers. The park also includes Missouri's first Braille trail.

Located just west of Taum Sauk Mountain, swimmers love the maze of chutes, pillars and ledges that the Black River eroded into a shelf of granite at Johnson's Shut-Ins State Park, which is expected to reopen in 2008 (see page 92).

Contact: Elephant Rocks State Park (573/546-3454, mostateparks.com). Johnson's Shut-Ins State Park and Taum Sauk Mountain state parks (573/546-2450, mostateparks.com). Nearest lodgings: five miles northeast of Taum Sauk Mountain in Ironton and adjacent Pilot Knob (573/546-7117, ironcounty.org).

Grand Gulf State Park

A roller-coasterlike road (County-W) dead-ends at this south-central Missouri park, where the ceiling of a mammoth cave collapsed aeons ago, creating a giant chasm called the "Little Grand Canyon." You'll gasp when you step to the edge of this plunging gorge (75 miles west of Poplar Bluff).

Surrounded by a forest of oaks, maples and sycamores, four overlooks, each a short stroll from the parking lot, provide views of the nearly mile-long, buff-colored chasm. Walls tower as high as 130 feet. Exhibits describe how rivulets honeycombed the rock in these Ozark hills with gigantic caves.

At one end of the canyon, a natural bridge looms where a section of the cave's ceiling remains intact. Adventurous souls can follow boardwalks partway into the chasm or hike steep dirt paths to its rocky floor. In some places, you ease between sheer walls a few feet apart. The air turns cool beneath the natural bridge's span. Visitors also can picnic in the woods and hike other trails in the 320-acre park.

Contact: Grand Gulf State Park (417/264-7600, mostateparks.com). Nearest lodgings: twenty-five miles northwest in West Plains (888/256-8835, westplains.net); limited options six miles east in Thayer (417/264-7324, thayerchamber.com).

Katy Trail State Park

(See previous section of this chapter.)

Lake of the Ozarks

Vacationers flock to this 92-mile-long silvery lake with arms twisting deep into forested hills (50 miles south of Jefferson City). Boats zip across the channels, and anglers fish for bass in the coves. On the lake's east side, attractions, restaurants and shops line US-54 near the busy resort towns of Lake Ozark and Osage Beach.

Two shoreside state parks provide access to the lake. South of Osage Beach, nearly 17,500-acre Lake of the Ozarks State Park is Missouri's largest. Its 85 miles of shore includes beaches, boat launches and a marina with boat rentals, plus a buoy-marked boat trail. You can fish, explore a cave, hike 10 trails, ride horses from the stables and join seasonal naturalist programs. Visitors camp and stay in cabins.

Near the lake's southern reaches south of Camdenton, follow a bluff-top trail to ruins of a 1920s mansion at Ha Ha Tonka State

Park. At this smaller day-use park, with two boat docks, trails also lead to lake overlooks, caves, a gurgling spring and natural bridge, even an Ozark savanna.

Contact: Lake of the Ozarks State Park (573/348-2694, mostateparks.com). Ha Ha Tonka State Park (573/346-2986, mostateparks.com). Lodgings all around the lake (800/431-4117, funlake.com).

Mark Twain National Forest

Scattered across Missouri's Ozarks, this forest promises endless outdoor recreation. In nine units, its 1.5-million acres stretch from prairie lands near the Missouri River to rugged granite formations in the northeast near St. Louis to grasslands, hills, deep hollows, streams and a huge meandering lake in the south.

Visitors hike, mountain bike and ride horses along nearly 750 miles of trails. Serious backpackers tackle the 180-mile Ozark Trail, starting at Berryman south of St. Louis. An 18-mile hiking loop, with camping along the trail, leads into the forest's 16,500-acre Irish Wilderness near Doniphan.

The vast forest encompasses lakes for swimming and fishing. Spring-fed canoeing rivers include the Current and Jacks Fork (see Ozark National Scenic Riverways, page xx), plus the Eleven Point River near Thomasville. You can sightsee along roads such as the 24-mile Blue Buck Knob National Forest Scenic Drive between Cabool and Siloam Springs. It's one of three designated scenic drives. The forest's southwestern unit, between Kimberling City and Cassville, surrounds twisted arms of Table Rock Lake, where largemouth bass abound and marinas rent boats.

Contact: Mark Twain National Forest (573/364-4621, www.fs.fed.us/r9/forests/marktwain). Lodgings: near or in all nine units (573/751-4133, visitmo.com).

Meramec State Park

The Meramec River stars as the main attraction at this popular state park almost within the shadows of St. Louis (65 miles northeast). Vacationers congregate at the nearly 6,900-acre preserve to canoe, raft and tube the river's riffles.

Stop at the visitors center to get oriented and learn about the river's variety of aquatic life, including several rare mussel species. You also can rent canoes and rafts at the park (plan a weekday visit for the most solitude). Riverside forests conceal clear-running springs, as well as fishing and swimming holes. About 16 miles of hiking and backpacking trails include the 10-mile Wilderness Trail. Spring through fall, naturalists lead tours of some of the park's 40 caves. Visitors can camp or stay in cabins and motel-style rooms at the park.

Contact: Meramec State Park (573/468-6072, mostateparks.com; 573/568-6519 for lodging and canoe and raft reservations). Nearest lodgings: four miles west in Sullivan (573/468-3314, sullivanmo.com).

Mingo National Wildlife Refuge

Traveling the winding two-lane highway a mile north from little Puxico, nothing prepares you for what's ahead. A vast, green and mysterious swampland awaits at this nearly 22,000-acre southeastern Missouri refuge (40 miles southwest of Cape Girardeau).

Lily pads carpet the surface, and bald cypress poke their knobby knees skyward along a mile-long boardwalk into the wetlands, where the Mississippi flowed before changing course long ago. Late November through early December is peak viewing season for some 150,000 ducks and geese that stop on their migrations south. The seven-mile Red Mill Drive is the best route for waterfowl viewing. You'll also see herons, egrets, ospreys and owls among nearly 250 types of birds. Bald eagles nest here in

TOP TO BOTTOM: Water coursing through rocky chutes at Johnson's Shut-Ins State Park. Tree-loving, nonvenomous rough green snake, Meramec State Park.

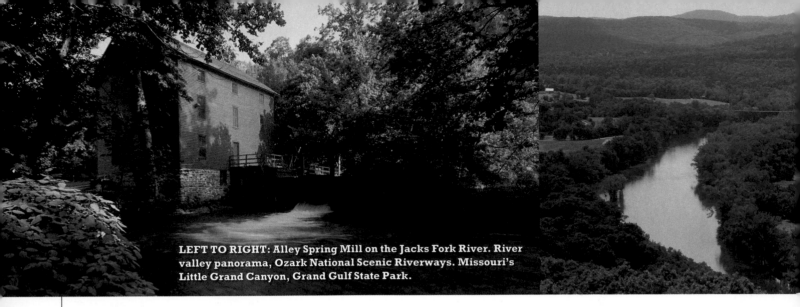

LEFT TO RIGHT: Alley Spring Mill on the Jacks Fork River. River valley panorama, Ozark National Scenic Riverways. Missouri's Little Grand Canyon, Grand Gulf State Park.

spring and summer. Amphibious creatures, including turtles, toads, snakes and salamanders, also call the swamp home.

Stop by the visitors center for maps, tour information, and details about fishing and wildlife viewing. You can drive the 18-mile Auto Tour Route in April and May, when spring songbirds migrate and wildflowers put on a show, and again in October and November to view fall foliage and waterfowl migration. From overlooks, you'll see the Ozark Mountains to the west and the marsh below.

Contact: Mingo National Wildlife Refuge (573/222-3589, www.fws.gov/midwest/mingo). Nearest lodgings: twenty-two miles southwest in Poplar Bluff (573/785-7761, poplarbluffchamber.org).

Ozark National Scenic Riverways

Canoes loaded with campers round the bend as a whisper of breeze stirs the air. That's the usual sight on southeastern Missouri's 134-mile Ozark National Scenic Riverways, including the Current River and its major tributary, the Jacks Fork. You can skirt riverbanks dotted with limestone bluffs and caves. Then, pull onto a sandbar and take a swim before feasting on fresh fish and pitching your tent for the night.

Ranging from sleepy crawls to quick tumbles, the riverways extend from the Current's headwaters at Montauk State Park (20 miles southwest of Salem) south through Van Buren to near the Carter and Ripley county lines. Natural springs, including gorgeous Alley Spring along the Jacks Fork west of Eminence, keep the water cool. In spots, dissolved limestone lends the river a brilliant jade cast. Canoe liveries and outfitters operate along the banks. Canoeists also can pitch tents at National Park Service and private campgrounds. An 18-mile stretch between Akers Ferry and Round Spring samples the riverways' variety. You'll maneuver among limestone bluffs and paddle through a dark cave along the way.

Contact: Ozark National Scenic Riverways (573/323-4236, nps.gov/ozar). Nearest lodgings: at Montauk State Park (573/548-2201, mostateparks.com; reservations 573/548-2234), midway along the riverways in Eminence (573/226-3318, eminencemo.com) and in Van Buren to the south (goto vanburen.com).

Prairie State Park

The state's largest public native grassland preserves a piece of Midwest heritage in southwestern Missouri just south of Liberal (35 miles north of Joplin). Prairie State Park's sea of tall grasses and wide-open spaces, bobbing with wildflowers, resemble the landscape that greeted early settlers.

For perfect solitude, hike some of the more than 10 miles of trails. You can get maps at the visitors center to explore on your own or join monthly naturalist-led hikes May through September. Wildflowers begin blooming early in spring. Yellow stargrass, shooting stars, bird's-foot violets and Indian paintbrush create the setting for colorful courting rituals of prairie chickens late March into April. Every season stages its own wildflower spectacle. By fall, big bluestem and Indian grasses tower above your head.

Spring also starts other birds and wildlife stirring. You might see a coyote warily

watching from a distance as grasshopper sparrows flit nearby. Elk and bison roam parts of the park. Visitors can overnight at primitive campsites. The park's fall Prairie Jubilee features interpretive programs and guided walks.

Contact: Prairie State Park (417/843-6711, mostateparks.com). Nearest lodgings: sixteen miles east in Lamar (417/682-5554, cityoflamar.org) and 15 miles southwest in Pittsburg, Kansas (620/231-1212, visit crawfordcounty.com).

Stockton Lake

Breezes lift your spirits as you zip across the open waters of this 25,000-acre southwestern Missouri lake south of Stockton (40 miles northwest of Springfield). Visitors can explore the V-shaped U.S. Army Corps of Engineers lake for hours, hardly encountering another person. Roads dip and climb among bluffs and forests along the nearly 300 miles of shore. Stop at one of three marinas or six beaches to learn where black bass and walleye are biting or to ask about favorite picnic spots and hiking trails at the 11 U.S. Army Corps of Engineers

recreation areas around Stockton lake.

On the northeastern shore, Stockton State Park's 2,200 acres never seem crowded. A haven for powerboating, sailing and water recreation, the park includes a marina renting all kinds of boats, plus a swimming beach, a campground and cabins, a motel and a dining lodge. Many visitors overnight on their sailboats and powerboats docked at the marina.

Contacts: Stockton State Park (417/276-4259, mostateparks.com; 417/276-5329 for lodging reservations). U.S. Army Corps of Engineers (417/276-3113, nwk.usace.army .mil/stockton/lakefact.htm). Nearest lodgings: in Stockton (417/276-5213, stockton lake.com or stocktonmochamber.com).

Squaw Creek National Wildlife Refuge

The whir of snow geese wings breaks the stillness at Squaw Creek National Wildlife Refuge (35 miles northwest of St. Joseph). During the fall migration, visitors gaze at thousands of the white beauties gliding like ballerinas into the refuge's wetlands.

More than half a million birds stop at this

7,300-acre preserve on the Missouri River floodplains. Besides snow geese, you'll see mallards by the thousands and other waterfowl. Visitors can bicycle or drive the 10-mile self-guided loop road. In October (prime viewing time), you'll travel through forests turning gold and past large pools covered with snow geese at midday.

On fall weekends, interpreters at the visitors center conduct nature programs about topics ranging from snow geese flyways to monarch butterflies. Among three hiking trails, the 1.5-mile Eagle Overlook Trail links the two largest wetlands. You'll probably also see muskrats building their lodges and deer traipsing through the woods. The snow geese disappear by December, but bald eagles remain all winter, commanding stark branches—their profiles etched against the sky.

Contact: Squaw Creek National Wildlife Refuge (660/442-3187, fws.gov/midwest/ squawcreek). Nearest lodgings: limited five miles north in Mound City (660/442-3447, moundcitychamber.org); more options 35 miles southeast in St. Joseph (800/748-7856, saintjoseph.com).

NEBRASKA

The shimmering Niobrara River flowing past towering bluffs near Valentine.

A hidden canoeing wonderland

CANOEING IN NEBRASKA? Isn't it terminally flat, dry and boring in the Cornhusker State? Prepare to stand corrected while exploring one of America's largely undiscovered ecological Brigadoons: the clear, cool waters of the Niobrara National Scenic River as it riffles beneath towering bluffs through a pine-banked valley along the northern edge of Nebraska's vast, awesomely empty Sandhills region.

Getting there is always half the fun, and that's certainly the case as I cruise along busy interstates and forgotten rural highways to Valentine, the jumping-off point for my Niobrara floating adventure.

Eugene T. Mahoney State Park
My first stop en route is a compact (just 740 acres) "resort" park right off busy I-80. You can't miss it: Just watch for the 65×40-foot U.S. flag atop a 185-foot pole in front of the main lodge at Exit 426! Deliberately situated about a half-hour's drive equidistant from the state's two largest cities, Omaha and Lincoln, Eugene T. Mahoney State Park honors the late former state senator and state parks commission director who championed the project. It's pretty enough, perched on wooded (mostly hand-planted oak and hickory) bluffs along the braided channels of the broad, shallow Platte River. But this park wasn't created because of any specific scenic wonder hereabouts. In fact,

Photography by Bob Stefko

LEFT TO RIGHT: Nebraska's grassy, undulating Sandhills. Kerry and Lisa Krueger at their Heartland Elk Guest Ranch. Dan and Kerry on a horseback-riding trail along the river. Chief Ranger Stuart Schneider and a hitchhiking Niobrara crayfish.

the site was cornfields prior to the development of the park, which opened in 1991.

I spend the night in a brand-new, home-like, four-bedroom "cabin" (one of 54 cabins and 149 campsites in the park) on a landscaped cul-de-sac that's more up-to-date than my neighborhood back in Des Moines. The hilltop, 40-room, log-style Peter Kiewit Lodge and full-service restaurant crown the park. During my brief stay, I dabble in miniature golf, horseback riding and paddleboating and visit the crafts center, a big water park and an indoor theater, scene of live performances year-round. Just a stone's throw away are yet more attractions, including the massive, glass-fronted Strategic Air & Space Museum. You won't believe the huge SR-71 Blackbird reconnaissance plane upended just inside the entry, one of more than 30 military aircraft on display in a space equivalent to six football fields.

There's also the Lee G. Simmons Conservation and Wildlife Safari, which is affiliated with Omaha's acclaimed Henry Doorly Zoo. Keep your eyes peeled on the 4.5-mile driving loop for some of the 200 species of birds and 25 types of mammals, including lots of bison and elk and even a few wolves and bears, living relatively unfettered here.

Oh, and did I mention there are seven golf courses nearby? As a result of this thoughtfully planned nexus of enticements, Eugene T. Mahoney State Park nets fiscally tight-fisted Nebraskans more than $1 million per year. (Other states pinched for park funds: Take note!)

Sandhills and Springs

Forging on toward Valentine (named for a 19th-century Nebraska U.S. congressman), I sense myself breathing deeper as soon as I enter the grass-covered—but just barely—dunes that comprise Nebraska's rolling, almost 20,000-square-mile Sandhills cattle country. Like this entire state, the Sandhills region is as much about surprises as it is about the expected.

At oasislike Victoria Springs State Recreation Area near Anselmo, a grove of towering cottonwoods, leaves quaking in the breeze, surrounds a small, spring-fed lake hidden away in a corner of this largely treeless realm. *Is this a mirage?*

Here, Eager Assistant Rob (who's about as far removed from his teeming urban environment—the Bronx—as you can get) and I meet up with our good-natured, impossible-to-rattle Sandhills rancher/state

tourism host, Twyla Witt. Twyla grew up on the remote Sandhills spread she and her husband, Tom, now run. It fascinates me that, like many other locals, she had to board in town during the week to attend high school. Indeed, we pass several still-operating one-room elementary schools as we travel down empty highways so solitary that it's customary to give a friendly nod or wave to the driver of an approaching vehicle.

Like a pioneer wagon train, our mini caravan forges northward on State-2. (Remember, I also travel with a TV and photography crew that usually numbers six.) We cross the misnamed Dismal River, which like the Niobrara is rated as one of the nation's top canoeing streams. At tiny Halsey, we enter Nebraska National Forest (yes, forest), which staggers even my jaded imagination: Here 22,000 acres fairly sing with trees—ponderosa pine, eastern red cedar, Rocky Mountain juniper and more.

In a place where Mother Nature otherwise forgot trees, humanity has created a wooded wonderland by lovingly hand-planting each one I see. The forest was founded in 1902, largely as an experiment in cultivating commercial lumber. The

scheme didn't pan out, but over the years, forestry workers, Depression-era CCCers and area volunteers kept planting. What a tribute to Nebraskans' determination to "foliate" their state! I'm sure all the antelope, deer, wild turkeys, prairie chickens, grouse, quail and other critters often spotted along the 30-mile drive through the forest would concur heartily. A nursery here has provided millions of seedlings that now are mature trees in many other federal, state and local parklands around the region.

My final stop en route to Valentine and the Niobrara is another Sandhills revelation: the 72,000-acre Valentine National Wildlife Refuge. Everything is big here in cattle country, where land costs only about $350 per acre and it takes 16 acres to sustain just one cow-calf pair. Within the refuge, more than 30 shallow, sand-bottomed lakes ringed with cattails dot the terrain. Sand doesn't absorb water the way soil does, so much of the Sandhills' scant 20 inches of annual rainfall collects in these jewellike magnets for 230 species of birds, 60 types of mammals and 20 kinds of amphibians and reptiles.

I suddenly brake as a huge but harmless brown-and-tan bull snake slithers across the road, and again later when a big Blanding's turtle lumbers across my path. Spiny yucca plants with their spikes of creamy blossoms, prickly pear cactuses and low sand cherry bushes interspersed with mixed prairie grasses remind me I'm not in Midwest corn country any longer. I only wish I could return for the famed springtime mating dance of the prairie chickens, which attracts birders here from afar.

Niobrara National Scenic River

Something's definitely up, topographically speaking. We near the town of Valentine (population 2,820). I tell Rob that hereabouts, this is the equivalent of being in Times Square on New Year's Eve! We glimpse the Cowboy Trail Bridge, a 1910-vintage former railroad trestle over a deep canyon traversing the Niobrara River. That bridge is now part of Nebraska's 200-mile-long biking/hiking/horseback-riding rail-trail, soon to become the nation's longest such recreational path.

Time to rendezvous with our local contacts briefly at the Bunkhouse Saloon, which actually is a very tame family restaurant (I highly recommend the chicken-fried steak with white gravy, followed by homemade pecan pie for dessert). Then it's on to the 1,000-acre Heartland Elk Guest Ranch, where we'll bivouac the next few days in a modern stone-and-log cabin overlooking one of the many small canyons that feed into the Niobrara Valley.

The ranch is situated about 15 miles northeast of Valentine on State-12 and several gravel-road miles south of Sparks (population 3), where the highway sign cheekily proclaims "Sparks: Next two exits!" We pick up the keys to our cabin at a big white farmhouse surrounded by elk pens. Cowhand-friendly Kerry and Lisa Krueger (he's from Colorado; she's a native of Southern California) have owned the ranch since 1996. I learn the 80 elk on this high-fenced property are confined here for hunters (many of them from the East), but primarily for commercial purposes—meat, as well as velvety elk antlers, which wind up in products such as the glucosamine chondroitin many arthritics swear by and and potency boosters consumed mainly in Asia.

At nighttime we hunker down at the horse barn for a dinner of marinated, tenderized elk steaks, Sweet & Spicy Baked Beans (recipe, page 111), and a so-good berry crunch dessert. I chat with fellow guests, including several families from Omaha also lodging in the Kruegers' spiffy, secluded cabins for a week of horseback riding and canoeing. "We've had guests from as far as the Philippines and Germany," Kerry says.

As daybreak sweeps over the valley, I awaken to the sight of a deer grazing outside my bedroom window. Soon, we're off on a three-mile ride over rocky trails that trace several canyons down to the river. My quarter horse is a patient, 16-year-old bay named Charley, whose only fault is a tendency to detour for a snack whenever he spots some tasty-looking grass. Even as a very inexperienced rider, I handle him with ease.

Charley is sure-footed, which is a good thing as we descend these scenic, steep-walled canyons. Mule deer and jackrabbits spot us and dash away. Chatting with Kerry on the way down to a meadow beside the

currently summertime-shallow, we don't run aground once—and that's not due to any expertise on my part. "Just hop in up front and follow my instructions," Stuart tells me in a measured, reassuring way.

"The Niobrara can run fast sometimes, but it's very safe," he says. Stuart explains that the river is only 2–3 feet deep on average, and only knee- to hip-high at most during summer, so there's nothing to fear except banging my head on a rock if we should happen to overturn (hmmm—maybe I should have worn a bicycle helmet?). I learn that, because it's primarily spring-fed, the reliable Niobrara usually varies just 6 inches up or down in depth.

I've only canoed a couple times before—once when my now-grown son, Adam, was a Boy Scout, the other time with three other couples my wife, Julie, and I joined

its unique biology and ecology, two topics I'll learn much more about firsthand with Stuart. The Niobrara also remains remarkably unpolluted and almost all free-flowing—there are only three dams on the whole river—somehow having escaped the dam-builders and developers who've straitjacketed so many of America's once-unfettered waterways.

Something else noteworthy about the Niobrara: waterfalls. Stuart says there are 230 in just one 30-mile stretch, and new ones still are being discovered. Most are unnamed. They're fed by the clear, cool waters that filter down through the region's sandy soil and rock (there's relatively little soil to sop it up here in the Sandhills). What doesn't wind up tumbling into the Niobrara keeps on filtering to the incredible underground Ogalala Aquifer, the huge, 200- to 500-foot-thick bedrock water reserve that extends all the way south to Texas and enables many Great Plains farmers to irrigate fields otherwise too dry for crops.

About a mile downstream, we beach our canoes and climb a trail past 45-foot-high Fort Falls, named for the long-gone 1879 outpost now occupied by the 19,000-acre Fort Niobrara National Wildlife Refuge. A bat-filled barn is all that remains of the fort these days—and the bats are welcome because they eat lots of pesky insects during their nocturnal forays. Here we meet up with Chuck Melvin, a refuge officer, to survey the panorama from the rim.

Chuck tells me the original idea behind the fort was for the cavalry, many of them African-American buffalo soldiers, to keep an eye on the restive Sioux back in the late 1800s. But cattle rustlers turned out to be the troops' main preoccupation, and when the fort was vacated in 1912 it soon became a sanctuary for migratory waterfowl. Now the property is also home to herds of buffalo and elk and 8,000 prairie dogs, plus

The Niobrara remains remarkably unpolluted and almost all free-flowing— there are only three dams on the river.

river, I learn that Charley's job prospects are diminishing, at least in the ranching world: Three-wheeled, motorized ATVs are fast replacing cow ponies here and elsewhere.

Before long, Rob and I are shuttling back to a landing near the Cornell Bridge, just northeast of Valentine. Our hosts for a five-hour, 11-mile canoe trip are a congenial group of National Park Service staffers who efficiently organize our combined group into five plastic-composite canoes (birch bark went out with Hiawatha and the voyageurs, I'm afraid). My canoe mate is a burly yet soft-spoken Missourian named Stuart Schneider, who's the chief ranger here. Between us, I estimate we weigh, ahem, something approaching 500 pounds. To my amazement, even though the river is

for a weekend getaway on the Upper Iowa back home. As I get the hang of it, Stuart offers a briefing: The Niobrara (the word means "running water" in the Sioux language) is one of 180-odd national scenic rivers across the United States. Originating in the high plains of eastern Wyoming, it's little more than a creek for most of its 435-mile journey to northeastern Nebraska and its confluence with the Missouri. The National Scenic River stretch, designated as such in 1991, extends about 76 miles east of Valentine, including about nine miles within the Fort Niobrara National Wildlife Refuge, where the river valley remains its most pristine.

The primary reason the Niobrara was awarded its protected status stems from

CLOCKWISE, FROM TOP LEFT: Elk at Fort Niobrara National Wildlife Refuge. Twyla Graham and Dan putting in near Berry Bridge. Upland sandpiper at the wildlife refuge. Smith Falls, Nebraska's tallest.

Easygoing paddling and ever-changing scenery along the clear, spring-fed Niobrara, where crowds are rare on summer weekdays.

wildlife including mountain lions, beavers, river otters, mink, bobcats and badgers, along with an array of birds such as hawks, ospreys, eagles, warblers and buntings.

The view from this breezy vantage point is stunning, all the more when Chuck points out specific examples of the various biomes that collide here thanks to the combined effects of topography, climate, weather and bygone glaciers. On cooler, shadier north-facing slopes, white-bark paper birch and aspen recall boreal forests. Ponderosa pine, juniper and aspen on hotter south-facing slopes represent species usually found much farther west. Intermingled are the American elm and box elder of eastern deciduous forests and the bur oak and green ash more common south of here. Also interspersed in this diverse botanical stew are grasses and other plants common to tall-, short-, and mixed-grass prairies. I'm more awed than ever!

We soon establish a pattern. Canoe a bit, then angle to shore so Stuart and his colleagues can lead us up leafy canyons beside burbling streams to those half-hidden veils of gushing water (the only real caution is poison ivy, whose "leaflets three" we soon learn to "let be"). These waterfalls are much friendlier than cataracts like Niagara, which I've visited several times but certainly never had the opportunity to stand underneath just to cool off!

The 60-degree water provides a delightful sensation on this 95-degree day. The most spectacular waterfall we encounter is 63-foot-high Smith Falls, Nebraska's highest and a state park in its own right. After following a wooden walkway and a short flight of steps, I head to a hidden corner for a clothes-on shower that soon leaves me breathless—thanks to 1,325 gallons of water per minute pouring over the convex-shaped precipice. What an experience!

Back on the river, Stuart grows more animated with each wildlife sighting (this guy is in the right profession, for sure). There's a great blue heron! An eagle! A mink! Several bashful turtles slip away as we near their sunning spots. On our hikes, Stuart identifies plants such as columbine, violet, parsley flower, horsetail, cowslip and wild grape and snags some delicious wild strawberries for me. He points out large rocks that are actually petrified logs. At one stop, he searches a rocky bank for bits of bone and tooth fragments from prehistoric bison, mastodons and three-toed horses.

In ankle-deep water, Stuart turns over rocks to identify some of the insect larvae and other invertebrates that constitute the lowest rung on the feeding chain along the Niobrara—even grabbing a crayfish that's soon adorning the bill of his cap. Canoeing along yet again, he mentions the brown, gray and muted rose-pink striations of rock that form the cliffs we pass, all indicating various layers of sandstone, siltstone and shale, with some volcanic ash thrown in for good measure.

"Ranchers and farmers have taken very good care of this valley for a long time. We want to keep it that way," Stuart says.

Western Wear and River Lore

Even though my objective in the Valentine area is to probe the Niobrara and related parkland gems, I can't resist snooping around wide-open, Western-feeling Valentine. People like to get their greeting cards postmarked here on February 14. Others get married in Valentine on that date. I wonder whether that has something to do with all the red hearts stenciled on the sidewalks up and down Main Street!

At Jordan's Fine Dining and Sports Bar (does that sound like an oxymoron?), I pack away a half-pound Huskerburger with cheese and bacon—I'm eating the way cowhands do! I also shop the way cowhands shop at Young's Western Wearhouse, an emporium stocking everything you can imagine in the way of saddles, ropes, chaps and other Western attire.

A couple blocks away, I pop into Plains Trading Company Booksellers, one of those fast-disappearing independent bookshops I love to browse. Owner Duane Gudgel, who grew up on an area ranch, steers me to several titles that address the Sandhills' natural history, as well as a collection of verses by noted cowboy poet Baxter Black (Valentine hosts a cowboy poetry festival each October). Just for fun, I also nose into a bungalow that houses the tiny Sandhills Boot Company, just a block off Main Street.

But I have to get back on that river for just one more float. At their headquarters on the outskirts of Valentine, we meet the Graham family (yet another Nebraska Twyla, her husband, Doug, and two of their three teenage offspring). They operate Graham Outfitters, one of 14 such concessions that offer soup-to-nuts canoeing packages on the Niobrara. Both Twyla and Doug grew up in the area, and they know this river as well as I know my computer keyboard.

Doug's day job involves raising fish at the state hatchery in Valentine, which stocks many of the catfish in this river, as well as bass, walleye and other species released in other Nebraska waters. We shuttle out to our put-in point near Berry Bridge, about 23 miles northeast of Valentine, for a fun three-hour, six-mile trip downstream.

Beyond the boundary of the Fort Niobrara National Wildlife Refuge, so much of the riparian land is privately held—another good reason to have a knowing outfitter as your guide. Although the scenery outside the refuge isn't quite as spectacular as it is inside, it's still pretty special. This is the more popular segment of the river, especially on weekends: Beer goes hand-in-mug with canoe-camping to many folks, and alcohol is permitted here outside the refuge. On the busiest summer weekends (in July and August), you'll find 2,000 people floating this stretch of the Niobrara. Still, there's plenty of space, especially on this relatively quiet weekday.

Twyla Graham is my canoe buddy. Once again, I'm placed right in front, which doesn't seem to be causing any problem, even though I'm guessing Twyla weighs about half what I do. "Just help keep the canoe in line with the current, don't lean over and stay in the middle of your seat," she advises in a soothing Nebraska country drawl. "We'll do just fine." She's right. Soon, we're nosing through a mildly turbulent passage called The Chute, reportedly the closest we'll come to shooting a rapids during my visit. It's a blast—although not all my companions make it through without a refreshing surprise soaking!

As we slip along, Twyla points out the barely visible remnants of a log cabin in a clearing where her 80-year-old father, retired rancher-farmer Roy Breuklander, spent his boyhood years. We hike up to Little and Big Cedar Falls, where we stop for a refreshing Jacuzzi-like break in a pool at its base. Soon we're exploring aptly named Stairstep Falls. "We love canoeing here year-round," Twyla says, "even in January—the blue ice formations on the bluffs are beautiful, and we see lots of bald eagles."

All too soon the twilight shadows begin to deepen, and we take our boat out at Sunnybrook, the Breuklander family's campground and canoe landing. There, Twyla's still-robust-looking father waits to greet us on the bank.

"I spent the first 10 years of my life on this river," Roy says. "All my life, I've come back down here just as often as I could with my family to camp or just spend the day. It's a lot busier here nowadays, but it's still pretty special here on the Niobrara."

Sweet & Spicy Baked Beans

Kerry and Lisa Krueger operate Heartland Elk Guest Ranch near Valentine. Tasty home-style meals are one way they make their guests feel welcome at the working elk ranch. The sweet flavors of brown sugar and ketchup blend nicely with picante and barbecue sauces, jalapeño mustard and a custom seasoning mix from Ben Mellor, a longtime friend.

½ cup packed brown sugar
½ cup ketchup
¼ cup bottled hot picante sauce or your favorite salsa
¼ cup barbecue sauce (Lisa uses Famous Dave's Devil's Spit BBQ Sauce)
¼ cup jalapeño mustard or spicy brown mustard
1½ teaspoons Sandhill Ben's Original Blend seasoning (to order: 402/291-6805) or a Kansas City-style steak seasoning
1 31-ounce can pork and beans in tomato sauce
1 16-ounce can butter beans, black beans or pinto beans, rinsed and drained
1 16-ounce can dark red kidney beans, rinsed and drained
1 medium onion, chopped

In a large bowl, combine brown sugar, ketchup, picante sauce, barbecue sauce, mustard and seasoning. Stir in pork and beans, butter beans, kidney beans and onion. Transfer bean mixture to a lightly greased 3-quart casserole.

Bake, covered, in a 350° oven for 1 hour. Reduce oven temperature to 325°. Uncover beans. Bake about 45 minutes more or until desired consistency, stirring occasionally. Baked beans will thicken slightly as they cool. *Makes 10 to 12 servings.*

TOP TO BOTTOM: Main Street in Valentine. Soaking-wet Dan enjoying a cool break at Smith Falls.

Dan's Travel Journal

FEATURED STOPS

Fort Niobrara National Wildlife Refuge Valentine. Six major plant com-munities converge on 19,000 acres, perfect for bison (350 head), elk and 48 other mammal species, along with 230 bird types. Drive the 3.5-mile auto tour; maps available at the visitors center (402/376-3789).

Niobrara National Scenic River Valentine. One of the nation's top canoeing rivers, the Niobrara stretches 76 miles east of Valentine; a 25-mile segment that starts just outside Valentine at Fort Niobrara Bridge is the most popular. Soak up the solitude, scenery and wildlife on an eight-mile paddle past Fort Niobrara National Wildlife Refuge; downstream, beach your boat at the star attraction, Smith Falls State Park. Well-spaced landings, plus outfitters offering canoe and tube rental, campgrounds and guided trips dot the route (402/336-3970).

Lodging, Dining and More

Bunkhouse Restaurant and Saloon Valentine. Family-pleasing homemade soups, roast beef dinners, fresh-baked pies and other comfort foods in the restaurant (402/376-1609).

Graham Canoe Outfitters Valentine. Canoeing, kayaking and tubing trips, half-day to two-day, and shuttle service along the Niobrara River. For the best experiences, visit in spring or fall. In summer, paddle midweek to avoid weekend crowds (402/376-3708).

Heartland Elk Guest Ranch Valentine. Fully furnished log cabins, a stone's throw from the Niobrara River. Elk roam the ranch; activities include canoeing, tubing, trout fishing and horseback riding (402/376-1124).

Jordan's Fine Dining Valentine. Breakfast and lunch in the cafe, Husker-sized steak dinners in the dining room and the Cornhuskers on TV in the sports bar (402/376-1255).

Peppermill Steakhouse Valentine. Ranchers Roger and Shelly Joseph wrangle up some of the best Nebraska corn-fed steaks in the territory. For dessert in the 100-year-old brick eatery, order a sinful slice of four-layer Chocolate Tower Cake (800/669-1440).

Plains Trading Company Booksellers Valentine. Locally owned store specializing in books about Native American and Western history, along with titles about the Sandhills and books by Nebraska authors (800/439-8640).

Sandhills Boot Company Valentine. Cobbler and former cowboy Kyle Rosfeld fashions fancy footwear for Sandhills ranchers out of shark hide, cowhide, lizard skin and other exotics (from $650; 402/376-5960).

Young's Western Wearhouse Valentine. "Cowboy up" at this 50-year-old Main Street landmark selling Western duds, saddles and tack (800/658-4398).

Related Area Event

Old West Days & Cowboy Poetry Gathering Valentine, early October—Hear cowboy poets, storytellers and musicians at this Sandhills shindig (800/658-4024).

More Information

Nebraska Travel & Tourism (877/632-7275, www.visitnebraska.org).

Valentine Chamber of Commerce (800/658-4024, www.visitvalentine.com).

DAN'S OTHER STOPS

(See also More Parks section that follows.) **Eugene T. Mahoney State Park** Ashland (402/944-2523), **Lee G. Simmons Conservation Park and Wildlife Safari** Ashland (402/733-8401), **Nebraska National Forest** Halsey (308/533-2257), **Strategic Air & Space Museum** Ashland (402/944-3100), **Valentine National Wildlife Refuge** Valentine (402/376-3789), **Victoria Springs State Recreation Area** Anselmo (308/749-2235).

More Nebraska Parks

Cowboy Recreation and Nature Trail

This trail just keeps getting better…and longer! Visionaries behind the hiking, biking and equestrian trail across Nebraska's northern reaches plotted 321 miles from Norfolk west to Chadron, following the right-of-way of the old Chicago & Northwestern Railroad. The finished rail-trail conversion will be among the nation's longest.

Though the route isn't complete, cyclists can pedal the smooth crushed-limestone trail for more than 160 miles through farmland and pleasant towns. Dramatic trestle bridges, refurbished with wooden decking and handrails, cross rivers and creeks. The longest, at the western end of the trail, spans a quarter mile from 145 feet up.

From the eastern trailhead in Norfolk, you can pedal 143 miles west to Ainsworth. A particularly scenic portion of the trail follows the Elkhorn River. At the trail's western end, an 18-mile segment stretches east from Valentine, where cyclists can access

the route at Trailhead Park, complete with a windmill and pond.

Contact: Nebraska Game and Parks Commission (402/471-0641, outdoornebraska .org). Norfolk Area Chamber of Commerce (402/371-4892, visitnorfolkne.com). Valentine Chamber of Commerce (800/658-4024, heartcity.com). Nearest lodgings: motels in Norfolk and Valentine (contacts above).

Eugene T. Mahoney State Park

Families converge at this 690-acre preserve near Ashland (halfway between Omaha and Lincoln), which combines wooded bluffs and open prairie, for hiking, horseback riding and water-park fun, plus theater during summer. Decks overlook the river from most rooms at the park's centerpiece, Peter Kiewit Lodge. Visitors also stay in secluded cabins along wooded ridges.

Next door, exhibits at the Strategic Air & Space Museum highlight huge restored aircraft from decades gone by, along with

interactive aviation games for kids and the sleek Lockheed SR-71 Blackbird suspended in a glass atrium. Drive through the nearby Lee G. Simmons Conservation Park & Wildlife Safari for close-up views of deer, buffalo, wolves, sandhill cranes and other creatures native to this region. Additional park activities include camping, fishing in two lakes, paddleboating, miniature golfing and dining at the wood-beamed restaurant.

Contact: Eugene T. Mahoney State Park (402/944-2523, outdoornebraska.org). Lee G. Simmons Conservation Park & Wildlife Safari (402/733-8401, omahazoo.com). Strategic Air & Space Museum (402/944-3100, strategicairandspace.com).

Fort Niobrara National Wildlife Refuge
(See previous section of this chapter.)

Lake McConaughy

Picture a topaz-colored sea and gleaming white sands in dreamy photographs of the Caribbean. Then, transport that image to western Nebraska at the state's largest and most popular reservoir. Lake McConaughy extends 23 miles through the North Platte River Valley (nine miles north of I-80 at Ogallala). Lake levels have dropped in recent years, but there's sill plenty of camping, boating and swimming along "Big Mac's" nearly 100 miles of beach.

Even on summer weekends, you'll feel as if you have the massive lake almost to yourself. You can pitch your tent or park your RV right on the sand or stay at state and private campgrounds around the lake.

Bright sails sparkle in breezes propelling sailboards and boats across the wide-open waters. Visitors can rent crafts from concessionaires around the 36,000-acre lake.

LEFT TO RIGHT: White-sand beaches and sailing at Lake McConaughy. Buffalo taking a rest at Lee G. Simmons Conservation and Wildlife Safari. Solitude at a pristine Sandhills lake, Valentine National Wildlife Refuge.

Just west, Ash Hollow State Historical Park interprets the area's history—from prehistoric times through the days of the pioneers. You'll see covered-wagon ruts from more than a century ago.

Contact: Ash Hollow State Historical Park (308/778-5651, outdoornebraska.org). Lake McConaughy Visitors Center (308/284-8800, lakemcconaughy.com). Nearest lodgings: limited around the lake (contact above); more options in Ogalala (308/284-4066, visitogallala.com).

Niobrara National Scenic River

(See previous section of this chapter.)

Pine Ridge Ranger District

This rugged wilderness defies the notion that Nebraska is all wide-open spaces. Sandstone buttes emerge from ponderosa pine forest in northwestern-Nebraska high country east of the Wyoming state line. Ridges and canyons supply stunning scenery for driving tours, hiking and mountain biking.

The district includes the Oglala National Grasslands, where visitors explore clay and sandstone formations resembling mushrooms at Toadstool Geologic Park. A three-mile trail leads to the Hudson-Meng Bison Kill Site, where more than 600 bison died 10,000 years ago. You also can drive to the site and take summer interpretive tours.

To the south, more rugged scenery awaits at Fort Robinson State Park, where the museum gives glimpses of cavalry days. Hikers head out on the trails, or you can join in historical tours, jeep rides and buffalo-stew cookouts. Visitors camp in the grasslands or at Pine Ridge Recreation Area, part of Nebraska National Forest just south of Chadron.

Contact: Fort Robinson State Park (308/665-2900, outdoornebraska.org). Pine Ridge Ranger District (308/432-4475, ngpc.state.ne.us). Nearest lodgings: cabins, refurbished officers quarters and other options at Fort Robinson State Park (contact above); in Chadron (308/432-4401, chadron.com); and about 25 miles southwest in Crawford (308/665-1462, crawford nebraska.net). Also Northwest Nebraska High Country, a group of ranchers and farmers with lodgings, camping and activities on their properties (nebraskahigh country.com).

Platte River State Park

Visitors to this wooded southeastern Nebraska enclave near Louisville huff and puff to the top of the Lincoln Journal Tower. The 85-foot climb is worth the effort. From the observation deck, you can view the rich Platte River Valley and the forested park (between Omaha and Lincoln about 20 miles from the Iowa state line).

You can settle into modern housekeeping and rustic camping cabins, or choose a Native American-style tepee. Because of its rough terrain, the park doesn't permit camping (sites two miles east at Louisville State Recreation Area). Activity choices seem endless. You can paddleboat on lakes, take guided horseback rides (horses provided), hike some 10 miles of trails, swim in the pool or head for the arts and crafts center to create your own masterpiece. For a night off from cooking, the park's expansive

lodge restaurant serves tasty fare, followed by screenings of nature films on weekends.

Contact: Louisville State Recreation Area (402/234-6855, ngpc.state.ne.us). Platte River State Park (402/234-2217, ngpc.state.ne.us).

Sandhills

Undulating dunes in North America's largest tract of mid- and tallgrass prairie define this region of north-central Nebraska called the Sandhills. One of the Midwest's best fishing lakes, two forests and a wildlife refuge attract outdoor and nature lovers.

Walleye, northern pike, panfish and bass make Merritt Reservoir an angler's dream. In the Snake River Valley 26 miles southwest of Valentine, white beaches line the lake's 44 miles of shore. Visitors also camp, water-ski, powerboat and sail.

The reservoir neighbors Samuel R. McKelvie National Forest, a 16,000-acre grassland with 2,200 acres of hand-planted trees. In 1902, Charles Bessey, a University of Nebraska botanist, convinced President Theodore Roosevelt to set aside two treeless tracts where pines could be planted.

The trees thrive here and 85 miles south at Nebraska National Forest. Campers, hikers and picnickers congregate at both.

Just five miles east of the reservoir, birdwatchers and photographers love Valentine National Wildlife Refuge. Some 200 types of birds, including herons and pelicans, have been spotted at this refuge of more than 71,000 acres.

Contact: Merritt Reservoir (402/376-3320, outdoornebraska.org). Nebraska and Samuel R. McKelvie national forests (308/533-2257, fs.fed.us/r2/nebraska). Valentine National Wildlife Refuge (402/376-1889, fws.gov/valentine). Lodgings: around Merritt Reservoir (contact above) and in Valentine (800/658-4024, heartcity.com).

Victoria Springs State Recreation Area

Pioneers stopped along central Nebraska's Victoria Creek more than a century ago. Next came the fountain-of-youth seekers, who sipped and soaked in the creek's mineral springs. The waters, which once were bottled and sold nationwide, still bubble at this shady 60-acre oasis surrounded by ranch country at the edge of the Sandhills (95 miles northwest of Grand Island). But today, campers claim the manicured landscape of towering hardwoods and a mirror-bright lake.

Campsites cluster on a grassy ridge overlooking the creek. At night, coyotes howl in the surrounding hills. Choruses of songbirds wake you at first light. Some visitors amble across a nearby footbridge to the five-acre lake and cast their lines for trout, bass, catfish and bluegill. Others take turns using the park's paddleboats. Hiking park trails, you'll discover an 1880s one-room school and two log cabins that date back 130 years.

Contact: Victoria Springs State Recreation Area (308/749-2235, outdoornebraska .org) Nearest lodgings: two housekeeping cabins at the recreation area (contact above); motels 20 miles south in Broken Bow (308/872-5691, brokenbow-ne.com).

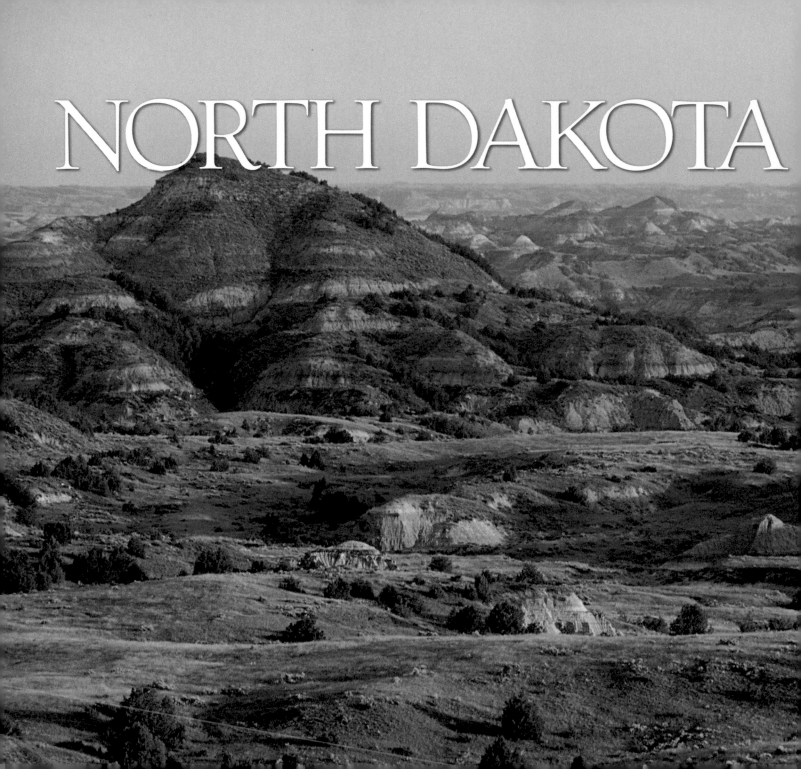

NORTH DAKOTA

Where the badlands cast their spell

AS I WRITE THIS CHAPTER, I'm gazing at a dazzling panoramic photo on my computer screen. One of our Parklands crew snapped the shot from the River Bend Overlook at Theodore Roosevelt National Park in far-west-central North Dakota. The scene encapsulates why this state and this park claim my heart so: limitless horizons with rugged rock formations tinted in subtle pastels, towering over lush green bottomlands. Aside from the activity here at the rustic log-and-stone shelter where we're standing, there's not a single hint of human endeavor as far as the eye can see. Surely this must be what captivated Theodore Roosevelt as well, back in 1883.

Way off the beaten path for most travelers, Theodore Roosevelt National Park comprises 110 square miles of untamed badlands and flinty grasslands. (To my eye, these eerie badlands are more painterly and less stark than the better-known ones in neighboring South Dakota.) Because I'm a history buff, I'm eager to probe our inimitable 26th president's brief but intense ties with the area.

My meandering route to "T.R." will take me to a wildlife refuge in central North Dakota, where I'll spend several hours continuing the birding education I began in Kansas on this journey. Then I'll renew my acquaintance with vast, man-made Lake Sakakawea ("Sacagawea" to most of us

Badlands panorama, Theodore Roosevelt National Park (South Unit).

Photography by Jason Lindsey

outside North Dakota) in the northwest part of this blessedly uncrowded state.

Two Prairie Lakes

Just 13 miles south of I-94 in the middle of the state, Long Lake is one of the nation's approximately 540 national wildlife refuges, most of them created for conservationists. It's fed by tributaries of the now-cosseted Missouri River, which flows 25 miles west of here. Birds are the big draw; more than 300 species have been sighted—prairie, marsh and shorebird in spring and summer and thousands of waterfowl in autumn. Mammals include white-tailed deer, coyotes, mink and Franklin's ground squirrels, which are more at home in these grasslands than their tree-loving cousins.

Extending 18 miles on an east-west axis, Long Lake is two miles wide and just 3 feet deep on average. Three large impoundments include almost 16,000 acres of a 23,000-acre prairie-wetland ecosystem. Birders armed with cameras and binoculars often zero in on the 35 species of shorebirds; several blinds are available, and many birders bring their own portable blinds.

My host, Refuge Manager Paul Van Ningen, helps me add to my now-swelling birding list by pointing out American avocets, marbled godwits and Wilson's pharalopes. I only wish I could catch a glimpse of one of the rare whooping cranes occasionally sighted here or the sandhill cranes during their spring stopovers or the wild mating dances of Long Lake grouse and grebes. As I fumble with my camera, Paul gives me two great tips for "shooting" birds: Invest in a camera with fast shutter speeds, and take photos during twilight when colors are most intense.

I ask whether the birds that flock here today are different from those Lewis and Clark observed when they were in the neighborhood more than 200 years ago.

Paul explains that some species from that era are extinct or nearly so, but others such as the flicker, nuthatch and cedar waxwing are now more commonplace.

Soon I'm back on the trail, loosely skirting the river Lewis and Clark paddled and stopping for a lunch of local German-Russian specialties at a Kroll's Diner near the interstate in Bismarck. About 75 miles northwest, near Pick City, I stand atop the huge, rolled-earth Garrison Dam that backs up Lake Sakakawea, the nation's third-largest reservoir. This engineering marvel is 2½ miles long and 210 feet high, and the lake it forms is 175 miles long and 180 feet deep at its maximum, with 1,500 miles of shoreline. But what really amazes me is that our crew is virtually alone here on a weekday. This has to be the least-crowded watery playground in the Midwest.

And it's all the more enticing when I consider the recreation menu here: powerboating, waterskiing, tubing, sailing, scuba diving, bird-watching and fishing (walleye, salmon, smallmouth bass, northern pike). This also is the western terminus of the North Country National Scenic Trail, which, when completed, will take hikers and bicyclists to Upstate New York (and link to the Pacific Northwest on the Lewis & Clark National Historic Trail).

Lake Sakakawea is just one of six such behemoth dam-building projects initiated back in the 1950s by the U.S. Army Corps of Engineers to tame the Missouri for flood control, power, navigation and recreation. It's a great tribute to the legendary young woman who joined the Lewis and Clark expedition near here.

T.R. National Park

Tucked into an open-ended canyon just off I-94 about 26 miles from the Montana line, Medora (year-round population about 100, but augmented by more than 150,000

visitors during the peak summer season) exists these days for one reason: It's the gateway to the South Unit of Theodore Roosevelt National Park. This town is the epitome of a Western movie set, with authentic-looking shops and cafes, a rustic old hotel and attractions such as a cowboy museum and a rootin'-tootin' Old West pageant showing nightly.

I've heard people sing Medora's praises for years, and now I'm finally here, quartered at the venerable nine-room Rough Riders Hotel right in the middle of town (all eight square blocks of it). My crew and I are famished, so the first order of business is a hearty meal in the rustic Rough Riders Dining Room, where I delight in watching Eager Assistant Rob devour a bottle of Moose Drool Ale and a buffalo tenderloin steak. Outside, local legend Cowboy Lyle Glass, who's rarely seen without his 10-gallon hat, rides Chocolate, his black-and-white pinto, down Third Avenue for one of his open-air demonstrations on topics such as branding, roping, cowboy attire and horse care and maintenance.

There's no Wal-Mart or McDonald's in Medora; in fact, I don't see a single sign I'd consider remotely garish. Thank vigilant locals for maintaining the authentic charm envisioned a half-century ago by a North Dakota inventor and businessman, the late Harold Schafer (ever heard of Mr. Bubble or Snowy Bleach?). Schafer had a lifelong love affair with Medora, which led him to restore the Rough Riders Hotel and launch the nonprofit Theodore Roosevelt Medora Foundation, which now manages two out of three buildings in town.

I stroll Medora's wooden sidewalks and poke my head into its cozy shops and eateries. But I'm here to check out the only national park named for a U.S. president, not to window-shop. My stop at the South Unit visitor center on the west side of town

CLOCKWISE, FROM TOP: Campers surveying the rugged landscape, Theodore Roosevelt National Park (South Unit). Greeting Cowboy Lyle and his horse, Chocolate, in Medora. Musical at Burning Hills Amphitheatre, Medora.

LEFT TO RIGHT: (All taken in or near Theodore Roosevelt National Park) Hikers observing wildlife. Where the buffalo roam. Horseback riding. Mountain biking the Maah Daah Hey Trail. BOTTOM: Roosevelt during an early visit.

quickly makes it clear why Theodore Roosevelt was honored by the designation of this park in 1978 (it had been a national memorial park since 1947). I learn that T.R. National Park consists of two units, along with a much smaller third unit in the middle that contains what once was Roosevelt's Elkhorn Ranch, now discernible only by remnants of its foundation.

Roosevelt spent only about four years, off and on, in the untamed badlands buttes, mesas, canyons and grasslands that surround Medora. But he often referred to those years as the defining period of his life. Roosevelt was America's first president to champion the budding cause of conservation. During his administration (1901–1909), he signed bills that set aside an astounding 230 million acres as national monuments, parks, forests and wildlife refuges.

Park Superintendent Valerie Naylor spins the Roosevelt saga as I wander the visitor center exhibits: Roosevelt came here an Eastern dandy looking for adventure and, subsequently, riches back in September 1883. He was a robust young man of 24 who'd overcome the "98-pound weakling"

syndrome caused by severe childhood asthma. Practically blind, his spectacles earned him the nickname Four Eyes, and his fancy Brooks Brothers-designed buckskin outfit and Tiffany Brothers hunting knife must have made the locals quake with laughter. But by the end of his North Dakota days in 1889, Roosevelt had their respect and the self-assurance that made him our youngest president, at age 42.

We head to a sturdy-looking log cabin in back of the visitor center. "Roosevelt came here to hunt buffalo and then decided to invest in a ranch," Valerie says. "This is the cabin from that first ranch, the Maltese Cross." Inside are three large whitewashed rooms filled with period furnishings, including Roosevelt's writing desk and trunk. Like its owner, the cabin has gotten around a bit: Originally constructed seven miles south of Medora, it was transported to the 1904 St. Louis World's Fair and later exhibited in Portland, Oregon; Fargo; and Bismarck before it landed back here in 1959.

Valerie continues the story: "After his first visit, Roosevelt's life took a tragic turn. On Valentine's Day of 1884, Roosevelt's young

bride, who'd just given birth to a daughter, and his mother both died of different causes in the same house in New York." I learn Roosevelt also suffered reverses in his political career at the time. He returned to North Dakota to put his shattered life back together. "I would not have become president had it not been for my experiences in North Dakota," T.R. often is quoted as saying. Now I get it.

The next morning, my crew and I head out on the South Unit's 36-mile loop road with its many turnouts where the park's 500,000 visitors annually might spot buffalo and lines of feral horses. I'm also on the lookout for the resident white-tailed and

mule deer, elk, pronghorn antelope, mountain lions, badgers, prairie dogs, coyotes and bighorn sheep, plus an array of birds that includes Spragues pipets, redheaded woodpeckers, various sparrows and sharp-tailed grouse.

I nose my car through the raw badlands landscape of clay, sandstone, siltstone and mudstone. It's greener here than in the almost totally barren South Dakota Badlands, perhaps because the 60-million-year-old rocks here have had twice as long to erode into soil as the much-younger (at 30 million years) upstarts there. Or perhaps it's because this area was the bottom of vast freshwater lakes, marshes and ponds, while the South Dakota Badlands were submerged in saltwater. These formations date back to the birth pangs of the Rocky Mountains. Like pastel-hued layered gelatin, the rocks reveal their volcanic, glacial and sedimentary origins, including ribbons of gray volcanic ash, red scoria clay and black coal.

About six miles into the South Unit, I pull up beside a log building that once served as park headquarters but now is the stable at Peaceful Valley Trail Rides,

the park's horseback-riding concession. It's operated by Neil and Laura Tangen, former Minnesotans who, with their three young children, trailered their horses here on vacation every summer and finally decided to settle here (Laura also is a high-school teacher in nearby South Heart; Neil now tends the horses full-time). Nine years later, they have 60 quarter- and paint horses. I'm off on the most memorable—and fun—horseback ride of my life, up and down canyon trails established by native buffalo, splashing through the shallow Little Missouri on Pete, who, like me, is an old-timer at the ripe age (for a horse) of 19.

Hiking and Biking Adventures

Like the young Theodore Roosevelt, I'm here for adventure. And I find it with the help of one of my hosts, Wade Westin, a Nordic-looking thirty-something who grew up on a North Dakota ranch, wound up a singer-dancer and emcee with the Medora Musical and now is marketing director of the Theodore Roosevelt Medora Foundation. We're off for a vigorous hike to a petrified forest (you heard right).

Sure enough, several miles into the park, I'm investigating what look like giant tree stumps and fallen limbs scattered like toys on the floor of a playroom. Upon closer inspection, they turn out to be deeply striated, solid rock fossils dating back 60 million years. Some seem to balance precariously on pedestals of softer rock that's eroded beneath. I also encounter several spectators along the route. Wade calls them "Lonesome George" buffalo—males who don't hang out with the rest of the herd.

I gingerly detour around the buffalo, and soon Wade and I are buzzing off to our next activity, at the Dakota Cyclery on Third Street back in town. Outfitted with fat-tire hybrid mountain bikes, we pedal a segment of the 96-mile Maah Daah Hey Trail (the term means something like "here to stay" in the Lakota language). Although the trail threads along both park units, biking is only allowed outside the park. The views of the badlands are great, but I'm more focused on surviving the hairpin turns we encounter. "Just stay in the middle gear most of the time and avoid the front brakes, or you might flip over," Wade cautions. I

Green Chile and Chorizo Strata Casseroles

Strata fans heartily applaud this innovative menu item at the Roughrider Hotel in Medora. It makes a wonderful brunch dish because it can be assembled the night before and baked in the morning. Bully!

6   ¾-inch-thick slices French bread
12   ounces uncooked chorizo, casings
      removed and chopped, or pork sausage
¼   cup finely chopped onion
1½   cups shredded Monterey Jack cheese
      with jalapeño peppers (6 ounces)
4   beaten eggs
2½   cups whole milk or half-and-half
1   4½-ounce can diced green chile
      peppers
1   teaspoon ground cumin
⅛   teaspoon salt
⅛   teaspoon ground black pepper
¼   cup snipped fresh cilantro or parsley

Grease six 1½-cup soufflé dishes or an 8×8×2-inch baking dish. Place a bread slice in each soufflé dish (or place all slices in baking dish, overlapping and tearing to fit).

In a large skillet, cook chorizo and onion over medium heat about 5 minutes or until sausage is cooked and onion is tender. Drain off fat. Sprinkle sausage mixture evenly over bread slices. Sprinkle cheese over sausage mixture.

Combine eggs, milk, undrained chile peppers, cumin, salt and black pepper. Pour the egg mixture over layers. Cover and chill for 2 to 24 hours. Place soufflé dishes on a large baking sheet. Bake, uncovered, in a 325° oven about 40 minutes for soufflé dishes (about 50 minutes for 8×8×2-inch baking dish) or until a knife inserted near center comes out clean. Sprinkle with cilantro. Let stand for 10 minutes before serving. *Makes 6 main-dish servings.*

manage to stay upright, and the ride is just as much fun as my horseback foray a few hours before.

What's a Chateau Doing Here?

I'm ready for a more pedestrian interlude here in T.R. country so, once again, I indulge my appetite for history. Perched on a mesa overlooking Medora is a rather improbable (for this setting) 26-room, gray-painted, red-roofed mansion maintained by the State Historical Society of North Dakota. It's known hereabouts as the "chateau" whose mistress gave the town its name.

An interpreter fills me in on one more chapter in this region's short-lived but fascinating 1880s cattle boom: Medora von Hoffman de Mores (MORez) was the German-American wife of a French nobleman, the Marquis de Mores. A real swashbuckler (he once killed a cowboy in a shoot-out in town and almost dueled Theodore Roosevelt over a cattle dispute), the Marquis came here hoping to establish a meatpacking empire.

At that time, cattle were shipped live to Eastern markets, but de Mores reasoned that newly invented refrigeration railcars would make it possible to butcher the cattle here at a huge slaughterhouse he'd built with funds from his wealthy father-in-law and other Eastern investors. De Mores ignited a mini boom that led to the birth of the town of Medora and the arrival of other young and restless Gilded Age types such as Theodore Roosevelt.

The concept was a good one, but unfortunately, existing meatpackers in Chicago didn't go for it (surprise), and the biblically brutal winter of 1886–87 intervened, killing local ranchers' cattle by the thousands (Roosevelt, who knew the de Moreses, was one of those who was almost ruined financially). The de Moreses packed up their retinue and headed on to other adventures.

In 1896 the Marquis was murdered by treacherous Arab guides in the Sahara, and the lovely, talented Medora (I purchased a reproduction of one of her exquisite watercolors of the chateau in the gift shop) died in 1921 after having opened her home to Allied forces during World War I.

I wander the chateau's elaborately furnished formal rooms, including his-and-hers bedrooms and a big dining room where the de Moreses entertained Roosevelt, visiting Russian nobility and others of note during their April-to-December stays in Medora. How much more remote these badlands must have seemed in the 1880s!

Back in town, I get a whirlwind tour of the very impressive new Center of Western Heritage and Cultures, home of the North Dakota Cowboy Hall of Fame. Inside the contemporary, $4 million facility, I watch a brief film that explains how the Great Plains "horse culture" intertwines the badlands' previous residents: Native Americans, early settlers, cowboys and today's rodeo stars. Dinosaur-era fossils reveal that the original "horses" in the area had three toes and stood a full 18 inches tall (those introduced to North America by the Spaniards in the 1500s more closely resemble the ones we see today).

Upstairs, photos lining the hall of fame depict North Dakota rodeo greats astride their bucking broncos. In the exhibit area, I'm thrilled to view a regal, 130-year-old eagle-feather headdress worn by Lakota chief Sitting Bull, the fellow who helped do in Custer and his cavalrymen and later wound up performing in Buffalo Bill's traveling show. I hope Medora's own laconic Cowboy Lyle makes it into the hall of fame someday. During a sidewalk chat outside, I learn that he has been Medora's star horseman for nearly 32 years. He's appeared in 2,800 performances of the Medora Musical, missing only one show. He gives me an off-the-cuff roping demonstration that impresses me even more.

In the evening, my crew and I dine on pitchfork steaks and fixings under a pavilion not far from the Chateau de Mores. Each season, 15,000 succulent beef rib eyes are impaled 10 at a time and seared in sizzling kettles of 400-degree vegetable oil. Watching the process is as fun as the steaks are good to eat. Then we're transported down what has to be North Dakota's biggest escalator (well, outdoor elevator, anyway) to hillside seats in the 2,900-seat Burning Hills Amphitheater for a performance of the Medora Musical, a twilight rite witnessed by 110,000 patrons annually.

The original amphitheater was constructed in the 1950s and renovated in 1992. Far below, the set loosely resembles Medora itself, with a real-life backdrop of badlands terrain and, on this night, a dazzling full moon. I love the energetic singing and dancing, cowboy comedy shtick and the T.R. impersonator. Variety acts even include a magician-comedian and a gravity-defying troupe of acrobats from Kenya. Cowboy Lyle, astride Chocolate, gallops onstage waving the American flag. It's all very bully, as Teddy Roosevelt would have said.

Outlaw Tales and Overlooks

I have one more mission before I leave the area: to see the shamefully neglected (by most visitors) North Unit of the park, about 55 miles north of Medora and the South Unit. Each year, about 500,000 people visit Theodore Roosevelt National Park; only about one-tenth of them make it to the North Unit. At 24,000 acres, it's approximately half the size of its sibling but, to my mind, even more bizarrely beautiful. Here, craggy cliffs shaped like lions' paws loom up to 500 feet over the Little Missouri River as it abruptly twists toward the Missouri and Lake Sakakawea about 40 miles

to the northeast (thank a glacier for rerouting the river about 600,000 years ago).

Todd Stoeberl, district interpreter for the park, is my guide, and he's understandably eager to show off the North Unit. Todd really knows his geology, and he explains in detail how these awesome rock formations got here, as we cruise the 14-mile scenic drive. At one turnout, I study and even climb some aptly named "cannonball concretions." The huge outsize jawbreakers measure up to 4 feet tall and weigh several tons. They were formed like pearls in oyster shells, when minerals from melting glacial torrents glommed on to something as tiny as a seed or a shell. Over time, these harder balls of rock were exposed by the erosion of softer sedimentary rock.

At the River Bend Overlook, gazing at the actual scene where I began this chapter, I'm awed at the expanse before me. I haven't seen Arizona's Grand Canyon in person, but this one will do nicely for now. Bluffs and cliffs draped with juniper, green ash and accented with vivid hues of wildflowers such as yellow clover, purple coneflower, Maximillian sunflower and torch flower line the cottonwood-carpeted valley of the Little Missouri.

On our way back, Todd recounts another defining Roosevelt episode: the time the future president single-handedly "escorted" three thieves who'd made off with a boat from his Elkhorn Ranch to justice in Dickinson, approximately 80 miles away. By the time we return to the North Unit visitor center, a dozen buffalo are grazing on the lawn. There's also a demonstration herd of longhorn cattle in the park, a reminder of the days when this was the last stop on epic cattle drives. Now I know why this great president, conservationist and adventurer so loved it here, and I feel deeply thankful that this hidden landscape has been preserved to inspire others.

The Little Missouri River coursing through the remote wilds of the lesser-known North Unit of Theodore Roosevelt National Park.

TOP TO BOTTOM: (Both taken at Theodore Roosevelt National Park) Dan studying a fossilized petrified forest formation. Horseback riders exploring the winding Maah Daah Hey Trail.

Dan's Travel Journal

FEATURED STOP

Theodore Roosevelt National Park Medora (26 miles east of the Montana state line). Painted Canyon Overlook on I-94 (28 miles west of Dickinson) hints at the savage beauty ahead at this 70,447-acre park, divided between the distinctly different South and North units. Enter the South Unit at the Medora Visitor Center (museum, theater and Roosevelt's Maltese Cross Cabin) and drive the paved, 36-mile scenic loop past interpretive signs explaining the park's historical and natural features. In the less-visited North Unit (50 miles north of I-94 on US-85), a 14-mile scenic drive starts at the North Unit Visitor Center and leads to Oxbow Overlook and its sweeping vista of the Little Missouri River badlands. Both units offer campgrounds and ranger-led walks and talks, plus 100 miles of trails for hiking and horseback riding (701/623-4466).

Lodging, Dining and More

Bully Pulpit Golf Course Three miles south of Medora. Named for Theodore Roosevelt's reference to the White House as a "bully pulpit" (a terrific platform), this 18-hole course has been praised by golf magazines (800/633-6721).

Chateau de Mores State Historic Site Medora. Now a museum, this 26-room, two-story mansion was built by Marquis de Mores in 1883 as a hunting and summer residence for his family. Overlooking the town, the chateau remains authentically furnished (701/623-4355).

Chuckwagon Buffet Medora. Downtown all-you-can-eat buffet for breakfast, lunch and dinner. Open Memorial Day weekend–Labor Day (800/633-6721).

Dakota Cyclery Mountain Bike Adventures Medora. Bike rental, service and sales; shuttle service; and guided mountain-bike tours through the challenging badlands (two-hour "slowpoke" and four-hour "cowpoke" tours offered). Memorial Day weekend–Labor Day (701/623-4700).

North Dakota Cowboy Hall of Fame Medora. View an introductory film, then learn more about horse culture on the Great Plains in the Native American, ranching and rodeo galleries (701/623-2000).

Peaceful Valley Ranch Trail Rides Theodore Roosevelt National Park (seven miles from the Medora entrance), June–August. Saddle up to see the backcountry in the South Unit on basic 1½-hour rides (must be at least 7 years old) or on longer 2½- and five-hour rides for experienced riders. Reservations recommended (701/623-4568).

Rough Riders Hotel Medora. Nine-room downtown inn with antique decor reminiscent of the days when Theodore Roosevelt stayed in the original 1884 hotel. Open mid-April–mid-October. $$$ (800/633-6721).

Related Area Event

Medora Musical Medora, nightly, first weekend in June through the day before Labor Day—Performers kick up their heels at this famous Western musical variety show. Before the show, chow down on rib eyes at the pitchfork fondue (800/633-6721).

More Information

Medora Information Center (701/623-4829, www.medorand.com).

North Dakota Department of Commerce Tourism Division (800/435-5663, www.ndtourism.com).

Theodore Roosevelt Medora Foundation (800/633-6721, www.medora.com).

DAN'S OTHER STOPS

(See also More Parks section that follows.) Lake Sakakawea State Park (701/487-3315), Long Lake National Wildlife Refuge (701/387-4397).

More North Dakota Parks

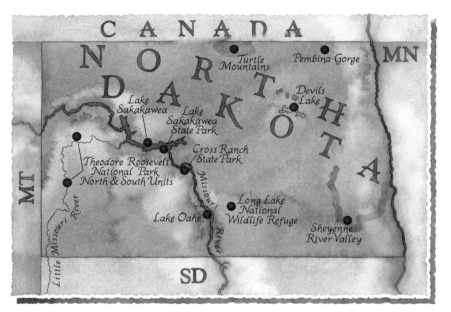

Cross Ranch State Park

Age-old cottonwoods sway above this state park, which extends seven miles along one of the last free-flowing, undeveloped stretches of the Missouri River. About 50 miles north of Bismarck between tiny Hensler and Sanger, the 560-acre park opened 15 years ago adjacent to 6,000-acre Cross Ranch Nature Preserve, where buffalo roam the upland prairie. You can boat, fish, swim and camp at the park, where canoes and kayaks are for rent. A network of 15 miles of hiking trails leads into the nature preserve for wildlife watching. Visitor center programs feature Native American and natural history.

About 10 miles north along the river near Washburn, the Lewis & Clark Interpretive Center tells the explorers' story. Adjacent Fort Mandan State Historic Site re-creates the stockade where the Corps of Discovery expedition met Native American guide Sakakawea and wintered in 1804–05. Interpreters give tours of the fort year-round.

Contact: Cross Ranch State Park (701/794-3731, ndparks.com). Lewis & Clark Interpretive Center and Fort Mandan (877/462-8535, fortmandan.com). Lodgings: two cabins at the state park; limited options in Washburn (701/462-3801, www.washburnnd.com) and motels in Bismarck (800/767-3555, bismarckmandancvb.com).

Devils Lake

Amid the wetlands, woods and grasslands of northeastern-North Dakota's prairie pothole region, the state's largest natural lake sprawls across Ramsey County (90 miles west of Grand Forks). Fishing ranks as the prime pastime at the 130,000-acre lake, where anglers reel in perch, walleye, pike and bass—often record catches. There's a fishing tournament almost every weekend.

On the lake's western shore, Grahams Island State Park and Black Tiger Bay State Recreation Area provide boaters lake access. You also can camp and hike in the wooded state park. Herds of bison, elk and deer graze at Sully's Hill National Game Preserve, where some 250 kinds of birds, including bald eagles, have been spotted. Visitors can take a four-mile drive and walk the mile-long nature trail.

To the south, plan to tour 16 original buildings at Fort Totten State Historic Site. This 1867 military outpost is the largest and best preserved from the Dakota-frontier era.

Contact: Devils Lake Visitors Bureau (800/233-8048, devilslakend.com). Fort Totten State Historic Site (701/766-4441, nd.gov/hist). Grahams Island State Park (701/766-4015, ndparks.com). Sully's Hill National Game Preserve (701/766-4272, fws.gov/refuges). Nearest lodgings: four cabins at the state park; motels in Devils Lake (800/233-8048, devilslakend.com).

Lake Oahe

A swath of blue, Lake Oahe (OWAHhee) meanders through grasslands for 80 miles from south of Bismarck into South Dakota. The immensity of this U.S. Army Corps of Engineers' impoundment on the Missouri River seems to swallow the hundreds of thousands who annually congregate for boating, fishing, swimming and other water recreation. Campgrounds, boat ramps and two marinas pepper the shore. You can hike and mountain bike trails as antelope graze distant hillsides and eagles ride the wind.

From the northern end of Oahe, detour 15 miles east to Long Lake National Wildlife Refuge, a migratory-bird preserve. In

LEFT TO RIGHT: Sailing Lake Sakakawea's vast, uncrowded waters. Lake Sakakawea shoreline. Grassy ridges and wooded ravines along the Sheyenne River Scenic Byway.

fall, geese, ducks and sandhill cranes fill the sky with flapping wings.

The Native American National Scenic Byway traces Lewis and Clark's route for 35 miles through the Standing Rock Sioux Reservation along Lake Oahe's west side before continuing into South Dakota (see page 160). Highlights include Sitting Bull's original burial site, Standing Rock Monument and the Fort Yates Stockade.

Contact: America's Byways (800/429-9297, byways.org). Long Lake National Wildlife Refuge (701/387-4397, longlake .fws.gov). U.S. Army Corps of Engineers, Bismarck (605/224-5862, usace.army.mil). Nearest lodgings: limited along the lake; motels in Bismarck (800/767-3555, bismarck mandancvb.com), plus Prairie Knights Casino & Resort near Fort Yates.

Lake Sakakawea

Outstanding fishing and near-perfect solitude draw visitors to this vast inland sea of the Great Plains. Following the course of the Missouri River, the 185-mile-long lake arcs northwest from the U.S. Army Corps of Engineers' Garrison Dam near the middle of the state almost to Montana.

Besides fishing, visitors can boat, sail, hike, camp, even scuba dive—all crowd-free—at the nation's third-largest man-made lake. Three state parks, Lewis & Clark, Fort Stevenson and Sakakawea, plus a host of recreation areas, marinas and boat ramps, anchor the lake, which includes more miles of sculpted shore than California. You'll also discover abundant isolated coves amid a landscape that varies from rugged buttes to open prairie where lithe grasses ripple in the breeze. Near the dam, an eight-mile drive leads through Audubon National Wildlife Refuge, home to 200 varieties of birds.

Contact: North Dakota Tourism Division (800/435-5663, ndtourism.com). U.S. Army Corps of Engineers, Riverdale (701/654-7411, usace.army.mil). Nearest lodgings: scattered along the lake, including state park cabins, motels in Williston (800/615-9041, willistonndtourism.com), a few options in Garrison (800/799-4242, garri-sonnd.com) and New Town (701/627-4812, newtownnd.com), including Four Bears Casino & Lodge.

Pembina Gorge

The Pembina River carves a deep, steep-sided valley known as the Pembina Gorge, rushing from Manitoba across the state's northeastern corner. Terrain varies from forest to wetland thickets in North Dakota's largest uninterrupted tract of woodland wilderness and longest unaltered segment of river valley—12,500 acres total.

Hiking, mountain biking and horseback-riding trails take you into the unexplored region from Tetrault Woods State Forest just south of Walhalla, the state's second-oldest community. The forest, which harbors wildlife such as moose and elk, plus plants rarely found elsewhere in North Dakota, also provides access to the Pembina River. Canoeing the 70-mile river is a good way to appreciate the panorama of hills, valleys and unbroken woods. Near Walhalla, one of the best stretches for canoeing flows over rapids and riffles.

You also can sightsee along county and township roads throughout the valley. A scenic 12-mile drive on County-55 goes west along the river from just east of Walhalla.

Contact: North Dakota Division of

Tourism (800/435-5663, ndtourism.com and turtlemountains.org). Nearest lodgings: in Walhalla (701/549-3939, tradecorridor.com/walhalla).

Sheyenne River Valley

On a winding 300-mile course, the Sheyenne River loops southeast between Lake Ashtabula and the Red River. Parks and preserves of southeastern North Dakota's Sheyenne River Valley line its banks. You can drive highways of the Sheyenne River Valley National Scenic Byway from Lake Ashtabula (north of Valley City) downriver 63 miles to Lisbon. Little towns, farms and historic bridges paint scenes of Americana.

Native Americans camped around the lake at Clausen Springs. At Fort Ransom State Park, popular for hiking, fishing, mountain biking and camping, visitors rent canoes and kayaks to float the river. Fort Ransom State Historic Site, across the river, is the location of an 1860s military post.

Northwest of Lisbon at Sheyenne State Forest, you can canoe, fish and hike. From trailheads near Lisbon, 25 miles of the North Country National Scenic Trail takes hikers, mountain bikers and horseback riders into the Sheyenne National Grassland, 70,000 acres of wildflowers and grasses patrolled by butterflies (maps at the ranger's office in Lisbon).

Contact: America's Byways (800/429-9297, byways.org). Fort Ransom State Park (701/973-4331, ndparks.com). North Dakota Tourism Division (800/435-5663, ndtourism.com). Sheyenne National Grassland (701/683-4342, fs.fed.us/r1/dakotaprairie/sheyenne). Nearest lodgings: in Valley City (701/845-1891, hellovalley.com) and Lisbon (701/683-5680, lisbonnd.com).

Theodore Roosevelt National Park

(See previous section of this chapter.)

Turtle Mountains

Traveling the Turtle Mountain State Scenic Byway, a stone's throw from Canada, you'll sample some of this timeworn range's best scenery. The 53-mile byway (State-43) twists and climbs west from tiny St. Johns past farmsteads, recreation areas, woods and lakes before descending into the foothills for prairie views. Plan to detour four miles north to the International Peace Garden. Straddling the border, the gardens and wilderness, campsites and trails celebrate peace between two neighboring nations.

The lakes and woods of Lake Metigoshe State Park make it a popular stop. You can fish, swim, canoe, bird-watch, hike, camp, join summer naturalist programs and visit the Outdoor Learning Center. West of the park, trails for hiking, horseback riding and mountain biking lead into 7,700-acre Turtle Mountain State Forest, North Dakota's largest. Deer and moose roam the woods surrounding Strawberry Lake, which has a beach and campground. Other pastimes include fishing and canoeing.

Contact: America's Byways (800/429-9297, byways.org). International Peace Garden (888/432-6733, peacegarden.com). Lake Metigoshe State Park (701/263-4651, ndparks.com). North Dakota Tourism Division (800/435-5663, ndtourism.com and turtlemountains.org). Nearest lodgings: three cabins in the state park; about 10 miles south of the byway, motels in Bottineau (800/735-6932, bottineau.com).

OHIO

Scenery and transportation history at Cuyahoga Valley National Park.

A rare jewel of nature and history

OHIO OFFERS THE NATURE LOVER so much to see and do: The state-park system is among the best, and there's a one-of-a-kind national park, among America's newest, that I can't wait to explore first-hand. I'll start in southwest Ohio and cruise northeast to the Cleveland-Akron urban corridor and Cuyahoga Valley National Park. But first, two very different types of Ohio state parks beckon en route, including my first experience at…paintball!

Hueston Woods State Park
I didn't stop at Hueston Woods State Park near the Indiana line, just six miles north of Oxford (population 22,000), expecting to be handed a carbon-dioxide-powered "gun"—especially one that fires plastic balls filled with a "paint" mixed from vegetable oil and food coloring! But after getting my safety instructions and securing my face mask, I blast away at a series of stationary targets. Splat! Powie! Gotcha!

Paintball is just one of the unexpected diversions waiting at this 3,600-acre family-focused resort park. I take a deep breath as knowledgeable Assistant Manager Pat Boryca (on staff for 25 years) rattles off the list: an 18-hole golf course, an archery range, a basketball court, and indoor and outdoor pools. You can go hiking or horseback riding, rent a mountain bike, pitch horseshoes, or ply 2½-mile-long, 600-acre Acton Lake in a

Photography by Randall Lee Schieber

LEFT TO RIGHT: Louis Bromfield's still-working Malabar Farm, now a state park. (Both taken at Cuyahoga Valley National Park) Vintage lodgings in an 1848 farmhouse. Bicycling the serene Ohio & Erie Canal Towpath Trail.

rented sailboat, pontoon, canoe or kayak.

You also can hang out at the beach or fish for largemouth bass, crappie, bluegill, saugeye and catfish in a rented fishing boat. Then there's the nature center where you can get up close and personal with rescued wild critters such as a bashful cougar, a bobcat, a bald and a golden eagle, several hawks, a turkey vulture and an owl. And the park's winter lineup sounds just as awesome: sledding, cross-country skiing, ice-fishing, ice-skating and bow-hunting for deer.

Named for a pioneer family that lived here from the early 1800s to the 1930s, Hueston Woods is one of Ohio's nine top-notch resort parks. The A-frame main-lodge lobby, completed in 1967 and still one of America's largest such structures, provides a breathtaking view of Acton Lake. The lodge offers 92 rooms, including two luxury suites with such amenities as full-body shower, whirlpool bath, and plasma TV (am I really at a state park?). If you prefer something more primitive, head for one of the 450 campsites and 37 cabins.

I'm fascinated by the 200 acres of old-growth beech-maple forest, which has been designated a national landmark. Pat tells me that Ohio once had 25 million acres of such uncut forests; now there are just 1,600 acres. We hike through a grove of towering beeches and sugar maples as well as cherry, walnut, tulip poplar and red oak, a big attraction for scarlet tanager, indigo bunting, pileated woodpecker, red northern cardinal and various warblers—as well as the birders who flock here to ogle them.

I peek into the nature center, a pioneer farm museum and the Hueston family's 1905 sugar shack, where a popular maple syrup festival is held each March. We park Pat's truck and hike down a steep ravine to a spillway for some fossil hunting.

He tells me the rocks at our feet are part of the Cincinnati Arch, a huge outcropping of Ordovician limestone formed up to 500 million years ago when Ohio was covered by a shallow sea. The fossils themselves are everywhere, precursors of modern-day clams and snails. "These are wonderful examples of brachiopods and bryozoans," Pat explains. Say what? I just think they're nifty, like this whole park.

Malabar Farm State Park

A couple interstate-highway hours later, I'm in the pastoral hills of north-central Ohio in the Mansfield area (population 50,560). I'm a history buff, so my next park—Malabar Farm, home of Pulitzer Prize-winning writer and farmer Louis Bromfield—is going to be pure heaven. It adjoins another popular Ohio state park, Mohican, where campers and canoeists flock to the hemlock forest and dramatic gorge. Park Manager Louie Andres greets me at the imposing main house and summarizes Malabar's story:

Louis Bromfield grew up 10 miles from here in Mansfield but spent a lot of his boyhood on his grandparents' farm outside town. Always eager to learn, Bromfield headed off to study agriculture at Cornell, but his mother didn't want him to become a farmer, so he switched to journalism at Columbia. For a decade he lived as a renowned author and screenwriter in France, where he and his wife, Mary, began raising three daughters and hobnobbing with literary expatriates such as Gertrude Stein, Ernest Hemingway and F. Scott Fitzgerald. In 1938, looming World War II

sent the family back to the United States, and Bromfield decided to pursue his heart's desire full bore, purchasing several forlorn farms in Pleasant Valley near Mansfield.

Louis Bromfield was a high-energy guy (sleeping only three or four hours a night) who loved people and his ever-present boxer dogs. Hollywood friends visited often. Louie tells me it was nothing for the Bromfields to have 15 people to dinner, both farm workers and stars, including James Cagney and Kay Francis (interestingly, Bromfield required all his guests to do some sort of farm chores while staying here). On May 21, 1945, Bromfield's pal Humphrey Bogart wed ingenue actress Lauren Bacall in the grand foyer of the handsome 32-room home (10 bedrooms and 10 baths) that Bromfield painstakingly renovated and enlarged from 1938 until his death at age 59 in 1956. The house is just as he left it, oozing 1940s-ish modern decor, memorabilia and vintage celebrity photos at every turn.

The picture-perfect, 900-acre property also includes a tiny cemetery where Bromfield and other family members lie at rest. But it's clear this still is very much a working farm: livestock, vegetables, cut flowers, and the ingeniously spring-cooled produce stand (Bromfield's design, of course). I survey the panorama from atop a hill known as Mount Jeez (as in a friend's lament to the demanding Bromfield, "Jeez, Louie...."): fertile fields of oats, corn and soybeans intermixed with lush woods—all of it on land once barren because of overcultivation and subsequent erosion.

It's all a testament to Bromfield's mission to promote sustainable farming, self-sufficiency and stewardship of the land. Those themes and more are explored at the park's brand-new $1.4 million Louis Bromfield Education Center, designed to echo the tidy farm's other white-and-green structures. The vitality I witness here 50 years after Bromfield's death is a grand tribute to his larger-than-life personality. Over a Malabar Farm-raised lunch at the park's historic restaurant, a former stagecoach inn, I ask Louie why there's still so much interest in Bromfield. He replies, "I think it's his visionary ideas and his ability to write and speak about agriculture in such an engaging, inspiring way."

Cuyahoga Valley National Park

Cuyahoga (KYaHOga) Valley ranks as one of America's most-visited national parks; as many as 2.5 million patrons per year roam its narrow realm, just one to five miles wide and 20 miles long. The park teems with natural attractions, history—notably the legacy of the Ohio & Erie Canal—culture, recreation and pure escape from the urban world. On another level, it is inspiring because of the partnerships, innovation and volunteer spirit I witness here.

All told, 33,000-acre Cuyahoga Valley is one of the most unique and all-encompassing parks I'll visit on this journey. First, it's right in the heart of the Cleveland-Akron metro area of just under 3 million people who live in almost 150 cities, towns and villages in eight once-highly industrial counties. For a variety of reasons, including rugged terrain, a lack of potable water and effluent-disposal challenges, developers mercifully bypassed the valley.

The diminutive Cuyahoga River itself flows for only 100 miles, beginning just 13 miles northeast of the heart of Cleveland and taking a northward U-turn on its way

to emptying into Lake Erie in the shadow of downtown Cleveland's towers (hence its name, which derives from a Native American word for "crooked"). The river valley reveals an amazing concentration of spectacular rock formations and waterfalls, along with wildlife havens, plant ecosystems, historic sites, cultural venues and more. What began as a national recreation area in 1974 received the national park designation in 2000. I recall when the once-sludge-filled river literally ignited in 1969 in downtown Cleveland. Though it's still not pristine, the Cuyahoga is vastly cleaner these days.

About 125 miles of trails knit the park together and, although there's no camping in the park, campgrounds abound nearby. I'm lucky to stay right inside the park at the Inn at Brandywine Falls, a rambling, antiques-packed 1848 Greek Revival farmhouse managed for 18 years by George and Katie Hoy. In the elegant dining room, George explains that the name Brandywine came from an early settler recalling the famous southeastern Pennsylvania river and the 1777 Revolutionary War battle that was fought there.

Long-gone grain mills once perched beside my first stop, the eponymous waterfall just 100 yards from my bedroom window (its low-key roar lulled me to sleep). I'm joined at breakfast by Interpretive Park Ranger Travis White, a Southern California native who liked what he saw when the National Park Service transferred him here and stuck around, with his wife, to raise three daughters.

Soon Travis and I are on a woodland walkway, descending 69 steps to a viewing platform for a better look at the 65-foot-tall and 30-foot-wide Brandywine Falls cascading behind a leafy curtain of sugar maples. The stunning falls, formed 10,000 years ago, spill over a geologic layer cake of rocks ranging up to 400 million years old: Berea

Sandstone, Bedford Shale and Cleveland Shale. This is the backdrop for about 30 weddings each year.

Beauty Born of Rocks and Water

From a natural standpoint, Cuyahoga Valley National Park stars two basic elements: rocks and water. Over the aeons, the river and its tributaries shaped some of the most breathtaking scenery: escarpments, rocky outcrops and waterfalls, from ephemeral trickles to gushing torrents. Travis and I are off to explore Tinker's Creek Gorge in the Bedford Reservation, a spur adjoining the north end of the park.

The 2,200-acre Bedford Reservation actually is a part of Cleveland Metroparks, one of the nation's oldest and best urban park systems. Founded in 1917, the 16 "reservations" (three of them adjoining the national park) are often referred to collectively as Cleveland's 21,000-acre Emerald Necklace because of the way the interconnected parks ring the city. It's impossible to tell here where Cuyahoga Valley National Park ends and Cleveland Metroparks begins, but who cares? I like to think of the national park as the gleaming pendant hanging from the Cleveland Metroparks chain.

At the brink of the almost tropically lush Tinker's Creek Gorge, Nature Center Manager Carl Casavecchia of Cleveland Metroparks wows me with a view from 200 feet above the Cuyahoga River tributary. It's so dense with tulip poplar, red and white oaks, sugar maples, hickory, birch and sycamore that I can't imagine how intense the autumn colors must be. "It was so farsighted of our civic leaders to preserve these canyons at a time when Cleveland was rapidly developing," Carl says. "They wanted people to have a place to escape the city in these peaceful valleys. Now, almost 90 years later, we're carrying on their vision with all kinds of picnic areas, overlooks, parkways,

outdoor education facilities and programs and more than 100 miles of trails."

We move on about a mile to broad, gently flowing Bridal Veil Falls. Another short hop away, in suburban Bedford, I hike with Carl to the Great Falls of Tinker's Creek, where a newly developed interpretive walk demonstrates how, in the 19th century, the falls were first harnessed for a sawmill, then a gristmill, then for electric power.

Later, I view another result of the Cuyahoga's rocks and water, in the south end of the national park, with Interpretive Park Ranger Rebecca Jones. It's gently misting, adding to the air of mystery as we hike down a sandstone escarpment known as the Ledges, formed 320 million years ago by slow-motion primeval geologic forces. I'm reminded of Canada's boreal forest as I look at hemlock trees banked with ferns, mosses and lichens thriving in a microclimate left behind when the last glacier circle retreated about 14,000 years ago.

As we hike the plateau's two-mile perimeter, Rebecca points out an example of such a microclimate: At the entrance to Icebox Cave, its opening the size of a huge cathedral door, I can see and feel the chilly vapors rising up from ground level, naturally air-conditioned by water that's filtered through the forest-shaded sandstone. The spot is absolutely silent except for the chirping of a hermit thrush and a winter wren. Looking back up at the formation from a tiny canyon on the lower trail, I'm awed at the sheer size of the rocks, which look like building blocks quarried for an ancient monument.

My next park host is Paul Motts, a ranger who grew up in Massachusetts and transferred here 15 years ago. As we set out, Paul tells me his family originally settled in this area in the 1800s, traveling on a boat from Cleveland south to Massillon, near Canton on the Ohio & Erie Canal. I ask him about the plants and animals that inhabit the

park. In addition to the hemlock are sugar and red maple, yellow birch, green ash, slippery elm and, along the river bottoms, cottonwood. The ever-changing array of wildflowers includes pink-streaked spring beauty, white trillium, wild geranium and trout lily.

All those trees and plants attract birds, which I quickly learn are Paul's passion. His eyes light up when he talks about all the bird species found here—more than 160 sighted—especially the signature hermit thrushes, black-throated green warblers and oven birds, all neotropical songbirds. "We have some great viewing spots around here, so we average two bird walks a month," Paul says. And despite its urban-corridor setting, the Cuyahoga Valley also is home to droves of white-tailed deer, beaver, coyotes, muskrats, mink, turtles and salamanders.

In the far-south end of the park, we leave Paul's truck at the Ira Trailhead and tramp a quarter mile on a boardwalk to Beaver Marsh, a waterlily-blanketed natural area. It sounds like the songbird department of a pet store as Paul hands me his binoculars. "Birds really like it in our park because of the mix of habitats: grasslands, woodlands, meadows and thickets," he says. A family of wood ducks navigates single file past a beaver lodge, while a red-bellied woodpecker hammers away overhead. Paul shares with quiet pride that his own life list includes more than 300 species, as he points to barn and tree swallows, warblers, red-winged blackbirds, belted kingfishers, eastern phoebes, cedar waxwings, willow flycatchers, spotted sandpipers and a great egret.

Soon we're back in the truck, pulling off the road yet again to view two of the area's three great blue heron rookeries, encircled by a swampy moat. Out come the binoculars. I'm awed by the park's tallest avians, whose long, pointed beaks and thin, crooked necks give them an exotic, primordial air. Their 4-foot height and 7-foot wingspans explain why their treetop nests are so incredibly huge.

Transportation Heritage

Much of the Cuyahoga Valley National Park story is intertwined with a canal: the Ohio & Erie, begun in 1825 and operational until 1913, when a flood destroyed the already declining system. The entire park lies within the Ohio & Erie Canalway National Heritage Area, which continues south to New Philadelphia. The canal led to the rise of two great cities—Cleveland and Akron—by providing relatively easy transportation for goods and passengers as far as Portsmouth on the Ohio River (308 total miles), giving financial hope to a wilderness region mired in poverty.

Today's Towpath Trail is where rope-tethered mules on shore once pulled along barges (one of those mule drivers was future president James Garfield). Now it's a recreational gem for walkers, hikers, joggers, bicyclists and horseback riders that eventually will extend 110 miles through the state.

Parts of the German- and Irish-immigrant-dug canal still look the way they did back in the 1800s. I see remnants of 15 locks in the park that raised and lowered boats, all required because of the 395-foot elevation change between Akron, in aptly named Summit County, and the terminus at Lake Erie. At Lock No. 38, I study a scale model of the ingenious system at the Canal

Much of the Cuyahoga Valley National Park story is intertwined with a canal: the Ohio & Erie, begun in 1825.

CLOCKWISE, FROM TOP: (All taken at Beaver Marsh, Cuyahoga Valley National Park) A misty morning. Great blue heron. Bird-watching, a park pastime. Native waterlilies.

Fruited Oatmeal Soup

Nestled in the scenic woods of Cuyahoga Valley National Park, the Inn at Brandywine Falls has a rich history dating back to 1848 when it was built as a farmhouse. Keeping with the theme, the inn's menu touts a rich food history. Innkeepers Katie and George Hoy offer guests bowls of creamy oatmeal embellished with fruit. It's fitting because Akron, at the south end of the park, was formerly the home of Quaker Oats.

2¼ cups milk
1½ cups chopped and peeled apples, pears or peaches
⅓ cup stone-ground oats, steel-cut oats or regular rolled oats
⅓ cup oat bran
⅓ cup dried cranberries, raisins, snipped dried cherries, snipped dried apricots or snipped pitted whole dates
⅛ teaspoon salt
Whole milk, half-and-half or light cream
Brown sugar
Granola, yogurt, dairy sour cream or toasted sliced almonds (optional)

In a large saucepan, combine milk, apples, oats, oat bran, cranberries and salt. Bring to boiling; reduce heat. Simmer, uncovered, about 10 minutes or until desired doneness and consistency, stirring often.

Serve with additional milk and brown sugar. If you like, top with granola, yogurt, sour cream or almonds. *Makes 4 servings.*

Visitor Center, which at various times was a tavern, a general store and a residence. A canal boat, which often served as home to the operator's entire family, carried up to 50 tons of freight: Grain, flour, livestock and whiskey went out; glass, furniture and farm equipment came in.

An interpreter in period dress demonstrates how one person single-handedly opened and closed the delicately balanced, 2-ton wooden lock gates with an iron wicket wrench. I'm impressed by the engineering savvy it took to conceive such an ingenious system. Soon Ohio was booming and railroads, the next transportation era, were coming.

Ohio's locomotives first chugged along the Cuyahoga in 1880. Those steam engines are long gone, but Cuyahoga Valley Scenic Railroad (CVSR) still conveys a sense of railroading's glory days. Its trains rumble on 51 miles of track, half of it in the park. These are real trains, not mini wannabes: nine early-1950s-vintage diesel electric engines and 20 passenger cars that clack along at 25 mph on a regular schedule year-round except for January.

There are nine boarding stations along the Cuyahoga Valley Scenic Railroad route through the park. I linger at the Brecksville depot, tucked away near the park's signature State-82 Bridge, a valley architectural landmark that CVSR trains pass under. My ride begins at the historic village of Peninsula (population 600), where the depot also serves as an interpretive center, and takes me to Indigo Lake Station, where I'll hop a tram to Hale Farm & Village.

My fellow passengers include dozens of preschoolers getting their first taste of train travel. Out my window, I watch hikers, joggers and bicyclists on the towpath as I relive my own childhood memories of train rides in cars like this one. I'm sure it's the same for many of the 113,000 rail-riding visitors

each year. I chat with a couple of teachers from Seattle who have a lifetime goal of visiting all the national parks (they've been to 34!). Several boarders put their bicycles in the baggage car for a one-way train trip and a return by bike on the Towpath Trail.

It's a pleasant interlude I'd love to repeat with my wife, Julie, come autumn, during one of the railroad's wine-tasting excursions—or during the holiday season with my grandson, Luis, when 21,000 youngsters in pajamas crowd the line's Polar Express to Peninsula, which is brightly decorated as the North Pole, bringing the popular children's story to life.

Cuyahoga Valley National Park's treasures also include a number of other historic gems. I walk the Everett Road Covered Bridge in the south end of the park, a replica of one of the 2,000-plus covered bridges Ohio boasted in the late 1800s, reconstructed in 1986 after an 1869 design. The state is known for the bridges, whose design helped protect them from the elements and made them stronger.

Another jewel is the 1826 two-story brick home of early pioneers Stephen and Mehitable Frazee. Unfurnished to highlight its design and construction, the Frazee House exemplifies the vernacular Federal style; creaky floors and tilted corners reveal its age. The Frazees, who settled here in 1806, eventually accumulated 190 riverside acres of what is now national parkland.

The Cuyahoga Valley's farming history comes to life even more vividly at Hale Farm & Village, owned by the Western Reserve Historical Society. In the 1700s, this entire northeast corner of Ohio was "reserved" for settlement by the state of Connecticut, which explains the still-evident vestiges of New England: village greens, pillared mansions and white-steepled churches. All told, 32 historic structures spanning the early- to mid-1800s were relocated here from other

CLOCKWISE, FROM TOP: (All taken at Hale Farm & Village) Sheep grazing near a relocated Western Reserve period home. Costumed interpreters re-creating mid-1800s rural life. A reconstructed kiln.

LEFT TO RIGHT: (Both taken at Cuyahoga Valley National Park) Romantic Everett Road Covered Bridge. Front-row view: sunset attracting an audience at a Ledges overlook.

sites in the Western Reserve, but only after being threatened with demolition. These 90 acres are part of a former 500-acre farm operated until 1958 by the descendants of Jonathan Hale, whose family's stately three-story brick home still is the focal point of the parklike grounds.

I duck (literally) into an 1805 one-room log home where interpreters tell me nine children lived with their parents. Other restored structures reflect various architectural styles found in the Cuyahoga Valley: a Greek Revival dating to 1845, an 1830 New England-style saltbox. Although no Civil War battles were fought here, that watershed period in American history is a recurring theme, as when an interpreter costumed as a Union soldier shows me how to load an 1855 Harper's Ferry Springfield musket and bayonet. More strolling leads me to a smithy, a schoolhouse, a

meetinghouse and a lawyer's office.

At the big barn, I glimpse heritage breeds of livestock, such as Tunis sheep, American shorthorn cattle and Percheron draft horses. Craftspeople demonstrate glass-blowing, blacksmithing, candle making, basket weaving, brick making, spinning, weaving and pottery making. Hale Farm & Village is all about the past, but it's presently a very busy place!

Park Partnerships, New and Old

Although the Frazee House and Hale Farm & Village represent the Cuyahoga Valley's agricultural past, innovators here are moving forward in a totally new way. Over lunch at the canal-side Park City Diner in Valley View, longtime Park Superintendent John P. Debo Jr. tells me about an idea born while he was on a sabbatical in Europe: "Back in the 1800s, this valley was filled with small

farms," he says. "We want to re-create some of that." The eventual goal is about twenty 20- to 30-acre farmsteads (there are seven now). The owners will lease their property from the National Park Service for 60 years and abide by park guidelines. I think it's a splendid idea: The small-scale, locally grown, high-value crops they'll produce, such as grapes and other fruits, vegetables, herbs and even goats and chickens, are all the buzz these days among those who tout sustainable agriculture.

I get a flavorful taste of what the vision is all about across the road from a cultural crown jewel adjoining the park: Blossom Music Center, the covered, 5,500-seat (with lawn seating for 13,500 more) summer concert venue of the world-renowned Cleveland Orchestra that was renovated to the tune of $17 million in 2003. I enjoy wines at Sarah's Vineyard, which Mike and

Margaret Lytz, an Akron couple pursuing their passion, will open in 2007. The Lytzes have chosen their location wisely: What accompanies an outdoor concert better than a bottle of wine?

Partnerships and alliances—and the level of volunteer involvement—are another of this park's innovations. National park volunteers donated more than 5 million hours throughout the United States in 2005; here at Cuyahoga Valley, I meet several of these unsung heroes at Cuyahoga Valley National Park Association's Administrative Office conference room.

The Administrative Office is a unique restored private residence whose previous owner incorporated architectural salvage into frequent remodeling projects. In the conference room, I learn that 1,300 volunteers ranging in age from 8 to 86 help make this park tick, as interpreters, trail workers,

bike- and hike patrol and wildlife-survey assistants, among other roles. The enthusiastic volunteers I meet include a retired NASA scientist, a local college professor of fashion merchandising and a freelance writer. All I can say to these and the other volunteers I meet is, "Thank you from all of us who love our parks."

It's getting late, and I'm back in the charming village of Peninsula, founded when the valley first was settled in 1806 and now on the National Register of Historic Places, for an unexpected dinner I won't soon forget. I'm at the home of one of the park's early patrons, architectural designer and environmentalist Robert Hunker. Over stuffed peppers and vichyssoise in an architecturally stunning and beautifully landscaped former barn filled with Hunker's eclectic objets d'art, I hear how Cuyahoga Valley National Park began.

"Back in the 1960s, a group of us were sitting in my living room here trying to figure out how to retain the Episcopal church building at its location down the street [they got the job done, in what became known as 'the battle of the belfry']," recalls the world traveler, preservationist and civic leader, who now owns many of Peninsula's repurposed structures. One of the activists was John Seiberling, descended from the Akron tire-manufacturing family that built Stan Hywet Hall, an imposing mansion now open to the public near the south end of the park. "John went on to become our congressman and was a major backer of what became this national park."

How pleased Hunker, Seiberling (who served in Congress from 1971 to 1987 and still resides in Akron) and the rest of that seminal group must be with the priceless national park they launched all those years ago.

Dan's Travel Journal

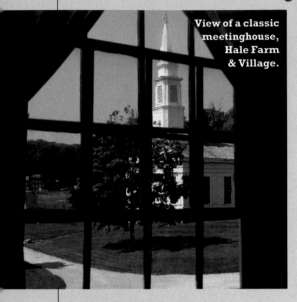

View of a classic meetinghouse, Hale Farm & Village.

FEATURED STOP

Cuyahoga Valley National Park Brecksville. Just a short drive from the Cleveland and Akron metro areas, this 33,000-acre park and its wealth of flora and fauna, spectacular rock formations and waterfalls sit worlds away from urban sprawl. Get oriented at the Canal Visitor Center at the park's north end (six visitor centers, all housed in historic buildings, dot the park, but only the Canal Visitor Center remains open year-round). From there, set out to hike and bike the trails, including the Ohio & Erie Canal Towpath Trail; ride the Cuyahoga Valley Scenic Railroad; go bird-watching; or browse the quaint canal village of Peninsula that lies within the park. Park rangers lead canal hikes, bird-watching trips, campfire programs and other outdoor adventures (216/524-1497).

Lodging, Dining and More

Blossom Music Center Cuyahoga Falls. In Cuyahoga Valley National Park, the summer home of the Cleveland Orchestra and its July–

Labor Day (weekends only) Blossom Festival of orchestral music (800/686-1141).

Century Cycles Peninsula. Bike rental and sales for rides on the Towpath Trail or a one-way trip aboard the Cuyahoga Valley Scenic Railroad (board at the Peninsula Depot and pedal back on the Towpath) (800/201-7433).

Cleveland Metroparks Cleveland. Urban park system with 16 "reservations" and 21,000 acres encircling the city, including Brecksville, Bedford and Ohio & Erie Canal reservations that adjoin Cuyahoga Valley National Park. Activities include golfing, hiking, fishing, swim-ming, winter recreation and exploring wildlife areas and nature centers (216/635-3200).

Cuyahoga Valley Scenic Railroad Peninsula. All aboard for a nostalgic train trip through the heart of Cuyahoga Valley National Park, along the historic Ohio & Erie Canalway connecting Cleveland, Akron and Canton. Choose from 1¾-hour to all-day excursions along the historic 1880s rail route. In the park, board at either the historic Peninsula Depot or Rockside Station in Independence, or outside the park in Akron and Canton (800/468-4070).

Hale Farm & Village Bath. Surrounded by Cuyahoga Valley National Park, an outdoor living-history museum with 32 historical buildings, costumed artisans and interpreters depicting life in the Western Reserve during the Civil War era (330/666-3711).

Holiday Inn Hudson Five minutes from Cuyahoga Valley National Park, near Hudson. A 239-room, full-service hotel with indoor pool, lounge and restaurant. $$ (330/653-9191).

The Inn at Brandywine Falls Sagamore Hills. Adjacent to Brandywine Falls in Cuyahoga Valley National Park, six antiques-appointed rooms in an 1848 Greek Revival farmhouse and a carriage barn out back. $$$–$$$$ (888/306-3381).

Lockkeepers Valley View (across from Park

City Diner). Sophisticated dining along the Cuyahoga River, a Cleveland award winner for its innovative American cuisine and wine list of more than 700 labels (216/524-9404).

Park City Diner Valley View. Hip 1940s-style diner with comfort food—thick shakes, cheeseburgers, hand-cut fries, pastries—and creative cocktails. Slide into a retro booth or overlook the Ohio & Erie Canal from the outdoor patio (216/328-0575).

Sarah's Vineyard Cuyahoga Falls. Opening in 2007, a winery on an 1840s farmstead, with tasting room, vineyards, art studio and gallery. Across from Blossom Music Center in Cuyahoga Valley National Park (330/929-8057).

Stan Hywet Hall & Gardens Akron. Tour the 65-room Tudor Revival manor house, built by the Goodyear Tire & Rubber Company founder in 1915, and 70 acres of manicured gardens (330/836-5533).

Stanford Hostel Peninsula. Part of Hostel-ling International, inexpensive (under $20) dorm accommodations and two private rooms (30 beds total) in a restored 1843 farmhouse. In Cuyahoga Valley National Park on the Ohio & Erie Canal Towpath Trail. $ (330/467-8711).

More Information

National Park Service Volunteers-in-Parks Program (www.nps.gov/volunteer).

Ohio Division of Travel and Tourism (800/282-5393, www.discoverohio.com).

DAN'S OTHER STOPS

(See also More Parks section that follows.)

Hueston Woods State Park College Corner (513/523-6347), **Malabar Farm State Park** Lucas (419/892-2784).

Lodging, Dining and More

Malabar Farm Restaurant Perrysville. Home-style cooking using fresh farm produce, in an 1820 stagecoach inn at Malabar State Park (419/892-2784).

More Ohio Parks

Atwood Lake Park

Surrounded by 3,000 acres of woods, Atwood Lake (45 miles south of Akron) is one of eight lakes in the Muskingum Watershed Conservancy District. Covering 18 counties, the district provides recreation, conservation and flood control along southeastern Ohio's Muskingum River.

Colorful sailboats skim across the mile-wide waters of Atwood, known as one of the state's best for all kinds of boating. Vacationers also hit the beach, swim and fish the more than seven-mile-long lake. Days in the outdoors include hiking and bicycling, tennis, swimming in outdoor and indoor pools and golfing on 9- and 18-hole courses. The lodge dining room makes the perfect spot for watching sunsets across the lake.

Park visitors can stay at the top-notch Atwood Lake Resort, which sprawls along the shore, or rent modern cabins with lake views or camp at 500 sites. Two marinas handle boating needs (boats for rent).

Contact: Atwood Lake Park (330/343-6780, mwcd lakes.com). Atwood Lake Resort and Conference Center (800/362-6406 atwoodlakeresort. com). Nearest lodgings: limited just east of the lake in Dellroy; more options 15 miles east in Carrollton (877/727-0103, carroll countyohio.com).

Beaver Creek State Park

On its way through the Appalachian foothills, Little Beaver Creek, designated a state and national wild and scenic river, rushes through this state park (30 miles south of Youngstown). Besides floating the river and admiring the scenery, park visitors explore the area's pioneer past.

Amid the park's more than 2,700 acres of forested wilderness, swift currents challenge canoeists on trips through Little Beaver Creek Gorge (canoes for rent). You can picnic at water's edge or sleep high above it at a campground ringed with pines. Bass is a popular river catch.

Hiking and biking trails lead through the gorge and woods. Cliffs and rock walls, decorated with waterfalls, drop to wildflower-dotted stream banks. For a perfect panorama, hike a short trail from the campgrounds to Oak Tree Point. Paths also lead to abandoned canal locks, once part of the Sandy and Beaver Creek Canal, and to the park's pioneer village. A working gristmill, built in 1837, stars among the village's 10 reconstructed buildings, which range from a chapel to a blacksmith shop.

Contact: Beaver Creek State Park (330/385-3091, ohiodnr.com). Nearest lodgings: less than 10 miles south of the park in Calcutta (330/386-6060, calcuttaohiochamber .com) and East Liverpool (330/385-0845, elchamber.org).

Cuyahoga Valley National Park

(See previous section of this chapter.)

Grand Lake St. Marys State Park

When developers created Grand Lake St. Marys as a feeder reservoir for the Miami-Erie Canal back in 1845, the man-made lake reigned as the world's largest. Today, along the 52 miles of shore of the state's largest inland lake, you'll discover one of Ohio's oldest state parks (75 miles northwest of Dayton).

Surrounded by a prairie landscape, this nearly 600-acre park is a surprising gem. Swimmers, boaters and anglers head for the water, while sunbathers get comfortable on wide stretches of sand (boats for rent). You can spend a pleasant afternoon just breezing around the nine-mile-long lake, stopping for a picnic and exploring quiet coves. The water never seems crowded.

Summer nature programs include wildlife walks and movies about the park's past. Along a major migration route, the lake is a popular stop for Canada geese, ducks and other waterfowl. The campground includes more than 200 sites and a full-service store.

Contact: Grand Lake St. Marys State Park (419/394-3611, ohiodnr.com). Nearest lodgings: at small lakeshore resorts; also, just north of the lake in Celina and just east of the lake in St. Marys (800/860-4726, see more.com).

Hocking Hills

Amid these forested hills and rugged valleys, you'll glimpse what much of America looked like before European settlers reshaped it. Time and water have worn southeastern Ohio's Appalachian foothills into towering humps and soft-shouldered ridges (beginning about 40 miles southeast of Columbus). Along winding byways, communities such as Logan, Nelsonville and Athens have endured. They form a 30-mile chain through the Hocking River Valley.

At the heart of the region, you'll discover 2,300-acre Hocking Hills State Park and neighboring 9,400-acre Hocking State Forest southwest of Logan. Trails lead to breathtaking cliffs, waterfalls and sandstone caves and recesses, the most famous called "Old Man's Cave." Ancient giant

hemlocks tower in the cool hollows. Seasonal nature programs at the park focus on the area's natural history. The 17-mile paved Hockhocking Adena Bikeway runs between Nelsonville and Athens, often near the Hocking River. In Logan, you can rent canoes to float the river.

Visitors can camp at nearly 160 sites and stay in 40 cottages at the park, which includes a dining lodge and outdoor swimming pool.

Contact: Hocking Hills State Forest (740/385-4402, ohiodnr.com). Hocking Hills State Park (740/385-6842, ohiodnr .com). Nearest lodgings: cabins and country inns—rustic to luxurious—around the park, plus accommodations in Athens, Logan, Nelsonville and other communities (800/462-5464, 1800hocking.com).

Hueston Woods State Park

A three-story chalet-style lodge provides a memorable view of Acton Lake at southwestern Ohio's Hueston Woods, one of the state's nine premier resort parks (30 miles northeast of Cincinnati). The park's center-

piece lodge isn't far from a 200-acre stand of virgin timber that's part of the 3,000-acre park's Hueston Woods Nature Preserve. Vacationers fish and boat in the 600-acre lake (boats for rent), swim along the beach or in outdoor and indoor pools, play golf on an 18-hole course and rent horses to ride the trails. There's also an archery range.

Hikers relish 10 miles of shady, easygoing trails, and mountain bikers tackle 20 miles of trails. Some of the paths meander through the nature preserve's stately old-growth beech and sugar maple trees, which the National Park Service has named a National Natural Landmark. The park's nature center conducts bird and wildflower walks. You can sign up for fossil hunts, too (a shallow sea covered much of Ohio ages ago).

Besides staying in rooms at the lodge, which includes a restaurant, visitors can take their pick of some three dozen cottages and nearly 500 developed and primitive campsites.

Contact: Hueston Woods State Park and Resort (513/523-6347, ohiodnr.com).

Nearest lodgings: just south of the park in Oxford (513/523-5200, cityofoxford.org).

Lake Erie Shore

Marshes and wetlands come alive with waterfowl and wildlife along the westernmost reaches of Lake Erie. In these natural areas of some 40 miles of shore, you can explore a region once dominated by the Great Black Swamp.

Canada geese, ducks and other waterfowl share nearly 2,000-acre Maumee Bay State Park with visitors who stay at the resort lodge, deluxe cabins and campsites (10 miles east of Toledo). Hiking trails lead into two wildlife areas. You can follow a boardwalk from the lodge through neighboring wetlands. The park also includes beaches, swimming pools, fishing ponds, hiking and biking trails, a golf course and Lake Erie marina (boats for rent).

A few miles east, bird-watchers and naturalists flock to Ottawa National Wildlife Refuge. You're sure to see herons and egrets along eight miles of trails in the 5,500 acres of wetlands. The refuge borders two other birding locations: Crane Creek State Park and adjacent 2,600-acre Magee Marsh. At the marsh's Migratory Bird Center, visitors learn that 100 types of birds have been spotted here in one week.

Contact: Crane Creek State Park and Magee Marsh Wildlife Area (419/898-0960, ohiodnr.com). Maumee Bay State Park (419/836-7758, ohiodnr.com). Ottawa National Wildlife Refuge (419/898-0014, fws.gov/midwest/ottawa). Nearest lodgings: in Toledo (800/243-4667, dotoledo.org) and 17 miles southeast of Ottawa National Wildlife Refuge in Port Clinton (800/441-1271, lake-erie.com).

Little Miami Scenic Trail

Quaint towns dot this 75-mile trail beside the Little Miami River, extending between the city of Springfield and Avoca Park (just north of Cincinnati). The popular bicycling route along a converted rail bed travels through quiet nature areas, farmland, rolling hills and near riverside cliffs.

As you pedal the paved rail-trail, you'll see canoeists paddling the Little Miami, a National Scenic River. Towering sycamores shade some stretches of the route. You might even spot herons. Warblers and other songbirds hide in the wildflowers, as families lollygag along and serious cyclists speed past in their neon togs.

Much of the trail, also a favorite with hikers and in-line skaters, is designated Little Miami State Park, a 50-mile long, 66-foot-wide corridor. You'll find picnic areas along the way. Two state parks not far from the trail—John Bryan near Yellow Springs and Caesar Creek near Waynesville—supply camping options, plus hiking trails. Picturesque communities such as Yellow Springs and Xenia make good stops for lunch or snacks.

Contact: Little Miami Scenic Trail (513/897-3055, ohiodnr.com). Nearest lodgings: in Xenia (800/773-9109, greenecountyohio.org) and Yellow Springs (937/767-2686, yellowspringsohio.com).

Little Muskingum River and Wayne National Forest

A sense of the past surrounds you as you

paddle the serene Little Muskingum River. In southeastern Ohio's Appalachian foothills northeast of Marietta, the river meanders through the 65,000-acre Marietta Unit of Wayne National Forest, one of three units in the state's only national forest.

Taking its name from the Native American word that means "muddy river," the Little Muskingum parallels the 35-mile National Forest Covered Bridge Scenic Byway. Canoeists slip beneath covered bridges and past green pastures, historic barns and century-old farmhouses mixed with more-rugged scenery, including bluffs and rocky outcropping. Four national forest campgrounds along a 35-mile stretch of the river lend themselves to multiday trips.

Within the forest, 100 miles of hiking and bicycling trails range from easy to challenging, as the rolling hills plunge through dense woods. River views highlight the Ohio View Trail off State-7 near New Matamoras (northeast of Marietta). Hikers and cyclists also can take advantage of two other forest campgrounds.

Contact: Wayne National Forest and National Forest Covered Bridge Scenic Byway (740/373-9055, fs.fed.us and byways.org). Nearest lodgings: in Marietta (800/288-2577, mariettaohio.org).

Mohican and Malabar Farm State Parks

Clear waters and the gentle current of the Clearfork River create a paddlers paradise at north-central Ohio's nearly 1,200-acre Mohican State Park (60 miles south of Cleveland). The river flows through hemlock forests and cuts beside the steep cliffs of a 400-foot-deep gorge in an area where the Delaware Indians once hunted.

But vacationers congregate at the park for other activities, too, including fishing, swimming, tennis and seasonal nature programs. You can hike and mountain bike

trails that link with those in surrounding Mohican-Memorial State Forest. Lyons Falls Trail leads through the Clearfork Gorge, with two waterfalls.

Visitors stay at the park's cedar lodge. Overlooking Pleasant Hill Lake, it's decorated with Native American murals and artifacts. Cottages and some 100 campsites tuck into the woods. You can dine at the lodge restaurant.

Just northwest of Mohican, Lauren Bacall and Humphrey Bogart spent their honeymoon at Malabar Farm. The one-time estate of Pulitzer Prize-winning Ohio author Louis Bromfield is now a state park, where visitors can tour the 32-room country house and working farm.

Contact: Malabar Farm State Park (419/892-2784, malabarfarm.org). Mohican-Memorial State Forest (330/339-2205, ohiodnr.com). Mohican State Park (419/994-5125, ohiodnr.com). Nearest lodgings: just north of Mohican State Park in Loudonville (877/266-4422, loudenville-mohican.com) and 10 miles northwest in Mansfield (800/642-8282, mansfield tourism.com).

Ohio River National Scenic Byway

The Ohio River becomes your companion on this 452-mile byway along the state's southern border (primarily US-52 and State-7). Bluffs border the river much of the way; bridges and car ferries cross it at several spots. You'll see tree-lined streets and hilltop mansions in historic communities such as Portsmouth, Ironton, Gallipolis and Marietta. Museums and antiques and crafts shops abound, and restaurants serve regional dishes. Scores of wide-spot-in-the-road towns also deserve stops.

Travelers glimpse Ohio's past at the new National Underground Railroad Freedom Center in Cincinnati. You can visit the

birthplace of Ulysses S. Grant in Point Pleasant just east of Cincinnati. About midway along the route, you'll discover Ohio's only Civil War battle site, at Buffington Island, and the George Washington Campsite near Long Bottom, where our first president stayed in 1770.

Barges ease through locks at Neville and Reedsville near Forked Run State Park. Views stretch for miles from Picnic Point along the 35-mile Panorama Scenic Loop through Shawnee State Forest (see Shawnee State Forest and Shawnee State Park, opposite page). You can explore the wilderness in two riverside units of Wayne National Forest (see Little Muskingum River and Wayne National Forest, page xx).

Contact: Ohio River National Scenic Byway (740/423-7233, ohioriverscenicbyway .com or ohiobyways.com). Nearest lodgings: all along the route (800/282-5393, discover ohio.com).

Pymatuning State Park

Traces of a vast, almost impenetrable swamp that once dominated the area remain at this more than 3,500-acre state park (about 50 miles north of Youngstown). But now, huge Pymatuning Lake, a reservoir straddling the Ohio and Pennsylvania state line in northeastern Ohio, draws vacationers for all kinds of water recreation.

Forests of hardwoods and pines surround the 14,000-acre lake, known for walleye and muskie fishing. Five boat launches speckle the shore (boats for rent), which includes a swimming beach. You can stay in cottages, canvas camping cabins called yurts or camp at more than 330 sites.

Easygoing trails lead through the woods. Ponds and marshes from long ago attract bald eagles and waterfowl. Summer nature programs sometimes explore the mysteries of the old swamp. At the Pymatuning Spillway, thousands of people stop each year to see the ducks "walk on fish." Visitors toss bread to the ducks and carp, which crowd together in such numbers that the ducks literally stand on the fish to catch the treats.

Contact: Pymatuning State Park (140/ 293-6030, ohiodnr.com). Nearest lodgings: twenty-five miles north in Conneaut and 35 miles northeast in Ashtabula (440/275-3202, visitashtabulacounty.com).

Shawnee State Forest and Shawnee State Park

It's easy to see why this area of south-central Ohio is called "Ohio's Little Smokies." Wooded ridges roll toward the Ohio River in a blue haze from Shawnee State Park and surrounding 63,000-acre Shawnee State Forest (10 miles west of Portsmouth).

Modern Ohio disappears in the state forest, Ohio's largest. A 60-mile backpack trail, with primitive campsites along the way, takes hikers to some of the state's best wilderness. Shorter trails also lead into the woods, which includes fishing lakes and 75 miles of horse trails.

But for "getting away from it all" in comfort, 1,000-acre Shawnee State Park, a full-scale resort, nestles in the forest. Visitors can stay at the lodge, with a dining room and heart-thumping views of wooded bluffs and sculpted valleys, or choose from among cottages and more than 100 campsites.

The marina provides access to the Ohio River. You can rent boats at the park campground to paddle and fish in Roosevelt and Turkey Creek lakes, both with swimming beaches. Hike seven trails and sign up for seasonal nature programs. Swimming pools, tennis courts and an 18-hole golf course round out recreation options.

Contact: Shawnee State Forest (740/858-6685, ohiodnr.com). Shawnee State Park (740/858-6652, ohiodnr.com). Nearest lodgings: in Portsmouth (740/353-1116, ohiorivertourism.org).

CLOCKWISE, FROM TOP LEFT: Canoeing the Little Muskingum near Wayne National Forest. Learning about owls, Mohican State Park. The Ohio River from Rankin House near Ripley, Ohio River National Scenic Byway.

SOUTH DAKOTA

Observing the buffalo during a jeep safari in Custer State Park.

Bigger-than-life adventures in the Wild West

MONTANA BOASTS THE slogan "Big Sky Country," but I believe South Dakota could stake a rival claim to the title, at least in the Midwest. With Eager Assistant Rob, I'm making my way across the state that residents divide according to "East River" and "West River," referring to the Missouri.

En route to my primary destination, Custer State Park, I'm transfixed by roiling black thunderheads and wan shafts of yellow sunlight, visible from miles away on these undulating plains. The state is so big and wide-open that it's an hour before I encounter any rain from those clouds.

Native American Scenic Byway

All told, 101 miles of several U.S. highways received the coveted National Scenic Byway designation in 2004, but the Native American Scenic Byway I'm on now is the only one that honors a cultural heritage as well as scenery. It's unique, both because of the surrounding spartan tableau of grassy, windswept buttes, breaks and bluffs along the Missouri River and the fact that most of it traverses a Native American reservation, the 250,000-acre home of the Lower Brule Sioux tribe.

I get chills whenever I travel along the Missouri and realize I'm viewing the same terrain that Meriwether Lewis and William Clark and their brave men probed in

Photography by Bob Stefko and Jason Lindsey

LEFT TO RIGHT: Sheldon Fletcher, a champion of wildlife and Lakota traditions, near the Native American Scenic Byway. (All taken at Badlands National Park) Fossil treasure. Climbing adventures. Tenacious Badlands flora.

1804–1806. U.S. Army Corps of Engineers dams built in the 1950s and '60s have tamed the once-feral river for flood-control, power and recreation purposes, primarily fishing and boating; on this drive I'll pass Lake Sharpe, created by the two-mile-long, earthen Big Bend Dam. Still, much of what I'm seeing is what the explorers viewed.

From South Dakota's friendly, pint-sized capital city of Pierre (population 14,000), I join the byway across the Missouri at Fort Pierre, where Lewis and Clark's journey almost ended during a confrontation with a band of Teton Sioux (fortunately, the standoff turned into a friendly parley). About five miles south on the byway, also labeled State-1806 hereabouts, is the contemporary new Buffalo Interpretive Center.

Inside, a short film titled *Return of the Buffalo* explains how vital the *tatanka*— that's "buffalo" in the Lakota Sioux language—were to the Lower Brule and other tribes, providing essentials from food to shelter, clothing and tools. No part of the buffalo was wasted; the bladder even was used for carrying water and the stomach as a cooking pot. Roaming the interactive exhib-

its, I punch buttons and watch videos that show how buffalo hides were prepared, how the Sioux fashioned bows and arrowheads and how they set up their tepees, those ingenious mobile homes of the Plains.

Soon I'm back on the road, skimming grassy ridges on the west side of the shimmering Missouri on my way to Lower Brule, the only town on the reservation. At the tribal wildlife center, I meet with Sheldon Fletcher. His Lakota name is *Tatanka Wicasa,* or Buffalo Man, and his features reflect his mixed European and Lakota ancestry. Sheldon is the conservation officer for the Lower Brule Wildlife Department.

Reservations such as the Lower Brule, with a population of about 1,500 mostly tribe members, are self-governing entities with their own law enforcement, fire protection and housing authorities. There are nine such tribal lands in South Dakota. Sheldon and his staff are responsible for managing the reservation's reintroduced herds of buffalo and elk, as well as keeping tabs on other wildlife and their habitats, including whitetailed and mule deer, coyotes and raccoons; geese, ducks and other waterfowl; and

game birds such as the sharp-tailed grouse, prairie chicken, pheasant and wild turkey. They're also nurturing small populations of black-footed ferrets and swift foxes, among other threatened and endangered species.

Sheldon spent four years in the U.S. Coast Guard, which took him to Puerto Rico, Miami Beach and other tropical ports before he returned to this harsh land he loves. Clearly, the 275 buffalo and 200 elk he husbands on these 5,600 fenced-in acres are his pride and joy. Especially the buffalo. "We have a saying, 'When the buffalo come back, our people will come back,' " he says.

Despite the progress I see in impressive new projects such as the tribal headquarters, justice center and recreation center, it's clear much of the reservation remains impoverished. Tourism, evidenced by the scenic byway and related projects, is one hope for the Lower Brule. Another is food processing; the tribe is one of the nation's largest popcorn producers, under the Lakota Foods label. Why did Sheldon come back? "The land," he says. "My ancestors were on this land for hundreds of years. It's hard to explain, but you can't deny it."

Nearing I-90 and the end of my byway ride, I make two final stops, in Chamberlain: the Akta Lakota Museum and Cultural Center (*akta* means "to honor") and the Lewis & Clark Interpretive Center. On the manicured grounds of St. Joseph's Indian School, a residential facility for 200 pre-high-school students from various tribes, the museum is rich with art, artifacts and educational displays. At the interpretive center, I hike to an overlook for a blustery view of the river valley, and I wonder: *Could Lewis and Clark ever have imagined the busy superhighway spanning the now-tame Missouri just two centuries after their trip?*

Inside the center, I learn how the explorers set up camp in the area, unloaded their boats to dry out their provisions following several days of rain, feasted on delicious plums and abundant wildlife and even came across a huge prehistoric fossil. But…back to the 21st century: Our crew crosses the river to Oacoma for lunch at Al's Oasis, a sprawling interstate highway truck stop where I purchase gas, groceries, several souvenirs—and a great slice of coconut cream pie—before heading west on I-90.

Badlands National Park

After a four-hour drive across the plains, I pull off at Exit 131 to revisit one of my favorite Midwest domains, Badlands National Park. First order of business: a late lunch at Cactus Flat (population 2). Here, Michael and Ellen Mulder run the Circle 10 Campground and Cafe, where our crew feasts on Indian tacos (seasoned ground beef and salad fixings in a fry-bread bowl) and a surprising dessert: the best chocolate raspberry cheesecake I've ever tasted. Reinvigorated, I hop into Bill Honerkamp's white van for a Badlands tour.

Bill is a great storyteller who knows these eerie sand-castlelike formations as well as anybody; he's lived in the area all his life, and he's been president of the Black Hills, Badlands & Lakes Association for 25 years. A quick stop at the Prairie Homestead sod house gives me an idea of how crude life was for the settlers who eked out their existence here after the area was opened to homesteading in 1890. Bill tells me human settlement in the Badlands dates back 11,000 years to mastodon fanciers, followed thousands of years later by

Native American buffalo hunters.

Soon we pull off the 32-mile Badlands Loop Road and hike a trail in this ever-changing Technicolor domain of red, purple, orange, tan, pink, white and gray canyons of clay, sandstone, volcanic ash and siltstone. Together, this layer cake of rock forms a 60-mile-long "wall" separating the area's high prairies from its low prairies. The Badlands, which was designated a national monument in 1939 and a national park in 1978, is one of the Midwest's most visited parklands, attracting 1 million tourists per year (in no other park on my journey do I note such a diverse collection of license plates, representing every corner of the United States and places beyond). Like me, most of them find this moonlike domain unforgettable.

The park is enormous, encompassing about 381 square miles that include a mixed-grass prairie preserve that's home to 60 varieties of grasses as well as brilliantly hued wildflowers and an array of critters. I've explored the well-marked trails that lace these "mini Grand Canyons" several times, yet I'm mesmerized anew by the park's raw beauty.

"Due to the porous nature of the clay and rock, the landscape changes every time it rains," Bill says. I ask how long these fabulous formations will be here. "Anyone who's planning to see the Badlands better make their travel plans for within the next 500,000 years," he advises with a wink. "After that, they could be gone."

The Badlands are like Disney World for all kinds of "ologists"—geologists, paleontologists, biologists and the like. For example, when it comes to studying fossils (as a paleontologist does), the Badlands are packed with reminders of the Golden Age of Mammals that flourished midway between the age of dinosaurs and the present. No dinosaurs resided here, because this was the bottom of a huge ocean when they were in their glory. But after that ocean receded, the Badlands became balmy and lush.

At the newly refurbished Ben Reifel Visitors Center, Park Educational Specialist Julie Johndreau points out some of her prized toothy skulls and drawings of the predecessors of today's horses, dogs, pigs, sheep, turtles and even rhinos, hyenas, camels and crocodiles—all residents of the Badlands when it resembled today's subtropical Florida.

offering travelers free ice water back during the Depression (those signs now can be found nearly everywhere, from South Dakota to Botswana and Singapore).

You still can get that free glass of ice water, as well as (believe it or not) a nickel cup of coffee at the complex, which now lines an entire block of Wall's main street. You'll also find a chapel, a soda fountain, several dining rooms, a Western art gallery and shops purveying merchandise from books to leather goods and jewelry (need some new cowboy boots or a Black Hills gold ring?). Oh yes, and there's still a drugstore somewhere in there.

Custer State Park

After a brief check-in stop at the big, modern Black Hills-area visitors center near I-90 on the east side of Rapid City, Rob and I make a beeline southwest to Mount Rushmore, just outside tourist-kitschy Keystone. Dinner is at the huge cafeteria overlooking the memorial, and later, the patriotic evening lighting ceremony in the jam-packed Rushmore amphitheater has us both ready to wave the flag.

Somewhere around 60 million years ago, molten magma from the earth's core gradu-

What a contrast within one state! No wonder the Lakota Sioux considered the whole 100×50-mile area sacred. Unfortunately, in 1874, civilians and Lt. Col. George Armstrong Custer and his 1,000 cavalrymen let the cat out of the bag when they discovered "gold in them thar hills." A stampede of settlement ensued that's still in progress (today, the settlers are mostly retirees, not gold rushers).

I believe the best place to experience the Black Hills these days is 71,000-acre Custer State Park. At 14 miles long and eight miles wide, this wildlife-packed Jurassic Park anchors the near-south end of the region (once-raucous Deadwood, the neighboring mining center of Lead and splendid Spearfish Canyon are in the somewhat wetter, greener northern end of the hills).

We all can thank South Dakota Governor and U.S. Senator Peter Norbeck (1870–1936) for creating one of America's best-known state parks. Norbeck, an early and ardent conservationist, devised an ingenious strategy: When South Dakota achieved statehood in 1889, two sections of land in each township were reserved for schools, way more than what turned out to be needed in this sparsely populated state. Norbeck proposed a trade with the federal government whereby unused school land would be swapped for a game preserve (the federal government still controls more than half of the Black Hills region, primarily within 1.2 million-acre Black Hills National Forest). In 1919, that game preserve became Custer State Park.

Now Norbeck is honored by having his name on the park's busy, Civilian Conservation Corps (CCC)-era rock-and-timber visitors center and on 70-mile Peter Norbeck Scenic Drive. The path gloriously wends through the region, encompassing the legendary 14-mile Needles Highway

''Anyone planning to see the Badlands better make their travel plans for within the next 500,000 years,'' Bill advises.

Nobody, but nobody, makes an official tour here without winding up at Wall Drug in the town of the same name. Wall (population 820) is named for the "wall" of rugged terrain people have to cross to get here. The famous shrine to retail chutzpah skyrocketed to fame when its new owners struck on the idea of plastering the state with signs

ally surged through sedentary rock, leaving behind a batholith (a mass of igneous rock that for the most part stopped in its rise a considerable distance below the surface). That dome of granite eroded over the ages into the forest-cloaked mountains, needles and pinnacles that now soar majestically over the South Dakota prairie.

CLOCKWISE, FROM TOP: (All taken at Custer State Park) Needles Highway panorama. Horseback excursion. Panning for gold. Dan exiting a rock passage at Sylvan Lake.

LEFT TO RIGHT: (All taken at Custer State Park) Sunning beside Sylvan Lake. Exploring a meadow. Rock-climbing interlude. Anything-but-bashful begging burro. BOTTOM: State Game Lodge.

I'll travel within the park (its tunnels and hairpin turns required 150,000 pounds of dynamite to blast through all the granite!). Wild game always has been the big attraction here, species native to the area, including those reintroduced after they vamoosed because of settlement—buffalo, elk, mountain goats, bighorn sheep, mountain lions and pronghorn antelope among them.

Hmmm…where do I begin? I peruse the rack of flyers offered at the front desk: "Buffalo Safari Jeep Tour," "Fly-Fishing School," "Mountain Bike Rentals," "Hydrobike, Paddleboat and Rowboat Rentals," "Hayride Chuck Wagon Cookout," "Panning for Gold," "Horseback Trail Rides," "Live Performances at the Black Hills Playhouse," "Rock Climbing." I'm daunted just considering the plethora of possibilities.

Rocks, Lakes and Critters
Situated along the Needles Highway several miles northwest of the main park, the Sylvan Lake area where I'm staying is one of Custer's crown jewels. The lake itself was created by an entrepreneur who dammed Sunday Gulch back in 1891 (all of the lakes in the area are man-made). The first lodge, which was built in 1895, became part of the park in 1921. After a fire in 1935, it was Frank Lloyd Wright (the Wisconsin-born high priest of modern architecture was touring in the area at the time) who suggested rebuilding on the present site. Great location suggestion, Mr. Wright! Stone-and-cedar Sylvan Lake Lodge, with its Deco-era Native American design motifs and stuffed critters glaring down from the lobby walls, is one of four historic resorts within the park. Each offers excellent dining facilities as well as a wide range of amenities and accommodations.

The surrounding ponderosa pine and Black Hills spruce-dappled rock formations seem more like a studio movie set than reality to me. After filling up at the ample breakfast buffet in the Lakota Dining Room and luxuriating a few moments on the pine-ringed terrace out back, it's time for a hike around Sylvan Lake. Later in the day, I return for dinner, and our crew feasts on specialties such as pheasant spring rolls, buffalo skewers, local rainbow trout, herbed pheasant and wild boar baby back ribs—all prepared by Head Chef Charles Etzrodt and served by a global waitstaff that hails from a half-dozen nations. There also are eight campgrounds and 350 campsites in Custer State Park, including French Creek Horse Camp, which caters to vacationers who bring along their own equines; they can ride horseback anywhere in the 71,000 acres of the park.

Sticking with the program, I'm off to the top of Mount Coolidge, one of the park's highest peaks, for a 360-degree view that encompasses Mount Rushmore, Harney Peak (the area's tallest, at 7,242 feet), the Crazy Horse Memorial being blasted from another mountain and, to the east, the Badlands and those endless prairies. There's a

fire-lookout tower here that's still in use. One reminder of that necessity is a mountainside that's green but devoid of mature trees due to the lightning-ignited Galena Fire of July 1988 (named for the creek area where it started). It took more than 1,000 firefighters five days to get the conflagration under control, and it will take Mother Nature a century to return the 16,788 burned-out acres to their former glory.

Next stop, the Peter Norbeck Visitors Center in the northeast quadrant of the park, where I browse exhibits about the park's history, geology and wildlife and chat with Craig Pugsley, Custer's energetic visitor services coordinator. Craig has been here for 30 years and lives with his family just down the road in the park; he says he's accustomed to spotting wildlife such as buffalo, deer and bighorn sheep right outside his living room window.

One thing I love about Custer State Park is its presidential connections. Practically across the road from the visitors center is the State Game Lodge and Resort. Here, "Silent Cal" Calvin Coolidge and his wife, Grace, set up their Summer White House

for 12 weeks back in 1927 (ask to reserve their room if you visit). It's interesting to note that Coolidge required accommodations for an entourage of 200 aides and reporters during his summer getaway; now, the swarm of staff and press numbers 2,500 when a president travels! Dwight Eisenhower stopped by for several days of trout fishing in 1953.

The homelike game lodge is always on my list when I'm at Custer State Park. Its initial 1920 lodge building (several more recent wings extend from the sides) enchants me with its original fixtures; vintage photographs, including dignified portraits of the Coolidges in the lobby; and broad front porch with a view of Grace Coolidge Creek across the road. I barely have time to nosh on barbecued buffalo ribs for lunch in the Pheasant Dining Room before I head off to drive the 18-mile Wildlife Loop Road that curves through the prairies at the south end of the park.

Craig has advised me that the best times for viewing wildlife are early morning and sunset, when animals are most likely to be feeding. We're still in the heat of the

afternoon; nonetheless, as we creep along in my vehicle with Rob at the wheel, we bag our unlimited photo quota of the park's buffalo (a line passes single file just yards away), pronghorn antelope, white-tailed and mule deer and uncounted little prairie dogs. I even get outside the car in the midst of a mini traffic jam to feed and pet some of the notorious, decidedly assertive but harmless "begging burros" that reside here. I don't see any elk, though; the park's herd of 1,000 prefers higher elevations at this time of year, as do the sure-footed mountain goats and bighorn sheep.

The Ones That Got Away

To a fly fisher, the Black Hills region is pure heaven. Approximately 800 miles of cool, clear streams and 22 deep, steel-blue reservoirs—four of them in Custer State Park—harbor pink-striped rainbow, red-spotted brook and wily brown trout. Although trout weren't introduced to the Black Hills until 1886, they certainly have taken to the place; in some streams, the count is estimated to be 300 trout per 100 yards. Because dry weather has made fishing for trout within

Black Hills Buffalo Stew

Located in Custer State Park, the State Game Lodge and Resort serves this savory Buffalo Stew in their popular Pheasant Dining Room. Discerning diners describe bison as rich and flavorful, similar to lean beef, and definitely not wild or gamey.

1   pound bison (buffalo) stew meat or beef stew meat; cut large pieces in half
1   large onion, chopped (1 cup)
3   cloves garlic, minced
2   tablespoons cooking oil
3   14-ounce cans beef broth (5¼ cups)
1½ teaspoons dried Italian seasoning, crushed
1   teaspoon dried oregano, crushed
½   teaspoon ground black pepper
4   medium potatoes, peeled and cubed (4 cups)
4   medium carrots, sliced (2 cups)
2   stalks celery, sliced (1 cup)
⅓   cup cold water
3   tablespoons all-purpose flour

In a 4- to 6-quart Dutch oven, cook meat, onion and garlic in hot oil until meat is brown; if necessary, drain fat. Add beef broth, Italian seasoning, oregano and black pepper. Bring to boiling; reduce heat. Simmer, covered, for 1 to 1¼ hours or until meat is nearly tender.

Stir in potatoes, carrots and celery. Return to boiling; reduce heat. Simmer, covered, about 30 minutes more or until meat and vegetables are tender.

In a small bowl, whisk together water and flour until smooth. Add flour mixture to stew. Cook and stir over medium heat until thickened and bubbly; cook and stir for 1 minute more. *Makes 6 (1½-cup) servings.*

the park uncharacteristically challenging (crappie, perch and bass still are biting nicely at Custer's Stockade Lake—but they're not trout!), I have a trout-fishing date at Rapid Creek in the National Forest west of Rapid City with Dave Gamet, head guide and instructor with Dakota Angler and Outfitter in Rapid City. We'll fly-fish just a mile below the 100-foot-deep Pactola Reservoir, where the rushing, incredibly clear 45-degree waters range from knee- to hip-deep. Outfitted in the vest, boots and waders provided, I practice casting under Dave's tutelage.

Nine years ago, Dave traded a career in restaurant management to pursue his life-long passion for fly-fishing. I'm a novice, so I ask, "What's the trick to fly-fishing?" The whole key, Dave advises, is NOT to cast with a flick of the wrist as you would when spin-fishing, but to keep your arm and wrist rigid, in effect, quickly catapulting the line back and forth. You also cast upstream, not down, he says, because trout apparently face upstream when it's time to grab a snack.

"Be careful not to spook the fish," Dave cautions me. "They're smart. You wouldn't reach for a T-bone if there was a bear in the room, would you? You're the bear in the room to these fish." He goes on to explain a lot that goes right over my head about nifty-sounding gizmos such as tippets, leaders, various types of lines, nippers and hemostats. He also shows me some hand-tied flies designed to resemble the little insects and aquatic critters trout like to eat, such as midges, mayflies and freshwater shrimp.

I don't catch a single trout, but I do a masterful job of entangling my line in a power line overhead. On the other hand, Dave effortlessly reels in five rainbow and brown trout measuring about 13 inches and weighing 1½ pounds each. That doesn't bother me as much as the fact that Rob,

who, like me, has never been fly-fishing before, reels in another six on his own. At any rate, everyone has a great time—me, most of all (as soon as we get my line disentangled from that power line for the second time). I think the fish are enjoying themselves too, because they wind up back in the stream, not in a frying pan (much wiser, I'm sure, for the experience).

Where the Buffalo Roam

Not far from the State Game Lodge, I rendezvous with Buffalo Herd Manager Chad Kremer, a former Minnesotan who's spent his entire career in the bison biz, here and elsewhere. How big are those critters I've been viewing (albeit from a respectful distance) on the Wildlife Loop Road? "A mature bull averages a ton in weight, up to 12 feet from nose to tail and 7 feet tall from hoof to hump, which makes the buffalo the largest land mammal in North America," Chad reports. Impressive!

Don't think they're slow; in spite of their size, Chad tells me, buffalo are capable of clocking up to 35 miles per hour. "I've seen them jump a 6-foot fence from a standing stop; our corrals and fences have to be pretty sturdy," he says. "If they're happy, they stay put. But if they're agitated, they can rearrange things in a hurry!"

For the most part, the Custer herd roams 18,000 acres of rangeland in the totally fenced park. Chad tells me the herd, which is one of the nation's largest, currently totals about 1,200. Reduced to near extinction at the turn of the 20th century from an estimated 30–70 million just decades before, buffalo now number approximately 500,000 in North America. There are 200 fewer in the Custer herd than a couple years ago because of long-term drought conditions that have heartily reduced the quantity of native prairie grasses available for the buffalo to consume.

CLOCKWISE, FROM TOP LEFT: Fly-fishing paraphernalia. Sunbathing denizen, Custer State Park. Dan at Sylvan Lake Lodge. Dave Gamet and Dan fly-fishing below Pactola Reservoir.

LEFT TO RIGHT: (Both taken at Blue Bell Lodge Chuck Wagon Cookout) Cowhand sing-along fun. "Bandits" on a hayride.

I only wish I could be here in October for the legendary buffalo roundup, which draws up to 10,000 visitors to observe 30 horseback riders and two dozen vehicles driven by staff and volunteers gather the herd for branding, vaccinations and sorting (excess buffalo are auctioned for breeding or slaughter). Oh, and Chad does mention an interesting behavioral quirk about buffalo: "A beef cow will moo and such. A buffalo grunts and even roars. It's just amazing to hear, like an African lion, if it's a bull buffalo in rut in late July or early August."

Time to meet up back at Sylvan Lake Lodge with Jessie Y. Sundstrom, a lifelong Black Hills resident and former reporter who wound up running the local newspaper in Custer with her late husband, Carl, for 40 years. Nobody knows the history of the region like this plainspoken woman, who even wrote a book about area pioneers. Jessie whisks me off in her blue-and-white 1991 Buick LeSabre (200,000-plus miles and counting!) a few miles west of the park to the town of Custer (population 1,900) and the reconstructed Gordon Stockade on French Creek.

As we walk the path leading up to the imposing log fortress, Jessie tells the tale of the Gordon party, a band of 25 men, plus a woman and child, who trekked here from Sioux City, Iowa, after word quickly spread that Custer's men had discovered gold. The interlopers arrived in late December 1874 and endured a harrowing winter. Unfortunately, their surreptitious presence riled both the U.S. government (settlement of the hills had been banned by a treaty with the Lakota, which later, sadly but characteristically, was ignored) and a band of about 3,000 Lakota led by one Lame Antelope. Enter the U.S. Cavalry! Just in the nick of time, the Gordon group was "escorted" to safety at Fort Laramie, Wyoming.

As we poke around the six primitive cabins re-created inside the stockade, I ask Jessie about the biggest modern-day battles she's witnessed in the region. "It's been the environmental issues, first with lumbermen, then with developers. There are more development pressures than ever, thanks to tourism and retirees moving in, but that's resulted in more restrictions on land use, which is a good thing for the most part."

On to my final stop: Rustic Blue Bell Lodge, nestled near French Creek at the base of Mount Coolidge. Blue Bell was named for the once-familiar Bell System logo by a former phone company executive who founded the sort-of dude ranch before it became part of the park in 1935.

Rob and I don the red bandanas and cowboy hats provided and hop aboard a long wagon towed by a pickup truck. Yahoo! Time for a classic "hayride" and chuckwagon dinner. During the hour-long ramble down winding roads, mellow cowboy entertainer "Wild Rod" Rice leads our crew and several vacationing families in songs I haven't sung since grade school, including *Home on the Range, Happy Trails* and *She'll Be Comin' 'Round the Mountain*.

Finally, we arrive at a shelter in a remote canyon and disembark to feast on grilled sirloin, baked beans, warm corn bread, watermelon and cookies. I ask a fellow Custer State Park visitor from Colorado, "Why do you come here when you have the Rocky Mountains right in your own state?" His reply makes sense: "These mountains just seem friendly." Indeed, they do.

Dan's Travel Journal

FEATURED STOP

Custer State Park Custer. Slender granite formations called "needles" punctuate the skyline, and grassy meadows carpet the valleys of these 71,000 acres. Go mountain biking, horseback riding, rock climbing and fishing, or drive on the twisting Needles Highway or the 18-mile Wildlife Loop Road past bison or begging burros. Lodging choices include scenic campgrounds as well as historic lodges. Park naturalists lead nature walks, or you can watch stage shows at the Black Hills Playhouse (605/255-4515).

Lodging, Dining and More

Blue Bell Lodge Chuck Wagon Cookout Custer State Park, Custer. At this lodge with guest-ranchlike amenities, a hayride leads to a secluded canyon for a chuckwagon feast (800/658-3530).

Dakota Angler and Outfitter Rapid City. Attend a fly-fishing class, then book a guided half- or full-day fishing trip to Black Hills streams (605/341-2450).

State Game Lodge and Resort Custer State Park, Custer. Set in a mountain valley, stately lodge rooms, motel units, cabins and dining in the historic Pheasant Dining Room. Also, Buffalo Safari Jeep Tours originate here. $$–$$$$ (800/658-3530).

Sylvan Lake Lodge and Resort Custer State Park, Custer. Sylvan Lake is the hub at this historic resort with lodge rooms and secluded cabins. $$–$$$$ (800/658-3530).

Related Area Event

Custer State Park Buffalo Roundup Custer, late September or early October—Annual roundup of the park's 1,200 buffalo for vaccinations and branding (some are sold at auction the third Saturday in November), along with the Buffalo Roundup Arts Festival and Buffalo Wallow Chili Cookoff (605/255-4515).

More Information

Black Hills, Badlands & Lakes Association (605/355-3600, www.blackhills badlands.com).
South Dakota Tourism (800/732-5682, www.travelsd.com).

DAN'S OTHER STOPS

Badlands National Park Rapid City (605-355-3600), **Buffalo Interpretive Center** Five miles south of Lewis (888/323-2260), **Mount Rushmore National Memorial** Twenty miles southwest of Rapid City (605/574-2523), **Native American National Scenic Byway** Chamberlain to Fort Pierre (800/429-9297).

Lodging, Dining and More

Al's Oasis Oacoma. Along I-90 (between Sioux Falls and the Black Hills), this expansive family-run oasis bustles with a restaurant and an adjacent motel (605/234-6054).

Best Western Ramkota Hotel Pierre. Full-service hotel on the Missouri River, minutes from the state capitol and Lewis & Clark Trail. $$ (605/224-6877).

Circle 10 Campground and Café Cactus Flat. At the east entrance to Badlands National Park, owner Ellen Mulder cooks up not-so-modest fare (pork tenderloin with raspberry chipotle sauce, and praline cheesecake) in her 40-seat cafe. Also: motel units and campsites (800/231-3617).

Wall Drug Store Wall. The third generation of Husteads runs this 75-year-old drugstore-turned-mega-tourist-attraction along I-90 on the northern edge of the Badlands (605/279-2175).

Related Area Event

Lower Brule Powwow and Fair Lower Brule (60 miles southeast of Pierre), the second weekend of August—Powwow featuring hundreds of dancers, plus a weekend rodeo (605/473-5561).

TOP TO BOTTOM: Western kitsch at Wall Drug, Wall. Scaling new heights, Custer State Park.

More South Dakota Parks

Badlands National Park

You might think you've landed on another planet when you arrive at this 244,000-acre realm of knifelike spires and buttes (50 miles east of Rapid City). In this savagely beautiful land, steep canyons open at the base of broad, grass-capped mesas, and barren-looking rock pinnacles rise in shades of red, gray and pink. A good place to begin your tour is the Ben Reifel Visitor Center, featuring exhibits and a film about the area. In summer, naturalists tell about the park's rich fossil history.

You can reach the Badlands' paved 30-mile Loop Drive from I-90. Rangers recommend that novice hikers stick to the eight well-marked trails along the Badlands Loop Road. The longest and least used, Castle Trail, encompasses 10 fairly flat miles round-trip. For more challenge, backpackers head for the rugged Sage Creek National Wilderness Area.

Visitors can preview the park in half a day, but most want to stay longer. Within the park, you can pitch a tent at either of two campgrounds or stay in a cabin at Cedar Pass Lodge or a motel-style room at the Badlands Inn.

Contact: Badlands National Park (605/433-5361, nps.gov/badl). Nearest lodgings: along I-90 in Wall just northeast of the park (888/852-9255, wall-badlands.com) and in Rapid City (605/343-1744, rapidcitycvb.com).

Custer State Park
(See previous section of this chapter.)

George S. Mickelson Trail
In the heart of Black Hills National Forest, this 109-mile crushed-limestone pathway winds through deep pine forests, cuts past sheer granite drop-offs and skirts remote canyons and lakes. Thanks to the trail's gentle slopes and easy access, bicyclists of all ages and abilities can enjoy the beauty of the Black Hills.

Cycling, you'll cross more than 100 converted railroad bridges and travel through four hard-rock tunnels between the historic northern Black Hills town of Deadwood, where you can experience the Old West and walk in the footsteps of Wild Bill Hickok, and trail's end in Edgemont to the south. Along the way, be sure to watch for wildlife, including deer and wild turkeys, even elk. You can rent bikes in Deadwood. Every September, the trail draws hundreds of cyclists from across the nation for the annual Mickelson Trail Trek.

Contact: George S. Mickelson Trail (605/584-3896, www.mickelsontrail.com). Nearest lodgings: in Deadwood (605/578-1876, deadwood.org).

Harney Peak
A Lakota Sioux holy man called Harney Peak "the mountain at the center of the world." From the lookout on top, that's what this massive granite peak resembles. It's the highest point between the Rockies and the Alps (7,242 feet above sea level). In the Black Elk Wilderness at the eastern edge of the Black Hills, Harney Peak towers above mirror-smooth Sylvan Lake and 35,000 acres of forested hills. You can hike, mountain bike or drive through spectacular mountain scenery. Maintained trails and unmarked paths wind through the preserve to the peak's summit.

Trail No. 9, a four-mile-long gravel tract known as Harney's "main street," starts at Sylvan Lake. The 4-foot-wide path climbs about 1,000 feet up the gentler southwestern slope, amid spruces, aspens and pines. Parts of the two-hour trek are challenging,

Dan experiencing a solitary
moment in a secluded corner of
exotic Badlands National Park.

but 6-year-olds and octogenarians alike conquer the trail. Guided horseback outings provide another popular way to traverse the mountain.

Contact: Black Hills, Badlands & Lakes Association (605/355-3600, blackhills badlands.com). Nearest lodgings: Sylvan Lake Lodge (605/574-2561, custerresorts .com) and Palmer Gulch Resort at the foot of the peak, with options from upscale cabins to camping, plus guided horseback rides (800/562-8503, palmergulch.com).

Lewis & Clark State Recreation Area

Cliff swallows spiral on updrafts above emerald waters and golden beaches of Lewis & Clark Lake, created by the U.S. Army Corps of Engineers' Gavins Point Dam along the Missouri River (four miles west of Yankton). Catamarans skim past the lake's bluffs near where Lewis and Clark shared a peace pipe with the Yankton Sioux in 1804.

Named for the explorers, 1,250-acre Lewis & Clark State Recreation Area lies along the north shore of the 25-mile-long lake, which separates South Dakota and Nebraska. Lake waters draw boaters, swimmers and anglers. You can rent crafts, from canoes and pontoons to Jet Skis and fishing boats, at the recreation area marina.

Other activities include bicycling and hiking some five miles of wooded trails to bluff-top views. Visitors also test their skill at an archery range and tour the Gavins Point National Fish Hatchery and Aquarium a mile east of the lake. You can stay at campgrounds or in cabins at Lewis & Clark Resort within the recreation area or in a scattering of other cabins and campgrounds around the lake.

Contact: Lewis & Clark State Recreation Area (605/668-2985, lewisandclarklake .com). Lodgings: a variety of options in Yankton (800/888-1460, yanktonsd.com).

Native American National Scenic Byway

Travelers feel a connection with the Sioux Nation, driving this byway across windblown plains the Sioux still call home. Markers, monuments, museums and sacred sites reveal history from the Native American perspective. The byway extends 357 miles up South Dakota's midsection before crossing the state line into North Dakota (see "Lake Oahe," page 125). With views of the Missouri River en route, you'll journey through reservations of four Sioux tribes.

Near the Crow Creek Reservation, the Akta Lakota Museum in Chamberlain displays authentic Sioux handicrafts. Visitors can relax along the shore of Lake Sharpe in the town of Lower Brule between the Lower Brule and Crow Creek reservations. In Eagle River on the Cheyenne River Reservation, murals depict tribal life, and the cultural center displays and sells Sioux artisans' works. Tours through the Tribal Tourism Division immerse you in Native American culture. Plan to view the grave of Sioux chief Sitting Bull on the Standing Rock Reservation near Mobridge.

Contact: America's Byways (800/429-

9297, byways.org). South Dakota Office of Tourism (800/732-5682, travelsd.com). Tourism Division, Cheyenne River Sioux Tribe (605/964-7812, sioux.org). Nearest lodgings: in Chamberlain (605/234-4416, chamberlainsd.org), Pierre (605/224-7361, pierre.org) and Mobridge (605/845-2387, mobridge.org).

Sica Hollow State Park

Sioux legends tell of spirits that haunted the hollows of this former northeastern-South Dakota reservation (11 miles northwest of Sisseton). Today, mysterious bogs and woods at the 860-acre park have become the domain of hikers, mountain bikers, horseback riders and other day-trippers.

The park is part of the glacial moraine, an accumulation of glacial deposits, running the length of this prairie *coteau* (a massive dirt mound pushed ahead of a glacier 10,000 years ago). Longfellow called the area "Mountain of the Prairie" in his poem "Hiawatha." The Sioux named it Sica (SEEcha) Hollow, or Bad Hollow,

and believed the bogs consumed people and animals.

Hiking across bridges, creeks and springs on the half-mile Trail of the Spirits, a self-guided interpretive foot trail, takes you to the heart of the bogs. More than 15 miles of additional trails lead high above both sides of the moraine and 800 feet down to its bottom. Hardwoods mix with marsh marigolds and other wildflowers along the way. You can't camp in the park, except at a horse camp, but campers are welcome 12 miles southwest at Roy Lake State Park.

Contact: Sica Hollow and Roy Lake state parks (605/448-5701, sdgfp.info). Lodgings: in Sisseton (605/698-7261, sisseton.com).

Spearfish Canyon National Scenic Byway

One of the Midwest's most awe-inspiring drives (US-14A) slips between the sandstone and limestone cliffs of Spearfish Canyon at the northern edge of Black Hills National Forest not far from the Wyoming state line. Motorists and cyclists who travel

this 20-mile route south from the town of Spearfish play tag with the tumbling waters of Spearfish Creek along the floor of the winding canyon.

Sheer rock walls soar 1,000 feet above the stream, known for trout fishing. Aspens and birch punctuate steep slopes carpeted in spruce and pines. Spearfish Creek alternates between placid pools and rapids that plunge over rock ledges. You can pull over at turnoffs to ponder wonders such as Bridal Veil Falls.

Wildlife abounds, including deer, eagles and coyotes. The D.C. Booth Fish Hatchery in Spearfish details the history of trout introduced into the Black Hills by the U.S. Bureau of Fisheries in the 1800s. Along the byway, you can stop for a trout lunch or dinner at the historic Latchstring restaurant.

Contact: Black Hills, Badlands & Lakes Association (605/355-3600, blackhills badlands.com). Lodgings: Spearfish Canyon Lodge in the canyon (877/975-6343, spfcanyon.com); other options in Spearfish (800/626-8013, spearfish.chamber.org).

WISCONSIN

Aerial view of Devils Island looking southeast,
Apostle Islands National Lakeshore.

Exploring a pristine island archipelago

WHAT A GEM WISCONSIN IS—as green as any state you'll come across, in terms of both the landscape and the environmentally progressive outlook of its citizens. I'm setting out to explore its natural riches in the eastern part of the state at the Northern Unit of Kettle Moraine State Forest. Then I'm off to Point Beach State Park, halfway up the coast between Milwaukee and the tip of Door County. Final stop: my star Wisconsin parkland, a Lake Superior jewel that glistens in a league of its own. It's Apostle Islands National Lakeshore, which forms the state's wild, rocky and forested northernmost plume.

Kettle Moraine State Forest

I'm at a state forest that represents a living tribute to the glaciers of the last Ice Age, which aeons ago shaped our Midwest landscape so profoundly. Kettle Moraine even takes its name from two glacial landforms. The 29,000-acre forest is 35 miles long and 10 miles wide, about 20 miles from Sheboygan and Lake Michigan. I'm touring the Northern Unit, but there's also a smaller Southern Unit southwest of Milwaukee.

My host, Assistant Superintendent Jason Quast, and I rendezvous at the circular Henry Reuss Ice Age Visitors Center, named for the late U.S. representative who helped found the Ice Age Trail. "It's all about glaciers here," Jason says. I orient via a film,

Photography by John Noltner

informative exhibits, models of the landforms in question and a panoramic view from a curving deck in back.

Dense stands of hardwoods camouflage the curious, slowly eroding calling cards of two lobes of the retreating Wisconsin Glacier, which collided in slow motion here. That glacier, which covered most of the state from 100,000 to 10,000 years ago, was a player in the still-mysterious global Ice Age that began as many as 1 million years ago, an era that also left behind the Great Lakes and smaller inland lakes in Wisconsin and Minnesota. Back then, this tranquil terrain was ruled by bear-size beavers, woolly mammoths, mastodons and musk oxen.

Wisconsin's Ice Age connection also is recalled in 35 miles of the 1,000-mile Ice Age Trail—one of only eight national scenic trails—which will someday snake 1,000 miles between Green Bay and the Minnesota line. Its hook-shaped route, marked by yellow signs, each with a woolly mammoth emblem, denotes the debris-rich edges of the one-mile-thick blanket of ice that covered all but the state's southwest corner.

Jason and I are working our way from north to south through land interspersed with privately owned farms and homes. The area's crops are thriving in the rich glacial soil, which reaches depths of up to 800 feet. We're on the Kettle Moraine Scenic Drive, a 115-mile picturesque wonder that wends through both units of the forest and six Wisconsin counties on a variety of roads (look for the drive's green acorn-shaped signs). Along the way, visitors picnic, hike, bicycle, ride horseback, camp, swim, fish, hunt, visit historic sites and ponder the glacial remnants. Winter brings cross-country skiing, snowshoeing and snowmobiling on some of the forest's 133 miles of trails.

Jason explains kettles: Large blocks of ice broke off and were buried in glacial till. As the hidden ice melted, sinkholes up to 200 feet deep appeared. At secluded Greenbush Kettle Overlook—reached by climbing a whole lot of steps to the top of Parnell Tower—we see eskers (long, narrow ridges of glacial deposits), moraines (hills formed by glacial debris), erratics (seemingly misplaced boulders and rocks dropped by the glaciers) and kames (cone-shaped deposits created by swirling glacial meltwater—nearby Dundee Kame, for example).

We wrap up our tour at Mauthe Lake, near the south end of the Northern Unit. The popular recreational lake is named for William Mauthe, a Fond du Lac businessman and conservationist who, in the 1930s, initiated the flood-control project that became this lake, a top draw for the Northern Unit's estimated 1 million visitors annually. Before we part, Jason says, "I grew up near here. We studied glaciers in school, but we never visited the Kettle Moraine to see these formations. What a shame. Now I'm helping to correct that."

Point Beach State Forest

Just north of the tidy, contiguous communities of Manitowoc and Two Rivers (combined population 46,700), I roam Point Beach, founded in 1937, a state forest that's really more of a park in recreational terms. At 2,900 acres, it's Wisconsin's smallest state forest, yet it's easy to see why the 350,000 visitors that come here each year love it so.

This gentle bump on Wisconsin's relatively straight-line Lake Michigan coast offers six miles of uninterrupted shoreline, dense woods and sunny meadows, plus a lighthouse and loads of shipwreck lore. It's a favorite of those who hike its 11 miles of trails, camp in one of its 127 campsites that handle rigs from tents to elaborate RVs, hunt and fish its woods and waters and revel in the beach with its café au lait-colored sand.

Forest Manager Guy Willman, who's lived in the area all his life, squires me to the now-automated Rawley Point Lighthouse, a U.S. Coast Guard enclave encircled by the forest. The skeletal steel structure, a relic of the 1893 Chicago World's Fair, was moved here and reerected beside the treacherous shoals in 1894.

Over the decades, more than 60 "sinkings" have been recorded in the Point Beach area. Perhaps the most famous was that of the *Rouse Simmons,* also known as the "Christmas Tree Ship," which was on its way from Michigan's Upper Peninsula to Chicago with a cargo of fresh-cut trees when it went down, claiming 16 lives in November 1912. In 1971, divers rediscovered the wreck. Guy tells me that denuded Christmas trees still occasionally wash up onshore! I learn more about the subject later in Two Rivers at the Rogers Street Fishing Village and Great lakes Coast Guard Museum, a repository of Lake Michigan shipwreck exhibits and information.

Back to nature: "We have a unique combination of ecosystems in a relatively small area: beaches, dunes, forests and meadows. It's quite unusual," Guy tells me. "There's a microclimate here thanks to the lake, which keeps us about 10 degrees cooler in summer and 10 degrees warmer in winter."

That tempering results in a mix of deciduous trees and conifers usually seen farther north—red, jack and white pine; balsam, fir and hemlock (whose tannin-rich bark once supplied the area's leather-tanning industry); beach, red oak and aspen. The dunes nurture their own ecosystem, including the sand dune willow and dune thistle, an endangered species. Farther inland, Guy points out various prairie species such as big and little bluestem, black-eyed Susan and blazing star. "In just 100 yards here, you go

THIS PAGE: Kayakers probing mainland sea caves at Apostle Islands National Lakeshore. OPPOSITE PAGE, TOP TO BOTTOM: Bicycling a Kettle Moraine State Forest trail. Lake Michigan sunrise at Point Beach State Forest.

from dunes to prairie to forest," he says.

Birders stalk a variety of shorebirds, great blue herons, bald eagles, owls and endangered piping plovers. Woods teem with deer, coyotes, foxes and black bears. Offshore, lake trout and king salmon beckon anglers. Native Americans were drawn to this abundance as many as 3,000 years ago and left behind buried artifacts, including beads, fishhooks and stone tools. Much of their history is related in the park's rustic WPA (Works Progress Administration)-era visitors center. "We have a lot to offer, but our big selling point is that long beach," Guy says. "Campers come here and head for the beach just to lie back and stargaze or watch the sunrise in the morning."

thought to derive from early Jesuit missionaries. In the 1800s, an official unsuccessfully pressed to have the name changed to the Federation Islands.

The national lakeshore covers nearly 70,000 acres spread across 700 square miles. A third of it is water, the remainder a 12-mile-long strip of mainland and those velvety-green islands that appear to float on plates of red sandstone. At 140 miles in circumference, the islands range in size from Gull Island, barely three acres and mainly populated with shorebirds, to Stockton, seven miles long and loaded with recreation opportunities. Madeline, the most populated and largest, isn't part of the national lakeshore proper.

park—and abundant photo opportunities.

For years, the Apostles' remoteness inhibited development. Except for Ashland, 24 miles south of Bayfield, Minnesota's cities are closest: Duluth is 85 miles east, the Twin Cities 220 miles southeast. The area slumbered after lumbering and fishing declined in the early 1900s. Now the region's virginal natural charm is prized by up to 200,000 visitors annually. In 2004, 80 percent of the park was designated a wilderness area honoring the late Wisconsin Sen. Gaylord Nelson (1916–2005). Nelson was the environmental advocate and founder of Earth Day who, along with President John F. Kennedy and others, helped establish the national lakeshore in 1969.

I'm starting out at the national lakeshore visitor center in Bayfield, a former county courthouse built in 1883 of locally quarried brownstone. Here, I meet with Neil Howk, the park's assistant chief of interpretation and education. Neil has been here since 1983, and he and his wife operate a bed and breakfast in the area. We head northwest on State-13 to the Lakeshore Trail near the village of Cornucopia (population 210).

Soon we're tramping through a North Country Eden, up and down a rocky trail toward the big lake. The fern-carpeted woods (eight species thrive here) seem tropically lush in the misty rain. Trees here and on the islands include regrowth eastern hemlock, sugar and red maple, yellow and white birch, oak and ash. Shrubs include Canada dogwood, blueberry and Canada yew (the latter only on the islands; deer decimate them on the mainland).

Not all the flora is wild. Neil explains that Bayfield Peninsula calls itself "Wisconsin's Berry Capital." Thanks to the climate-tempering lake effect, mainland growers raise bumper crops of blueberries, raspberries and strawberries, as well as apples, cherries and pears. Fresh-cut and dried

Even though they're called the Apostles (as in the 12 disciples), there are 22 islands in the archipelago all told.

Apostle Islands Lakeshore

Through the centuries, the islands that spangle the Great Lakes have afforded voyageurs safe havens from enemies and storms. They've served as way stations for trappers and anglers and surrendered timber riches to loggers. Each is unique: remote Beaver Island near the top of Lake Michigan, genteel Mackinac Island in the straits between lakes Michigan and Huron, Lake Superior's wild Isle Royale and history-rich Kelleys Island in Lake Erie.

I'm heading north from Ashland (population 8,300), at the foot of Lake Superior's Chequamegon Bay, to Bayfield, my mainland base for exploring the Apostle Islands, arguably the most scenic and unspoiled cluster of all Great Lakes islands. Even though they're called the Apostles (as in the 12 disciples), there are 22 islands in the archipelago all told. The appellation is

Besides being appreciated by those Jesuits and the native Ojibwe (who considered the islands sacred), as well as the voyageurs, fur trappers and traders, loggers and commercial anglers, this comparatively calm corner of tempestuous Lake Superior has been a favorite of tourists. Vacationers thrill at sailing, boating and kayaking the islands and the sandstone cliffs, caves and beaches that rim them. The interior of the islands reveals reminders of bygone inhabitants: logging camps, fishing communities and farmsteads.

As one of America's premier sailing getaways, the Apostles draw bird-watchers and wildlife watchers, hikers, divers and lighthouse lovers. They feature more than 50 miles of trails, camping on all but three of the islands, 18 known shipwrecks for scuba divers to discover, six 19th-century lighthouses—more than in any other national

CLOCKWISE, FROM TOP LEFT: (All taken at Apostle Islands National Lakeshore area) Map showing Madeline, the largest, and other islands. Hillside Bayfield and its picturesque harbor. Sailing the Apostles. Julian Bay beach, Stockton Island.

LEFT TO RIGHT: (All taken at Apostle Islands National Lakeshore area) Rocky shoreline near the Sand Island Lighthouse. Fern-carpeted pine forest, Stockton Island. Ferryboat making the mainland–Madeline Island run.

flowers also are a thriving industry.

We arrive at the edge of a 60-foot cliff composed of highly eroded, billion-year-old sandstone. Up the coast, I can see caves, arches and crevices exposed by aeons of glacial scouring and wave action. The lake itself is shimmering blue-green. Superior can be a chameleon: I've noticed she also can appear jade green, slate blue and a forbidding gray at various locations, depending on the depth and sunshine.

Once there were saber-toothed cats, cave-dwelling lions, mammoths and mastodons in the area. It's a lot tamer now. "We have 150 species of migratory birds and 100 types that nest here, including gulls, herons, cormorants and bald eagles," Neil says. "Smaller birds that rest in the area during their spring and fall migrations include sparrows, warblers, woodpeckers and thrushes. Our mammals include black bears, white-tailed deer, coyotes, timber wolves and red squirrels." Neil says the mammals on the islands frequently are swimmers, like the black bear. Fish include commercially fished whitefish, lake trout and herring, as well as sport fish found in shallower waters,

such as smallmouth bass, northern pike and chub.

Across the lake, Minnesota's cliff-top Split Rock Lighthouse perches 25 miles northwest; although I can't see it, I make out the faint hint of several islands that seem to beckon me offshore.

I return to my harbor-side condo unit (varied accommodation options in the area also include charming inns, bed and breakfasts, motels and entire houses) to change into dry clothes. Although not within the national lakeshore boundary, Bayfield (population 610) is the gateway to the Apostles, and the plucky village is marking its 150th anniversary in 2006. Early investors hoped the town, sheltered from Lake Superior's wrath by the Apostles, would become what Duluth is today; however, shipping-rich Duluth (population 87,000) at the far western tip of Lake Superior got the crown, and Bayfield declined and slumbered.

Bayfield has a bracing nautical ambience rarely experienced in the Midwest. Victorian homes and churches spill down hillsides toward the lake, and there's a busy harbor. I'm told development is a hot

issue here. Dave Strzok, author of an in-for-mative Apostle Islands travel guide, is waiting for me at the Bayfield Maritime Museum down by the docks. Cleverly housed in a building that stores sailboats in winter (when the exhibits get packed away), the nonprofit museum illuminates a range of topics related to boatbuilding, nautical crafts, commercial fishing, shipwrecks, light-houses and more.

A former central-Wisconsin high school teacher who moved here in 1972, Dave operates the Apostle Islands Cruise Service, one of several Bayfield enterprises offering visitors narrated tours, shuttles and water taxis. We talk about Bayfield's past, present and future. "We have to keep the special atmosphere," Dave says. "That's what attracts people." What islands are this expert's favorites? "Stockton—it has six miles of beaches. But I also love Sand Island for its lighthouse and natural beauty, and Outer Island for its remoteness."

My hike and Bayfield's "sea air" have aroused my appetite, and I stroll up the hill to the 1890 Old Rittenhouse Inn, an imposing Queen Anne mansion. This has to be

one of the Midwest's most photogenic inns: cream-colored brick, wine-red shingles, yellow trim and a profusion of hanging flowers all abloom. The Phillips family arrived here in 1974, and their inn soon won a national following. The award-winning restaurant opened in 1976. Today, the Phillipses operate five guest properties in Bayfield, with 25 rooms all told. In the opulently restored dining room, Innkeeper Jerry Phillips explains that the house was built by a General Fuller from Illinois, one of those early investors who'd earned his "general" title by heading a draft commission during the Civil War.

Fuller's summer home now entices guests year-round with a smorgasbord of themed weekends dedicated to wine and beer, chocolate, antiques and all types of music. And, oh, the food! Even breakfast is a treat, with specialties such as smoked-trout scramble, lamb sausage and Cinnamon French Toast with Apricot-Riesling Sauce (see recipe, page 170). (By the way, in the Bayfield breakfast department, I also can vouch for the delectable blueberry pancakes at Gruenke's, an 1865 restaurant, tavern and lodging establishment downtown.)

On the Water, at Last!

With 3 quadrillion gallons of sloshing water, 350-mile-long, restless Lake Superior is more of an ocean than a lake. The largest of the Great Lakes, it contains 10 percent of the world's freshwater and plummets to a startling maximum depth of 1,333 feet (it's 500 feet at its deepest in the sheltered Apostles). Untamed shores lap and snarl at the edges of Wisconsin, Minnesota, Michigan and Ontario, Canada. Superior's elevation, 602 feet above sea level, is the Great Lakes' highest, meaning its cold waters course through all four sister lakes, eventually reaching the Atlantic via the St. Lawrence Seaway. Scientists have somehow calculated it takes 191 years for the lake to completely "turn over," which means I'll be dipping my paddle into water molecules dating to 1815!

Mary Motiff of the local tourism office has lined up a full schedule for our crew: a motorboat tour, a kayaking expedition, a sailing adventure and a ferryboat ride under the stars to cap off our day. Our excursion starts at the harbor with Dave Locey, a former Twin Cities businessman who now

owns SeaFare charters. Like so many Apostles residents, Dave vacationed here, bought a condo, then retired with his wife Annie in 2000. I admire his passion for the North Coast Community Sailing Club, a nonprofit volunteer organization that teaches kids ages 9–13 about sailing and safe boating.

We board *Annie's Great Gatsby*, a 30-footer Dave refers to as a "picnic boat," and begin at a pace of 25 knots (about 28 mph). We'll thread the passages among Madeline, Michigan, Manitou, Stockton, Oak, Bear, Raspberry and Sand islands. "Lake Superior can be rough," Dave says. But here in the Apostles, "there's always someplace to hide if a wind comes up. You can always find an empty beach or hike an island or just enjoy a swim."

First we circle the southeast side of 14-mile-long Madeline Island, which has about 700 summer and year-round homes. We glimpse the beach at Madeline's popular Big Bay State Park, then head to Michigan Island. Dave docks the boat at the base of a 123-step concrete staircase at the foot of a bluff. At the top, I'm greeted by resident volunteers Doris and Max Loudenslager of

Cinnamon French Toast with Apricot-Riesling Sauce

Hungry vacationers and local residents in Bayfield head for Old Rittenhouse Inn. At this Victorian gem, Executive Chef David Miller wows the guests with this scrumptious French toast served with Chef Mark Wolslegel's sweet-tart sauce.

4 eggs
1 cup milk
¼ cup sugar
½ teaspoon vanilla
8 1-inch-thick slices cinnamon-swirl bread
2 tablespoons butter
 Apricot-Riesling Sauce (recipe follows)

In a shallow bowl, beat together eggs, milk, sugar and vanilla with a whisk. Dip bread slices into egg mixture, coating both sides.

In a 12-inch skillet or on a griddle, melt 1 tablespoon of butter over medium heat; add half of bread slices. Cook for 2 minutes or until golden brown. Flip each slice and cook for 2 minutes more or until golden brown. Repeat with remaining butter and bread slices. Top with Apricot-Riesling Sauce. *Makes 4 servings.*

Apricot-Riesling Sauce: In a small saucepan, bring 1½ cups Riesling wine or sweet white wine, ¼ cup sugar, 2 tablespoons lemon juice and 2 inches stick cinnamon to boiling; reduce heat, stirring to dissolve sugar. Simmer, uncovered, about 20 minutes or until mixture is reduced to ½ cup. Remove stick cinnamon; discard. Add 6 medium apricots, peeled, pitted and sliced, or stir in one 15-ounce can of apricot halves, drained and sliced. Remove saucepan from heat; let apricot mixture stand for 5 minutes before serving. Makes 2 cups sauce.

Tip: If you wish, substitute 1-inch-thick slices of white bread (Texas toast) and add 1 teaspoon ground cinnamon to the egg mixture. Continue as directed.

Kirkwood, a St. Louis, Missouri, suburb. The recently retired Loudenslagers are experiencing six weeks of relative isolation here at Michigan Island, helping with maintenance, giving lighthouse tours and assisting campers.

"We have two lighthouses, just yards apart," Doris tells me. The 64-foot white-washed stone-and-stucco original was built in 1857, but on the wrong island; it was intended for Long Island, another of the Apostles. Its successor is Wisconsin's tallest lighthouse at 112 feet. "It's an 1880 skeletal-frame metal lighthouse that was shipped here in 1919 from a site on the Delaware near Philadelphia," Doris explains.

Next we visit the keeper's cottage, where Doris and Max reside. From the outside, it's an attractive brick house that easily could fit into any older Midwest neighborhood. Inside, there's limited electricity and no hot water, laundry or indoor toilets. Drinking water has to be pumped up from the lake and filtered. The Loudenslagers hitch a boat ride to Bayfield every couple of weeks during their stint to shop and enjoy hot showers. Despite the no-frills lifestyle, Doris and Max tell me they love their annual island volunteering escape.

We bid farewell and soon nose past a watery island world of sandstone cliffs, dense green forests and terra-cotta-colored beaches. These waters are uncrowded, and bathers enjoy the shallow shelves that extend off some of the islands. After a lunch stop at the visitor center on Stockton Island, we note a bobbing buoy that marks the resting place of a lumber boat that sank in 12 feet of water in 1905.

Dave points out several sites with abandoned quarries whose brownstone helped rebuild Chicago after the 1871 fire, as well as Milwaukee, Saint Paul and other Upper Midwest cities that boomed in the late 1800s. We pass large Oak Island, with

its popular hiking trails and, at 1,100 feet above sea level, the Apostle's highest point. At Raspberry Island, an 1863 light station is being renovated.

Near the Meyers Beach kayak-launch area, Dave idles the motor, and Eager Assistant Rob and I gingerly hop into a tandem kayak that's been towed to our boat by Gail Green, who, with her husband Grant Herman, operates Living Adventure Inc., a kayak outfitter. As we secure our life jackets, Gail, clearly an infectious optimist, says, "Sorry we don't have time to train you on the beach, but it's going to be great!" I'm tentative at first, but soon we're bobbing along like seasoned veterans.

Gail relocated here from the Twin Cities and has been a kayaker for 20 years and a kayaking teacher for 15. "These are sea kayaks. They're much more stable than the river-running kind and better than canoes in these waters," she says. "Kayaking is more about finesse than strength, so it's for both men and women and people of all ages and abilities [later, I note a returning kayaker on the beach being assisted back to his wheelchair]. Just remember to try to stay in sync and use your whole upper body, not just your arms."

Any lingering apprehensions dissipate at the incredible sight before me: a water's eye view of that sandstone cliff we hiked atop earlier, pockmarked with caves, passages and arches, several of which we paddle under. The green-tinged water and clay-colored rocks mesmerize me, but it's soon time to reboard Dave's boat and head to our next adventure. First, I ask Gail what she loves about kayaking here. "It's the mystique of being able to island-hop. You see an island off in the distance and just paddle to it, explore it and then head to another."

Back in Bayfield, I join a vacationing Madison acquaintance, Gary Knowles, and his family in boarding the 34-foot *Esprit,* a

CLOCKWISE, FROM TOP LEFT: (All taken at Apostle Islands National Lakeshore area) La Pointe Light on Long Island. Big Bay Township Park, Madeline Island. Kayakers skirting a rocky shore.

Car ferry between Bayfield and Madeline Island.

charter sailboat that sleeps six, captained by John Thiel. John and his wife Mary operate Dreamcatcher Sailing Charters, as well as leading dogsledding expeditions in winter.

John maneuvers us out of the harbor, and we ply the waters to Basswood, the midsize island closest to Bayfield. John has been sailing all his life. A native of Fond du Lac, he's lived here for 13 years and been a U.S. Coast Guard-licensed captain for nine. He and Mary offer their clients half-day, all-day or even weeklong cruises. John assigns us a variety of tasks: manning the wheel, hoisting the mainsail, unfurling the jib, turning the sails in and out, cranking the winch. "It's a lot more fun when everybody gets involved, hands-on," he says. How true!

At a leisurely 6 mph, we nose toward Basswood. As we get farther into the passage, the water morphs from greenish blue to metallic gray. John tells me the water temperature today is about 68 degrees. "That's much warmer than the main body of Lake Superior, which averages about 40 degrees year-round." What does John love about the Apostles? "The sea caves, the beaches, the lighthouses. These islands are just so pristine. Sometimes I feel like I'm the first person who ever set foot on one."

Ferrying to Madeline

Our Saturday-night farewell to the Apostle Islands starts back at the dock in Bayfield, where we board the car ferry for Madeline Island, three miles and 20 minutes distant. I'm thrilled to be invited into the pilothouse by Captain Matthew Olson of Ashland. After my customary round of questions— How many cars can you handle? 25. What speed are we going? About 10 miles per hour. How many passengers, tops? 149— Matthew even lets me take the wheel under his vigilant eye.

"We have four ferries running back and forth. Most of our passengers are Madeline Island day-trippers," says Matthew, who's been a ferry captain for four years. "It can get pretty rough out here in November, with those storms from the northeast. In fact, we had some impressive waves during a storm just last week. Safety is always my top concern. Still, we only get shut down by weather three or four days a season."

We disembark at the ferry landing in La Pointe, a cozy collection of vintage homes, cottages, frame churches—and most of Madeline Island's eateries and bars. Madeline has about 250 year-round residents and up to 10 times that number during the busy summer season. (In winter, people drive and windsurf the frozen passage to Bayfield, ice conditions permitting.) Thanks to our tour with Dave Locey, we've already viewed much of Madeline's shoreline. Next time, I'll explore Big Bay State Park and the island's historical museum. Oh, and the island's elegant name? It's the Christian appellation of an Ojibwe chief's daughter who married a French fur trader.

After our brief ferry ride, we make our way to Lotta's ("lotta" food, "lotta" fun), an upscale yet resort-town-friendly dining spot where I sample a signature whitefish taco and blueberry cobbler dessert. Back at the dock awaiting our ferry ride home, I simply lie on my back to gaze up at the sky—the stars are amazing on this clear night! And so are the Apostle Islands!

Dan's Travel Journal

FEATURED STOP

Apostle Islands National Lakeshore Off the Bayfield Peninsula at the northernmost point in Wisconsin. Twenty-one islands and a narrow 12-mile strip on the mainland comprise this remote Lake Superior haven. Camping is allowed on 18 islands, and hikers can explore more than 50 miles of trails, some leading to century-old logging camps, fishing camps or brownstone quarries. Lighthouses still stand tall on a half-dozen islands. The most accessible, Raspberry Island Lighthouse, offers guided tours from mid-June to September. Visitors get to the islands by sailboat, powerboat, sea kayak, water taxi or cruise boat. Information and maps available at park headquarters in Bayfield (715/779-3397) and at seasonal visitor centers in Little Sand Bay (13 miles northwest of Bayfield) and on Stockton Island.

Lodging, Dining and More

Apostle Island Rentals Bayfield. Rentals at six condominium properties, including Reiten Boatyard on the lakeshore. $$$–$$$$ (800/842-1199).

Apostle Islands Cruise Service Bayfield. Scenic cruises and shuttles to the Apostle Islands. For an overview, take the three-hour narrated Grand Tour through the islands, past lighthouses and sea caves (800/323-7619).

Bayfield Maritime Museum Bayfield. Exhibits cover 150 years of Bayfield's rich maritime heritage, including lighthouses, shipwrecks, boatbuilding traditions, commercial fishing and boats (715/779-3925).

Bayfront Inn Bayfield. Private decks overlook Lake Superior at this 10-room waterfront motel adjacent to Pier Plaza restaurant. $$ (888/243-4191).

Blue Horizons Cafe Bayfield. A favorite morning stopover for coffee drinks and fresh-baked scones, cinnamon rolls and homemade granola (715/779-9619).

Dreamcatcher Sailing Charters and Wolfsong Adventures in Mushing Bayfield. Half-day, all-day and overnight sailing cruises among the Apostles. In winter, experience a daylong dogsledding adventure (800/262-4176).

Greunke's First Street Inn Bayfield. A boardinghouse in the late 1800s, the gray clapboard inn books guests in 12 quaint rooms and serves walnut-breaded trout and deep-fried whitefish livers in its restaurant (traditional fish boil served on patio in summer). $$–$$$ (800/245-3072).

Living Adventure Inc. Bayfield. On guided sea kayak trips, paddle past shipwrecks on half-day outings and sea caves on full-day outings, or opt for overnight kayaking adventures (from one to six nights). Also rent a kayak for paddling on your own (866/779-9503).

Lotta's Lakeside Café Madeline Island. An upscale bistro with ever-changing menu items (nut-encrusted lake trout is always a hit) using fresh ingredients supplied by local farmers and anglers (715/747-2033).

Madeline Island Ferry Line La Pointe. Car, bicycle and passenger ferry between the towns of LaPointe on Madeline Island and Bayfield (715/747-2051).

Maggie's Bayfield. This 27-year-old icon serves lunch and dinner (pizza, burgers, steak and fresh whitefish and trout) in a bright pink-and-yellow building bedecked inside with flamingos galore (715/779-5641).

Old Rittenhouse Inn Bayfield. At this late-19th-century Victorian mansion, stay in one of 12 antiques-filled guest rooms (some with fireplaces, whirlpools and views of Lake Superior), and dine on creative regional cuisine at the inn's restaurant. Other nearby Rittenhouse accommodations include a Victorian home, a guesthouse and two cottages. $$$–$$$$ (715/779-5111).

Rogers Street Fishing Village and Great Lakes Coast Guard Museum Two Rivers (920/793-5905).

SeaFare Bayfield. Custom boating excursions among the islands (715/779-5275).

Superior Rentals Bayfield. Choose from beachside cottages and houses (rent individual rooms or a whole house). $$$–$$$$ (866/779-5123).

What Goes 'Round Bayfield. Locally owned bookstore with 25,000 new and used books in stock, including titles about Lake Superior-area history, shipwrecks, lighthouses and nature (877/779-5223).

Related Area Events

Apostle Islands Lighthouse Celebration Bayfield, three weeks in September beginning the Wednesday after Labor Day—Special narrated lighthouse cruises and, on the islands, hikes and lighthouse tours (800/779-4487).

"Bayfield in Bloom" Festival Bayfield, mid-May to the end of June—A celebration of the area's blooming wildflowers and fruit trees, featuring gardening activities and lectures, plant sales, orchard and garden tours and entertainment (800/447-4094).

Big Top Chautauqua Bayfield, mid-June to early September—A summer season of 70 shows starring top national entertainers, historical musicals and variety acts, all under the big top (888/244-8368).

More Information

Bayfield Chamber of Commerce (800-447-4094, www.bayfield.org).

Manitowoc Area Visitor & Convention Bureau (800/627-4896, www.manitowoc.info).

Wisconsin Department of Tourism (800/432-8747, www.travelwisconsin.com).

DAN'S OTHER STOPS

(See also More Parks section that follows.) **Kettle Moraine State Forest, Northern Unit** (262/626-2116), **Point Beach State Forest** (920/794-7480).

More Wisconsin Parks

Apostle Islands National Lakeshore
(See previous section of this chapter.)

Buckhorn State Park
Just off the trail, sunlight floods a marsh where a doe stands knee-deep in the still water. A blue jay dives, and the deer disappears into the trees with a splash. This is Buckhorn State Park, a wilderness peninsula along the Wisconsin River, with 15,000 acres of water and seven miles of shore flanking it on three sides (about 75 miles east of La Crosse).

The park's 3,000-plus acres of prairie and mixed oak-and-pine forests conceal more than 40 walk-in campsites, plus 11 you can drive to. Transporting gear into most walk-in sites is easy. You load it into bicycle-wheeled carts you push or pull on wide paths. Backpackers can hike into eight sites. After setting up camp, lounge on the beach, fish or stroll marked nature trails. Along the park's eastern edge, an interpretive canoe trail circles an island (boat launch available). You will probably spot herons and otters and hear songbirds.

Contact: Buckhorn State Park (608/565-2789, wiparks .net). Nearest lodgings: limited in Necedah and New Lisbon north and southwest of the park, respectively (608/847-1904, juneau county tourism.com); more options 15 miles south in Mauston (608/847-4142, mauston.com).

Chequamegon-Nicolet National Forest
This 1.5 million-acre forest hopscotches the northern third of the state amid true Wisconsin North Woods. Dense forest surrounds hundreds of rivers and lakes. Five miles of the Peshtigo River attract rafters and kayakers. The Popple and Pine, state-designated wild rivers, supply spurts of rapids. Canoeists favor the Brule and Pine rivers for longer trips, camping along the banks (some canoe liveries).

More than 400 miles of hiking trails include segments of the Ice Age National Scenic Trail near Medford and North Country National Scenic Trail near Ashland, where you'll find the forest's visitors center. A 300-mile mountain-biking network runs in and around the forest. You can see 40 feet down to bottoms of lakes such as five-mile-long Lac Vieux Desert at the Wisconsin River's headwaters. Most of nearly 50 campgrounds cluster beside fishing lakes, many with beaches. Scenic drives crisscross the forest.

Contact: Chequamegon-Nicolet National Forest (715/762-2461 or 715/362-1300, fs.fed.us/r9/cnnf). Nearest lodgings: cottages and small resorts within the forest; other options nearby in Ashland (800/248-9484, visitashland.com), Eagle River (800/359-6315, eagleriver.org), Hayward (800/724-2992, haywardlakes.com), Medford (888/682-9567, medfordwis.com) and Park Falls (800/762-2709, park falls.com).

Copper Falls State Park
As it meanders to Lake Superior, the Bad River plunges into a steep canyon at Copper Falls. Just as spectacular, Brownstone Falls, Red Granite Falls and stair-stepped Tyler Forks also surge through this undiscovered 3,100-acre northwestern Wisconsin state park (25 miles southeast of Ashland). For some of the best views of the falls and the park, hike the nearly two-mile Doughboys' Nature Trail. Follow the trail along sheer cliffs and down 70 steps to the river. Other hiking, backpacking and mountain-biking trails meander among hardwood forests, marshes, gorges and beaver ponds. Trails also connect with the North Country National Scenic Trail, which extends nearly the entire length of the park.

Swimmers, anglers and canoeists head for Loon Lake. You can fish for trout, too, in the copper-colored waters of the Tyler Forks and Bad rivers. Two campgrounds provide more than 50 sites. Some visitors prefer the solitude of primitive backpack sites.

Contact: Copper Falls State Park (715/274-5123, wiparks.net). Lodgings: limited two miles south in Mellen (715/274-2330, mellenwi.org); more options in Ashland (800/284-9484, visitashland.com).

Door County Parklands

Green Bay and Lake Michigan caress this sliver of land, popular with vacationers for more than a century (130 miles north of Milwaukee). Beyond resort towns on the peninsula's bay side, you can escape to two Lake Michigan state parks, plus an island off the peninsula's tip.

Midway along the eastern shore, Whitefish Dunes State Park's nearly 900 acres rarely are crowded. The park harbors Wisconsin's highest dunes. You can fish and visit the nature center. Bring a picnic and spend the day on the beach (no camping). Farther north, 30 miles of hiking trails traverse rocky shore, dunes and woods at 2,400-acre Newport State Park (no cars permitted). Visitors canoe and kayak or backpack and mountain bike into 16 campsites. From Northport, ferries shuttle to four-mile-long Washington Island. Hop another ferry there for the 10-minute ride to supreme seclusion at Rock Island State Park, encompassing the entire forested island. Camping, fishing, and hiking are prime pastimes (no cars or bicycles permitted).

Contact: Newport State Park (920/854-2500, dcty.com/Newport or wiparks.net). Rock Island State Park (920/847-2235, wiparks.net). Whitefish Dunes State Park (920/823-2400, wiparks.net). Lodgings: throughout the peninsula, including along Lake Michigan in Bailey's Harbor and Jacksonport (920/743-4456, doorcounty.com).

Elroy-Sparta State Trail

In a state known for its trails along abandoned railroad beds, Elroy-Sparta, the nation's first rail-trail, spans 32 miles of wooded valleys, rural countryside and small towns in two west-central Wisconsin counties. The trail ranks among the most popular bicycling destinations in Wisconsin, which boasts more than 1,000 miles of rail-trails.

From Elroy, a community of 1,600 (about 60 miles northwest of Madison), the trail runs northwest to the county seat of Sparta. Bicycle tires hum on the hard-packed limestone surface as you sail by silos, campgrounds, farmhouses and small towns. Three century-old stone railroad tunnels add cool mystery to the easy ride. Plan to stop at trail headquarters in a restored historic train depot in Kendall, with bike rentals and drop-off service along the trail (May–October). Bikes fill the rack outside Gina's Pies Are Square in Wilton.

Contact: Elroy-Sparta State Trail (608/463-7109, elroy-sparta-trail.com). Nearest lodgings: in communities along the trail (contact above).

Great River Road National Scenic Byway

Cradled between bluffs and the Mississippi, this 250-mile route follows Wisconsin's southwestern border. You'll travel from just south of the Twin Cities at Prescott to the Illinois state line. Towns hug the bluffs and squeeze between hills. Historic buildings house shops and restaurants in communities such as Stockholm, Fountain City, Trempealeau and Prairie du Chien. A car ferry crosses the river in Cassville, once a frontier outpost, with a riverside park for picnicking.

Bluffs and bends make the drive a delight. You'll also see boats and barges easing through locks. Between Alma and Bay City, the Mississippi widens into Lake Pepin, a 25-mile-long boaters haven. Islands dot the river below Alma, where the main street parallels Lock No. 4. You'll pass parks, including Merrick State Park, with backwater bayous for boating, fishing and birdwatching. The Mississippi and Wisconsin rivers meet at Wyalusing State Park. Don't

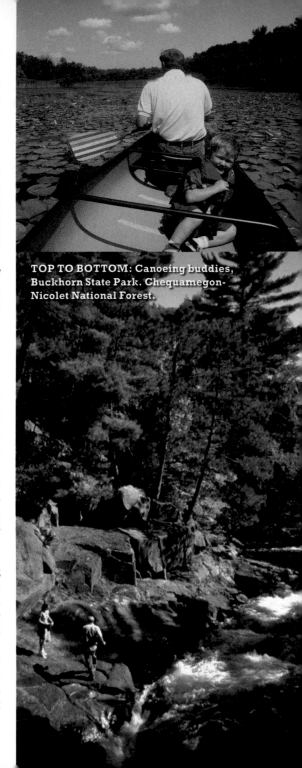

TOP TO BOTTOM: Canoeing buddies, Buckhorn State Park. Chequamegon-Nicolet National Forest.

LEFT TO RIGHT: Bicycling on the Elroy-Sparta State Trail. Peninsula State Park, Door County. Wyalusing State Park, overlooking the confluence of the Mississippi and Wisconsin rivers.

miss the burial mounds and river views at Nelson Dewey State Park. Nearby Stonefield Village State Historic Site re-creates a yesteryear settlement and farmstead.

Contact: Great River Road National Scenic Byway (800/429-9297, wigreatriverroad .org). Lodgings: all along the route (800/432-8747, travelwisconsin.com), including in the largest community, La Crosse (800/658-9424, explorelacrosse.com).

Horicon Marsh

Like ribbons streaming across the rosy evening sky, Canada geese and ducks by the hundreds of thousands wing above Horicon National Wildlife Refuge and adjacent Horicon Marsh State Wildlife Area (60 miles northwest of Milwaukee). The combined national refuge and state-managed marsh area—14 miles long and five miles wide—ranks as the nation's largest freshwater cattail marsh. On the 50-mile drive around Horicon's perimeter, you also might spot sandhill cranes, white pelicans, egrets and herons sharing their domain with muskrats, foxes and river otters. For close-up views,

hike the five miles of trails or bicycle the 34-mile Wild Goose State Trail.

Three small communities, Horicon, Mayville and Waupun, anchor the area. Visitors can board pontoons in Horicon for tours or rent canoes and kayaks. Early mornings and late afternoons mid-September through mid-November are prime viewing times. Just north of the area, the Marsh Haven Nature Center includes an art gallery, museum and nature program.

Contact: Horicon National Wildlife Refuge (920/387-2658, fws.gov/midwest/ horicon). Horicon Marsh State Wildlife Area(920/387-7860,dnr.state.wi.us/org/land/ wildlife/reclands/horicon). Marsh Haven Nature Center (920/324-5818, marshhaven .com). Nearest lodgings: in Horicon (920/ 485-3200, horiconchamber.com), Mayville (800/256-7670, mayvillechamber.com) and Waupun (920/324-3491, waupunchamber. com).

Kettle Moraine State Forest

In this nearly 52,000-acre eastern Wisconsin preserve, hiking and mountain-biking

trails dip and twist across miles of moraines. The larger Northern and Southern units dominate the forest's four areas, spanning three counties from 45 miles northwest to 35 miles southwest of Milwaukee. Paths lead atop hills and ridges, rising improbably from surrounding farmland. You can see for miles. The forest also shelters kettles formed by melting ice chunks. A combined 35 miles of mountain-biking trails in the two units climb through forests, then whoosh down into cool valleys. Easier trails wind through wildflower meadows.

Glaciers also scoured troughs that formed spring-fed lakes. Favorites for fishing and canoeing include Mauthe and Long lakes in the Northern Unit and Whitewater and Rice in the Southern Unit. In each unit, hiking trails encompass at least 30 miles of the Ice Age National Scenic Trail, plus other loops and paths. The Southern Unit's Stony Ridge Trail skirts a glasslike kettle. Visitors centers provide maps and information about campgrounds.

Contact: Kettle Moraine State Forest, Northern Unit (262/626-2116, wiparks

.net); Southern Unit (262/594-6200, wi parks.net). Lodgings: Northern Unit, in West Bend (888/338-8666, wbachamber .org); Southern Unit, in Delafield (888/294-1082, delafield-wi.org) and Mukwonago (262/363-7758, mukwonagochamber.org).

Lake Winnebago
Summer vacationers zoom past Wisconsin's largest inland lake to places farther north. But Lake Winnebago fans say those travelers don't know what they're missing at this east-central Wisconsin water playground, which covers more than 200 square miles (60 miles northwest of Milwaukee).

Along the less-developed eastern shore, nearly 1,200-acre High Cliff State Park and smaller Calumet County Park provide access to the lake beyond the larger communities at both ends and along its western shore. Cornfields, red barns and clover fields mix with parks and harbors on the quieter east side. Vacationers can camp, swim, fish and launch boats at both parks, where history and geology buffs explore the effigy mounds. Hiking and bicycling trails highlight dramatic rock formations known as the Niagara Escarpment. From limestone bluffs, High Cliff State Park provides lofty views. But don't miss getting out on the water to swim or fish in a bay.

Contact: Calumet County Park (920/439-1008, www.co.calumet.wi.us). High Cliff State Park (920/989-1106, wiparks.net). Nearest lodgings: along the eastern shore in Stockbridge and Chilton (888/576-9196, www.co.calumet.wi.us).

Point Beach State Forest
Looking for a treasure? You'll find it at this gem of a state forest jutting into Lake Michigan in northeastern Wisconsin (10 miles northwest of Manitowoc). Besides roaming six miles of sand and dunes, some beachcombers discover real treasure washed up from 26 sunken ships. The forest's Rawley Point Lighthouse, a 113-foot beacon, ended the tragedies when it was built in 1894.

As the rosy glow of sunrise drifts across the lake, you might see anglers heading out for deep-water fishing. Visitors can camp at some 125 sites and pedal the limestone-surfaced Rawley Point Bicycle Trail. It runs through pines and hemlocks for five miles before connecting with the paved seven-mile Mariners Trail into Two Rivers and Manitowoc. Cyclists also ride four miles of mountain-biking trails.

For hikers, the nearly 16-mile Ridges Trail from the lodge, housing a nature center and concessionaire in summer, includes three connecting loops. In the evenings, you'll hear croaking bullfrog choruses from trailside swales. Of course, allow plenty of time for lolling on the sand and splashing in the waves.

Contact: Point Beach State Forest (920/794-7480, wiparks.net). Nearest lodgings: in Two Rivers and Manitowoc (800/627-4896, manitowoc.info).

St. Croix National Scenic Riverway
Born in Wisconsin's North Woods, the 252-mile St. Croix River often tumbles into rapids in its upper reaches. Flowing southward, it forms the state's northwestern border from near Riverside until it joins

the Mississippi 20 miles southeast of the Twin Cities.

Canoeists and kayakers love the Upper St. Croix, paddling narrow stretches past cliffs, sandbars and forested shores. Looping southwest from Danbury, the river is a family favorite, with hundreds of picnic spots and campsites—some on islands. You'll also pass 20,000-acre Governor Knowles State Forest. State parks dot both banks farther south. Interstate Park, where the river rushes through a gorge, straddles the channel below St. Croix Falls, site of the riverway's new visitors center.

In the heart of the river valley, from St. Croix Falls to Prescott, historic lumbering towns cater to visitors. Cascade Falls tumbles into a glen at Osceola. The river becomes a haven for powerboaters as it broadens into Lake St. Croix around Hudson, where a beach park runs along the downtown riverfront. North of Prescott, Kinnickinnic State Park includes boat-in campsites.

Contact: St. Croix National Scenic Riverway (715/483-3284, nps.gov/sacn or saint croixriver.com). Nearest lodgings: all along the river (800/432-8747, travelwisconsin .com), including in the largest town, Hudson (800/657-6775, hudsonwi.org).

Turtle Flambeau Flowage

The dam that harnessed the Flambeau River 80 years ago swallowed nine lakes, three rivers and several creeks, creating this peaceful 19,000-acre realm in southern Iron County (about 10 miles south of the Michigan state line). The Turtle Flambeau ranks as Wisconsin's largest true wilderness.

Visitors fish, canoe and kayak solitary waterways and float a rowdy river amid nearly 200 wooded islands, never-ending waters and some 200 miles of shore. The best way to explore is by canoe or kayak, staying at one of five shore lodges or camping

on secluded islands (60 remote campsites are accessible only by water). Scenery and wildlife change with the seasons, from budding birches, fox kits and gleeful otters in spring to brilliant maples and aspens, bald eagles and ruffled grouse in fall.

For a livelier outing, paddle the Flambeau River, pitching your tent on its forested banks. Heading southwest toward Park Falls, the river includes 17 rapids (limited canoe and raft liveries).

Contact: Mercer Area Chamber of Commerce (715/476-2389, mercercc.com). Turtle Flambeau Flowage Association (715/ 476-2555, turtleflambeau flowage.com). Nearest lodgings: outside the flowage in nearby Mercer (715/476-2389, mercercc .com); more options 25 miles southwest in Park Falls (800/762-2709, parkfalls.com).

Wisconsin Dells

In this popular vacation area, sandstone bluffs loom above a 15-mile stretch of the Wisconsin River known as the Wisconsin Dells (50 miles northwest of Madison). The region centers on the towns of Wisconsin Dells, Lake Delton and Baraboo, where attractions range from water-park resorts to boat tours and the Circus World Museum. But to see the valley's natural side, visit its two state parks.

Nearly 20 miles of hiking and mountain-biking trails wind through forests and climb to overlooks at 2,200-acre Mirror Lake State Park. Pines and sandstone bluffs frame the park's namesake lake, where vacationers canoe, fish and relax on the beach. You can stay at some 150 wooded campsites.

More than 10,000-acre Devil's Lake State Park rolls across the timeworn Baraboo Range. Surrounding the lake, boulders piled on steep inclines of 500-foot bluffs make the landscape unique. Besides fishing, swimming, boating and mountain

biking, the park includes some 30 miles of hiking trails and a nature center. Campers choose from more than 400 sites.

Contact: Devil's Lake State Park (608/356-8301, wiparks.net or devilslake wisconsin.com). Mirror Lake State Park (608/254-2333, wiparks.net). Lodgings: in Baraboo (800/227-2266, baraboo.com) and in Lake Delton and Wisconsin Dells (800/223-3557, wisdells.com).

Wolf National Wild and Scenic River

For outstanding river rafting, travel north to Wisconsin's Langlade and Menominee counties (about 60 miles northwest of Green Bay). You'll careen through rounds of foamy "back rollers," souse holes and haystack rapids as the river booms like thunder. Then, tame again, the Wolf ambles through sun-drenched patches and pine woods.

With outfitters who supply gear and often guides, rafting and kayaking become memorable adventures for both first-timers and veteran paddlers. Along the river's quieter stretches, you can scan the shore for deer and watch ospreys scoop up fish. But you'll also want to practice paddling and steering for rougher water ahead. The Wolf drops 430 feet over 28 miles, making it among the Midwest's fastest. The river picks up speed beyond Hollister and Langlade and becomes rowdier the farther downstream you go. South from Langlade to the Menominee County Line, it rushes through rapids and boulder-strewn chutes, including menacing Horse Race and 20-Day rapids, plus a narrow chute called Gilmore's Mistake.

Contact: For Langlade County, Antigo Chamber of Commerce (888/526-4523, antigochamber.com). National Park Service, Rivers and Trails (414/297-3605, nps .gov/rivers/wsr-wolf.html). Lodgings: small cottage resorts in Langlade and White Lake (chamber of commerce contact above).

CLOCKWISE, FROM TOP LEFT: Horicon National Wildlife Refuge. Wolf National Wild and Scenic River. Turtle Flambeau Flowage. Interstate Park, St. Croix National Scenic Riverway.

Index

Acknowledgments
I am deeply grateful to the many Midwesterners who hosted me on my journey, including park professionals, tourism representatives, outfitters, guides and volunteers; my management at Meredith Corp., publishers of *Midwest Living*®, who have been so supportive of these road-trip projects; our itinerary coordinators, Nancy Singh and Joan Lynch Luckett; *Midwest Living* Creative Director Geri Boesen, who pulled this book together visually; the photographers who traveled with me (particularly Bob Stefko) and the many others whose work illustrates these pages; the talented and patient editors at Globe Pequot Press, most notably Mary Norris and Gia Manalio; the team at Iowa Public Television, including Duane Huey, Deb Herbold and my stout-hearted traveling companions, Peter Tubbs, Paul Hickey, Andrew Batt and John Torpey; Nancy McClimen, who so deftly polished my prose; and the capable assistants who gathered research and photography and transcribed my notes and tapes.

I also wish to acknowledge Barbara Humeston and Linda Ryberg, the award-winning travel writers who compiled the "More Parks" section at the end of each chapter; Debbie Leckron Miller, who wrote the "Travel Journal" listings; and Sandra Mapes Granseth, who tested and edited our recipes. I owe a huge and very personal thank-you to Rob Kaercher, who served as my travel assistant with boundless energy, good humor and infectious curiosity.

As always, my final tribute goes to my wife, Julie, for her steadfast support, without which I never would have reached the finish line on this project.

—*Dan Kaercher*

Contributors

Barbara Humeston and Linda Ryberg

These two contributors teamed up to produce the "More Parks" section at the end of each state chapter. Iowa native Barbara Humeston (left) is a former executive editor of *Midwest Living*® and former travel editor of *Better Homes and Gardens*®. Most of her favorite parks and preserves are found in the Great Lakes region, notably Wisconsin's Apostle Islands National Lakeshore. Linda Ryberg (right) lived in Michigan and Illinois before settling in Iowa. This project brought back memories of the many parks throughout the region she visited on assignment in her 13 years as a travel writer and editor with *Midwest Living*. Canoeing and birdwatching are among her top-rated outdoor pursuits.

Nancy Singh

Nancy Singh served as overall Parklands project coordinator, an assignment that included responsibilities from mapping out each day's travel itinerary from her home office in Des Moines to expediting and fact-checking the contents of this book. An Iowa native, Nancy attended Creighton University and lived in India and several other countries before returning to reside in her home state. Her Midwest vacations are spent visiting water-related parks with her family.

Photographers

This was the third *Midwest Living* summer road trip for Bob Stefko (pictured) of Evanston, Illinois, who photographed parks in five states from South Dakota to Indiana while traveling with Dan for this project. Bob specializes in images of travel, food and people and, with his wife, Holly, is an avid camper. Photographers Jason Lindsey of Champaign, Illinois, and Clint Farlinger of Cresco, Iowa, also accompanied Dan on segments of the journey. Jason's images are found in the Michigan and North Dakota chapters, Clint's in the Iowa chapter. (Please see page ii for the other talented photographers whose images are showcased in this book.)

Iowa Public Television Videography Team

A production-and-videography team accompanied Dan on his trip, documenting the journey for a public television Parklands special and subsequent series. Andrew Batt, a broadcasting journalism graduate of Iowa State University, acted as producer throughout Dan's travels. His most memorable park was Michigan's unique Sleeping Bear Dunes National Lakeshore. Peter Tubbs and John Torpey, both also on the Iowa Public Television staff, served as videographers on several legs of the project. Peter Tubbs' prized scene from the trip was a spectacular sunrise on the Ohio River near Golconda, Illinois. John Torpey's most cherished moments were unforgettable sunsets and filming Dan catching a king salmon in Lake Michigan. Paul Hickey, a freelance videographer, director of photography and lighting designer, accompanied Dan on the Great Plains leg of the trip on behalf of Iowa Public Television, revisiting many of his favorite parks and natural areas in the region.

Rob Kaercher

Rob Kaercher, a recent communications graduate of Manhattan College in New York City and Dan's cousin's son, served as the author's on-the-road travel assistant. His job entailed a variety of logistical support and editorial tasks, from driving to assisting with note-taking and lighting. Despite his affinity for big cities and oceans, Rob says he genuinely enjoyed the opportunity to experience America's Heartland and its people.